Whose Movie Are You In?

**Transform Your Intergenerational Trauma
Into Your Source of Light**

Michael Hsu

Cover Artist: Lika Kvirikashvili
Editors: Daniella Emrani & Kate Kennelly

The author of this book does not dispense medical advice or prescribe the use of
any technique as a form of treatment for physical or medical problems without
the advice of a physician, either directly or indirectly. The intent of the author
is only to offer information of a general nature to help you in your quest for
physical fitness and good health. In the event you use any of the information int
his book for yourself, which is your constitutional right, the author and publisher
assume no responsibility for your actions.

Publisher's Cataloging-in-Publication Data

Names: Hsu, Michael, author.
Title: Whose movie are you in ? transform your intergenerational trauma into your source of light /
By Michael Hsu.
Description: Includes bibliographical references. | San Francisco, CA: Heal From the Ground Up,
2020.
Identifiers: LCCN 2020914936 | ISBN 978-1-949593-06-8 (pbk.) | 978-1-949593-09-9 (ebook) |
978-1-949593-08-2 (audiobook)
Subjects: LCSH Post-traumatic stress disorder--Popular works. | Psychic trauma--Treatment. |
Anxiety--Treatment. | Depression--Treatment. | Anger--Treatment. | Intergenerational relations--
Psychological aspects. | Families--Mental health. | Dysfunctional families--Psychological aspects. |
Adult children of dysfunctional families--Psychology. | Families--Psychological aspects. | Resilience
(Personality trait) | Self-realization. | Psychic trauma. | BISAC SELF-HELP / Post-Traumatic Stress
Disorder (PTSD) | SELF-HELP / Emotions | SELF-HELP / Personal Growth / Self-Esteem | FAMILY
& RELATIONSHIPS / Dysfunctional Families | PSYCHOLOGY / Mental Health
Classification: LCC RC552.P67 .H88 2020 | DDC 616.8521--dc23

I dedicate this book to my son Zen Mikhailovich Hsu. My hope as a father is to lead the way in my own healing and transformation so you can lead the way in your own healing journey while discovering and sharing the light that you are to me and to all others.

Table of Contents

Introduction

Do you feel stuck in this vicious cycle of perpetual anxiety, worry, fear, anger, frustration, or depression and have no way of getting out no matter how hard you try to think your way out of it?

Do you have social anxiety and are you deathly scared of the perception of others?

Do you fear failure because you attach your self-worth to success?

Do you have anxiety over your health and worry if you will die?

Do you need to be in control all the time, or otherwise feel utterly powerless?

Do you feel immensely responsible for others because if you are not serving others or fail to do so, you don't know who you are? Or, do you make everything about yourself because you feel empty inside?

Is your relationship falling apart and no matter how much you work towards "communication" things only get worse?

Is your child experiencing emotional pain and struggles, leaving you lost and helpless about how to help them?

Is your mind thinking endless thoughts with no solution in sight?

Do you numb, suppress, and avoid your negative thoughts, emotions and feelings through your addictions to social media, overworking, overeating, alcohol, and the greatest addiction of all in overthinking?

What if I were to tell you that all of your pain did not belong to you?

What if you were living in somebody else's movie as your own, explaining that you suffer this horrific nightmare because it simply does not belong to you in the first place?

This book is about healing your negative emotions, feelings, and problems from the ground up, through intergenerational trauma healing. By finding "Whose movie are you in?" you can separate from all that and dedicate your life to creating and being the director of your movie and then sharing it with the world because that is why you exist.

You can easily and unknowingly find yourself in the movies of others if you are born with the gift of high sensitivity and high empathy: what I call emotional antennas. You can know if you have this gift by answering this key question:

"If someone around you is feeling anxious, angry, sad, or depressed, can you feel it, sense it, or pick up on it?"

If yes, then you are the one out of five people with the gift of high sensitivity and high empathy. Although this gift is incredibly powerful, it can be a double-edged sword, by having you subconsciously zap yourself into the movies of others as your own. In this scenario, it can be incredibly painful, confusing, and even traumatic, because no matter what you do in this movie, nothing ever changes, because this movie simply does not belong to you.

Important Note:

Although this book is primarily about intergenerational trauma, I am in no way negating the tremendous and pernicious impact of childhood trauma. My next book will be dedicated to this very topic.

This completely hidden and subconscious phenomenon is the very reason why you suffer and the very reason why the world suffers. This is the very reason why humanity as a whole suffers from anxiety, worry, or fear, anger or frustration, and depression, and at best can only manage it or contain it because what these emotions really are, are coping mechanisms to avoid feeling pain:

"Anxiety is how we run away from our pain, anger is how we protect our pain and depression is how we numb our pain."

This book is not about coping with your pain, resisting your pain, or even controlling your pain. All of these methods only exacerbate and intensify the pain of your anxiety, anger, and depression.

I hear all the time from clients that they want to "control" their anxiety, or "control" their anger, which is like trying to put out a fire by throwing fuel at it. All these negative emotions are forms of control. Anxiety (worry or fear) is how we try to control the future, anger is when we try to seek control but feel powerless so we try to mask it with a false appearance of strength and power. Depression is when we feel hopeless and powerless to change anything, curling up into a ball of sadness and numb it all. Thus when we try to "control anxiety," we are literally trying to control "control" and thus only to get more control and more suffering.

This book is not about controlling your pain, but rather, about healing your pain from the ground up and transforming it into your light, as you are guided through a revolutionary process and emotional toolkit that will heal the root of all of your negative emotions, feelings, and problems and transform it all into your light.

Your light is your purpose, your dreams and your movie in which you are meant to share with the world because it is why you exist and it is why you were created. You ultimately will realize that the "pain" and the "darkness" you experience will become the beacon of light you shine onto the world because the purpose of pain and darkness is to transform it into your light and the movie in which you will share with the world and change it forever.

I share this with you so you can understand where we are ultimately heading in this book and so you can see the light at the end of the tunnel. But before we get there, let's start from the very beginning and I will begin by showing you what intergenerational trauma healing is by first sharing my personal story.

On top of my personal story and experiences, this book is packed with real-life client examples and dialogues who volunteered themselves to be coached on my "Heal From the Ground Up" podcast, and for this book.

The real-life examples, stories, and dialogues are powerfully transformative because storytelling helps you understand the abstract almost instantaneously like a hot knife through butter because we process information best through stories.

We may try to escape into logic and overthinking but you cannot deny the essence of being human which is feeling and storytelling. In essence, stories are our connection to each other as humans and to what it means to be human, because without stories we are not human.

I will now begin sharing my personal story to give you a powerful example and help you begin to understand what intergenerational trauma healing is and how I was living in the traumatic experience of living in someone else's movie as my own.

Michael's Personal Story with Intergenerational Trauma Healing

Ten days before my baby boy was born, I started suffering from terrifying insomnia. I slept three to four hours and woke up because I had to either change his diaper or use the restroom. Immediately upon waking up, I feared that I would not be able to go back to sleep, which almost always turned out to be the case. My son was born in the Czech Republic, and we were there for two months before coming back to the US. During these two months of horrific insomnia, my worst fear was that if this lack of a full night's sleep continued, I would die.

The day we went back to the US, my parents picked us up at the airport and we all had dinner together to celebrate our family reunion. We all shared stories about how my wife and I raised our newborn and how my parents raised me as a newborn. It was then that I found out, for the first time ever, that my mother never took care of me throughout the night because she feared if she was woken up by me, she would not be able to go back asleep.

My mom obsessively fears death but avoids it by fixating on health and safety. Her home is in a very nice neighborhood but her windows are barred up, has an alarm system, and a surveillance system. Her bedroom door has a door lock, chain lock and she pushes a chair against the door handle. In essence, I felt and internalized my mother's pain and trauma as a newborn and then repeated that same exact pain and trauma, 39 years later, when I had my own newborn.

My mother's ultimate and underlying pain is feeling abandoned, which is what her fear of death is actually rooted in which is tied to the intergenerational trauma of being abandoned.

When my grandmother was five years old, her father, who was a high-ranking general in China, wanted a wife who was prettier and better educated, so he divorced my grandmother's mother. My great-grandmother was separated from the family and had to live a life of extreme poverty and was severed from her first child, my grandmother. This was the first experience of abandonment.

My grandmother's stepmother didn't want to be known as the step-mother, or the second wife, so my grandmother was raised by her grandparents. But this was all during the time of World War II. Communists invaded my grandmother's home, and while she was hiding in the barn, they lined up her family members in a line and killed them execution-style. My grandmother fled to safety to her father's new home with her step-mother, but he opened the door to my grandmother, his first reaction was disappointment, because he knew his second wife would be angry. Thus, with my grandmother's life on the line, she was not worth protecting by her very own father.

My grandmother is 93 years old now and for all the time that I have known her, during family lunches and dinners, she sits with her body facing outwardly because subconsciously she feels like she is not a part of the family.

Although it is true, my grandmother was influenced by the traditional culture of China, and heavily favored my uncle over my mother because he was a boy, my mother internalized my grandmother's core pain of being abandoned as her own, which explains why she is so fearful of death but avoids it all by fixating on health and safety.

I then internalized this pain and movie as my own with my fear of not sleeping because if I don't sleep, then I will die and if I die, I cease to exist. The fear of death is an extremely common fear for humanity, as it is the most extreme version of worthlessness, because if you die you cease to exist.

As much I hated this experience of insomnia and as much as not sleeping feels like my absolute worst nightmare, you wouldn't be reading this book if it weren't for that. This painful and horrific experience set off a major chain of events that transformed my life forever and helped me see what my true calling was; which is to lead a movement for humanity to separate from the movies of our intergenerational traumas so we can be the director of our own movies in which we are meant to share with the world to transform it.

Ultimately:

When we feel pain we normally want to avoid it, resist it, fight it, or numb it all together. However, doing so will deprive you and all others of the lessons you learn from pain that will make your movie into a masterpiece, ultimately transforming yourself, your family, and the world.

Note: I will talk later on, about how my father's side has impacted me, and it took me longer to connect the dots, because my father and the family he comes from suppresses their feelings and emotions tremendously. Although this made it difficult to consciously be aware of its impact on me, I was still subconsciously feeling it all as my own.

Other Examples of Intergenerational Trauma Healing

Now, before we delve deep into the healing process and apply the process onto you, I would like to share a couple more profound examples of what intergenerational trauma healing looks like, starting with Tia's story.

TIA LANDERS' STORY

Tia used to have a steady job and now is transitioning into a career as an entrepreneur. She feels extremely lost and worries all the time if she will fail or not. The ultimate feeling she feels is powerlessness as she needs to be in control. As an entrepreneur, nothing is set in stone and you have to create your way each and every day. Another example of Tia's need to be in control is with her daughter, for whom she has bought enough clothing to fit three weeks of unlimited outfits.

Her daughter will, for example, wear one outfit Monday, and then wear the same outfit Wednesday and Tia will lose it. She is constantly fighting with her daughter over similar issues. Tia is a single mother and another example of Tia's need to be in control and feeling powerless is when her boyfriend is not listening to her intently, as he may be distracted by something and Tia will lose it again, only to become infuriated with him.

Where does Tia's pain of feeling powerless come from? When she was one year old, her mother's sister was murdered by her very own husband, who happened to be a serial killer. He had strangled her to death. He did this many times before in other states. Thus, the trauma of feeling powerless is rooted in the whole family's trauma of feeling powerless by the fact that they were completely blindsided by their loved one being murdered by her husband who was a serial killer on top of that.

In the beginning of our session, Tia expressed the fear of failure a lot in this new endeavor as an entrepreneur, but what was really stopping her from having the success that she wanted, wasn't the fear of failure, but the fear of not being in control and feeling powerless.

Although, from the outside looking in, it may seem insignificant for Tia's daughter to wear the same outfit within two days, to Tia's subconscious, it means so much more, because in her mind, your loved ones die when you are not in control.

(You can listen and watch the full session on my Heal From the Ground Up podcast and YouTube channel and look for the episode titled, "The Trauma of a Family Murder".)

Looking at Tia's and my own example, it answers the question of "How could you internalize something from another that you were not even conscious of?" Your emotional antennas and high sensitivity is so powerful, that although consciously you may not be aware of it, subconsciously, you can feel every morsel of it all.

JAGRIT SINGH'S STORY

Jagrit is a college student living in Canada who is terrified of driving. He has only driven twice in his life and it was only in a parking lot. He is even scared of walking around moving cars. His worst fear is to be hit by a car and die. Where does this fear and trauma all come from?

His family is from India and Pakistan, at a time when they were still one country under Britain's rule. When Britain left in 1947, there was a partition that declared Pakistan as a Muslim state and India as a non-secular state. In this time, Muslims migrated from India to Pakistan and non-Muslims migrated from Pakistan to India. It is important to note that there were major contentions between these two groups. Thus, the migration that involved 15 million people, encapsulated a world of death, horrific violence, rape, murder, hunger, and starvation, leading to the deaths of 1-2 million people.

Nisid Hajari, author of "Midnight's Furies: The Deadly Legacy of India's Partition" wrote of the history of the Partition and its aftermath, "Gangs of killers set whole villages aflame, hacking to death men and children and the aged while carrying off young women to be raped. Some British soldiers and journalists who had witnessed the Nazi death camps claimed Partition's brutalities were worse: pregnant women had their breasts cut off and babies hacked out of their bellies; infants were found literally roasted on spits."[1]

When Jagrit is in a car behind the wheel, he is reliving his great-grandparents' movie as his own, as well as his grandparents, who were around five at the time; feeling like he is living in a world of death, violence, murder, and starvation while sitting behind a wheel and having no idea why.

When you subconsciously and unknowingly live in the movie of others as our own, your thinking mind, otherwise known as the "ego," just as with Jagrit's thinking mind, creates a present-day fear in your own life to make some kind of sense and normalcy of the trauma you unknowingly internalized as your own, otherwise you would think you are going crazy.

This is just like the case where my mother's thinking mind creates the fear of death by fixating on health and safety, to avoid the subconscious intergenerational trauma of her mother and her grandmother being abandoned.

APPLYING THE EMOTIONAL STRENGTH F.I.S.T. PROCESS TO YOURSELF, RELATIONSHIPS, CHILDREN AND FAMILIES

THE EMOTIONAL STRENGTH F.I.S.T. PROCESS

The Emotional Strength F.I.S.T. Process is a process and emotional toolkit that will heal the root of all your negative emotions, feelings, and problems from the ground up. Before you dive deep and apply the FIST process onto yourself, it is important to know that you do not exist in isolation. You have parents, children, and/or a life partner, all of whom can greatly affect you. The FIST process works remarkably well for relationships, especially for families with young or adult children.

The well-being of the family unit is crucial to the well-being of each individual within the family unit. If the well-being of the family unit is not in a good place or at least its issues are not understood, then these issues will secretly bleed into your personal life that is seemingly separate from the family unit.

The family unit relates to the relationship between both parents, the relationship between the parent and child, as well as the families that both parents come from and how they affect the family unit.

Although you may not be in a relationship or have children, it is still very helpful to read this section, because you still come from the family unit of your parents (and step-parents).

APPLYING THE FIST PROCESS WITH YOUR PARTNER

If you are applying the FIST process with your partner and you want to better your relationship and get to the root of your issues, do each step within the process together.

Most relationship problems act as the tip of the iceberg. Meaning these problems are happening at the surface level, and cannot be resolved by not uncovering what is happening deep down at the root level. For example, a lot of couples I work with, tell me they need to work on their "communication" but it really has little to do with communication.

Most relationships have issues because it's not just the two of you in the relationship. Both of you are subconsciously and unknowingly bringing your intergenerational trauma into the relationship and projecting the cause of one's pain onto each other, which is only rooted in one's intergenerational trauma.

RELATIONSHIPS ARE MEANT TO TEST YOU

Your relationship may feel like hell, especially if you are in a relationship with your life partner. Why is that? Because it's supposed to. Relationships, as well as having a family and children, are one of the prime mechanisms in your life that will bring up your most hidden and painful demons to the surface.

However, as hopeless as the relationship may feel, all of this is good and actually necessary, because both of your inner demons and really intergenerational trauma are coming to the surface so you can work through them and detoxify them out of yourself, your relationship and your current or future family.

APPLYING THE FIST PROCESS WITH YOUR CHILDREN

Note: Although you may not have children, it is very important for you to read this section as it is very helpful in you understanding your childhood, the family unit you come from, and something we will discuss later on, the importance of knowing the 4th generation, which are your great-grandparents.

I have a lot of parents who bring their children to see me and their main focus, and seemingly only focus, is the well-being of their child. Understandably so, as parents naturally love their children and want the best for them. Nevertheless, you cannot help a child by understanding them in isolation, for they are a singular puzzle piece within the entire puzzle of the family and the past generations they come from. In fact, the FIST process works best when you can do it together as a family unit, so you can see how all the different puzzle pieces of the family unit relate to and affect each other.

If you truly desire to improve the well-being of your child, the work has to include you, the parent. Mainly because, children are the emotional sponges to their parents' unresolved feelings. Your unhealed pain is the dark cloud hanging over your child's head secretly haunting their every step in life.

When you, the parent, decide to do the inner healing work along with your child, the once dark cloud hanging over your child's head, transforms itself into a ray of sunshine of warmth that your kid's faces can bask in.

THIS IS NOT ABOUT BLAMING THE PARENT

This in no way is blaming you, or casting judgment upon you, the parent, for your children's emotional issues. You are not the cause. When you see your child suffering through the same feelings you experience, I want you to visualize your own innocent inner child in them. Envision your inner child in your own child with this new lens of subconsciously taking on their parents' unresolved feelings and emotions as their own.

You are not to blame. Your ultimate priority is to uncover, identify, and separate from the intergenerational and ancestral cycle of pain and trauma, so that you and your children can stop living in the intergenerational movies of your past family members.

"EVERYTHING IS FOR MY CHILD"

When working with young families and after we identify the child's dreams, purpose and movie, we get to the stage where I then ask the parent "What is your movie, your dreams, and your calling?" Many parents respond by asking if I can just focus on their child in following their dreams. To which I respond, "How can your child truly follow their dreams and channel their struggle and pain into their movie of light to shine onto the world, if you don't do the same?" A parent is supposed to lead and guide their child.

I love my son with all my heart, and I devote so much of my life to him but I know I must be that beacon of light so he can know how to be his own beacon of light. There is no way he can be that beacon of light, if I'm still hiding in my shadows, and fear-based comfort zone.

When you do follow your dreams, and answer your calling, your deepest and most hidden wounds will come to the surface. However, in doing so, you can heal these wounds, and be free of them, while ultimately transforming these wounds into your beacon of light. If you do not follow your dreams while truly healing and transforming your deepest wounds, your child will continue to not only feel your wounds but take them on as their own.

Love yourself enough to do this precious work for yourself, because your family and your child are depending on it. How can you expect your child to love themself if you don't love yourself enough to honor who you are in your life's purpose and reason for existence? If you make "everything about your child" by sacrificing your dreams and neglecting your inner healing work, then, unfortunately, you will have failed your child. Lead the way and be the beacon of the light that you are, so that your child can follow your lead and be the beacon of light that they are.

APPLYING THE FIST PROCESS TO THE FAMILY UNIT

I want to remind you, as much as you are concerned about the issues and the well-being of your child, stay adamant in continuing to apply the FIST process (beginning with the PEWF process) onto yourself, the parent. Continually finding out your core negative feelings and intergenerational trauma are vital key links in understanding and resolving your child's emotional well-being.

In fact, it will amaze you how understanding your child's experience will help provide missing key links in your own personal healing journey. Your child's pain and struggles are mirror reflections and extensions of your unresolved feelings and intergenerational trauma.

Remember, in families, the FIST process is best done together as a family unit. To understand any singular puzzle piece (i.e. the child, the marriage, the parent) you need to view and understand the entire puzzle set, the family unit. You will get to see all the seemingly separate puzzle pieces together (the child, the parents, the marriage, the intergenerational trauma from each parent) and how they are all related and deeply mold each other.

part one

Feel

CHAPTER ONE:

"*Feeling is Healing*"

THE FIRST STEP TO HEALING IS FEELING

As mentioned earlier, the Emotional Strength F.I.S.T. Process is a process and emotional toolkit that will heal the root of all your negative emotions, feelings, and problems from the ground up. Take some time right now and think of and write down what you would like to focus on and how you are feeling:

_____

_____

_____

"F" in the F.I.S.T. process stands for "feeling" as in "feeling is healing." The antithesis to "feeling" is thinking, and overthinking.

THE ANTITHESIS TO FEELING: DO YOU THINK, THINK AND OVERTHINK?

Answer this question: are you constantly doing and constantly thinking? If yes, explain how so:

_____

_____

_____

Client Example: Scottie admits her problem is that she "tries to think her way through it". "It's hard for me to sit with that feeling and work through it and identify the feeling because I feel I think my way through it."

We are normally thinking, thinking and overthinking. I'm not saying thinking is not important, because it is. However, thinking must be balanced with the act of feeling, because they work like yin and yang and are supportive of each other, just as our minds and our hearts do.

Thoughts are important as thoughts and actions are the ship that helps you get to your destination. But your captain is "feeling." Without a captain, your ship has no direction. When you are only thinking, overthinking, and basically living in your headspace, you will find yourself in a neverending downward spiral with no solution in sight. The thinking mind acts as a carrot on a stick, giving you the illusion that the solution is almost within arms reach but actually leading you astray in the very opposite direction you wanted to go.

The thinking mind is like a motor that never stops, leading you to constantly think and constantly do as if your very existence depended on it.

Here is a mantra that is the first crucial step to centering the motor mind.

The thinking mind tells us a certain problem is causing our negative emotions and negative feelings, and gives us the illusion of telling us "If you fix the problem, you will fix the feeling." However, this does not work, because the reality is, our feelings preceded the problem. Thus, even if you fix the "problem," you will still have not fixed the core issue, which is your negative feelings.

These feelings that you will uncover are weeds. They will say something negative about you, but you need to remind yourself that these feelings are just "weeds" and they are not true about who you really are. You are just uncovering, identifying and pulling out the weeds so they don't overtake your yard and subconsciously control how you feel and think.

Next, you will see a client dialogue reflecting the notion that "Problems bring up feelings in us that existed before the problem ever happened."

COACHING DIALOGUE WITH ADRIENNE MACLAIN ON "FEELING IS HEALING"

Adrienne: I want to focus on feeling that I am enough. I am doing enough. I have enough. This is enough, you know.

Michael: Can you give me an example of a situation when you don't feel you are enough?

Michael: Okay. And can you give me an example where that feeling comes up?

Adrienne: Like the opposite of that feeling?

Michael: Because that's what you want, but then probably you're feeling the opposite. (Adrienne: Yeah, exactly.) What situation is happening that brings up that feeling?

Adrienne: Yeah. So I'm working on some voiceover work for somebody, and he is very exacting. He wants it, you know, a very specific way.

And so he keeps sending me this feedback that's very abrupt and very negative. Letting me know that my equipment isn't good enough, my delivery isn't good enough. It's just not good enough for him. And so that's hard for me as a creative type. I think I'm sensitive, and it just hurts my feelings a little bit when I'm like, "I spent two hours trying to get this perfect for you, and it's still not good enough." And it just feels really demoralizing.

I'm really wanting to get more of the right kinds of clients. Do you know what I mean? Like when I have that right client who really appreciates what I do and just thinks that I'm brilliant. And when I come up with something, they're like, "I love this. This is great."

Just wanting to pull more of that energy into my life and not ending up with these clients where I'm like bending over backwards to try to make them happy, and often not succeeding anyway.

Michael: Having this type of difficult client brings up these negative feelings (in you that you want to uncover and identify so you can let it go). There's a mantra that I use, and it'll help you center yourself. So you want to say this mantra to yourself, "Problems bring up feelings in us that existed before the problem ever happened."

I ask Adrienne to stretch this all the way to her worst fear and worst-case scenario, to which she says she will be so busy with paying off debt that it will take away time from her family and daughter. She continues explaining:

Adrienne: That I'll never be able to pay off the debt. That it's just gonna mount and mount and I'm never going to be able to, you know, own my own land or home or anything like that. That I'm just going to be kind of like a slave to the debt for the rest of my life. Just trying to pay it off.

And feeling like I'm not bringing real value, or I'm not bringing my gifts to the world, because I have to do whatever I can to, you know, work to pay off this debt. And so therefore I'm not really taking the risks I would need to take to create a business and a life for myself that is really using my real gifts.

Michael: I'm going to say something. This sounds really bad but I'm here just to identify the feeling, just to uncover the feeling. So I wonder even if you were to pay off the debt and then were allowed to have the free time with your daughter and also to pursue your passion that makes you happy...what if, even though you had the free time and the money, you still failed?

Would that get to you even more? Because it's one thing to be like, "Oh, I'm able to do it. I have the ability to do it, but it's just I don't have the time and the money." But what if you had all the time and the money to do so, but when you did, you actually failed.

Adrienne: Yeah...that...that hurts. That hurts to think about that. Yeah.

As you can see, the "problem" of being a slave to debt, and not being able to pursue and live out her passions and gifts because of it, is the distraction and excuse to avoid feeling like a failure if she had all the time and money in the world and yet still failed. Obviously, Adrienne is not a failure, but she needs to first identify her feelings so they don't control her on a subconscious level.

She goes on to admit that she fears failure mainly because of the fear of judgment. For instance, when Adrienne receives criticism for her voiceover work, her worst fear is that it will lead to many negative reviews, making her lose her business and eventually become homeless. Interestingly, the worst thing for Adrienne about being homeless is encountering the judgment of others, as she describes:

Adrienne: Especially in this society, we blame people for being poor. And we judge them for being poor. And so once you get to this kind of threshold of poverty, it's like nobody even wants to try to help you anymore because it's like, "Well, obviously, even if I gave you charity, you wouldn't even do something good with it, if you've gotten to this point of helplessness or hopelessness."

HEALING YOUR FOUNDATION
THROUGH THE ACT OF FEELING

You don't need to figure things out for the moment, as you will begin to do that soon in the next step of the process. Let the motor mind take a rest from its constant motion of thinking like the pulsating pistons of an engine.

I'm not saying the act of feeling is the end all be all, but you want to first establish a critical foundation for all other levels of healing and awareness to be possible.

"FEELING IS HEALING" BECAUSE IT CONNECTS YOU TO LOVE

We normally don't like to feel, because we associate "feeling" with "feeling pain." I want you to reframe what pain is as an emotional wound. "Feeling is healing" because it connects you to love, therefore when you feel your emotional wound, you begin the healing process because you are giving it the medicine of love in order to heal.

What happens when you choose to avoid your emotional wound through constant thinking and constant doing? Your emotional wound, when avoided, will do what all wounds do when you ignore them: it will only grow and consume you, very much acting like cancer.

Interestingly, cancer has a strong emotional element of avoiding our feelings. In a study done in the 1960's, psychotherapist Ronald Grossarth-Mticek observed 1353 inhabitants of Crvenka, Yugoslavia over a decade and found that 9 out of every 10 cases of cancer was attributed to an "overly rational, anti-emotional attitude." People with high anti-emotional scores were 29 times more likely to develop cancer than people with low anti-emotional scores.[2]

What I took away from this study was that cancer can be considered the physical manifestation of what we are doing on an emotional level. When we try to avoid and suppress our feelings and our emotional wounds, they only grow and consume our lives, just as cancer kills by "metastasizing" and spreading to others parts of the body.

"FEELING IS HEALING" EXERCISE

It is virtually impossible to purely, mentally, and logically understand the importance of the act of feeling without having to practice it and actually allowing yourself to "feel."

I have clients who are so much consumed in their headspace that when I tell them about the healing importance of the act of feeling, they respond by asking, "HOW do you feel?" The logical mind is always trying to figure things out by figuring out the "how." But you cannot figure things out and find the root of it all until you establish the foundation of "feeling is healing," so all other levels of healing and awareness can be possible.

Now let's do an exercise to take a moment to practice the act of feeling. Close your eyes for a moment and find the "tension" in your body (or the anxiety, worry, fear, anger, frustration and depression) either in your throat, chest, top of your stomach or the bottom of your stomach.

Note: Many of my clients often will say they feel their negative emotions and tension in their head. Remember that we overthink in order to avoid our feelings. I personally believe headaches are caused very much by thinking too much to avoid our feelings.

If you noted that your negative emotions and tension are in your head, close your eyes once more, and feel where your negative emotions lie by scanning your throat, chest or top and bottom of your stomach.

Once you find the tension and negative emotions in your body, just feel safe in feeling it, knowing that "feeling is healing" and you're thereby giving this emotional wound the medicine of love in order to begin the healing process. Gently remind yourself, you don't need to figure things out right now. You will do that soon, but for now establish the foundation for all other levels of healing and awareness to be possible.

WHAT IS OVER-POSITIVITY?

Angie was feeling very down because she feels like absolutely nothing ever good happens to her and it's to the point where she feels like she doesn't even deserve good things to happen to her.

Angie: I'm a very optimistic person, but lately just the things that happen to me, I just sometimes laugh because it gets to the point where it's just laughable. You know, it just gets to a point. I'm an optimistic person. Sometimes I'm too optimistic. So it just came to a point where I think it's making me a little bit more realistic, but it's bringing my self-worth down.

Michael: Optimism is really important, but we still want to be conscious of optimism because it can be a way to avoid the negative feelings. You want to feel these negative feelings so you can identify them, and then truly separate from them and let go of them.

It is very common to be overly optimistic and positive in order to avoid feeling your negative feelings. Optimism entails positive thinking, but the reason why positive thinking has its severe limitations in correcting negative thinking is because negative thoughts are rooted in negative feelings. Thus, if you try to simply transform your negative thoughts into positive thoughts, doing so just symbolizes a bandaid that masks the problem and does nothing to address the root of the negative thought which is the negative feeling. Consequently, when you don't acknowledge your negative feelings, over-positivity is just a coping mechanism to avoid feeling and suppressing your negative feelings, allowing the pain of your emotional wounds to fester.

PAIN IS YOUR GREATEST TEACHER

How do you truly feel safe in feeling your feelings when these feelings feel like your worst nightmare?

Whatever pain you are feeling, I want you to close your eyes now and feel safe in feeling it, because the universal truth is:

> The avoidance of pain is the creation of all pain.

You wake up in the morning feeling this pain and you want to avoid it by immediately checking your phone.

You can avoid your pain through any drug of your choice: alcohol, social media, overeating, binging on non-stop thinking, and action. There are infinite ways you can avoid your pain but always remember:

> The avoidance of pain creates all pain.

At the core of pain is light, because the purpose of pain and darkness is for it to be transformed into light that you will share with others and the world.

As we discussed earlier, anytime you feel pain or any negative emotion and negative feeling, I want you to repeat the mantra,

> *"Pain is my greatest teacher. The lessons I learn from pain will transform me, my family and the world."*

When you choose to resist, defeat, fight or numb pain, but you deny yourself and all others the lessons you will learn from pain which will transform yourself, your family, and the world.

I will talk about how to channel your pain into your movie in great detail in the last phase of the book which is about uncovering your movie, your true self, your light and sharing it with the world, but I wanted to let you truly feel safe in feeling this pain, because pain is your greatest teacher.

Remind yourself, time and time again:

"Feeling is healing. Avoiding is suffering."

"Feeling is healing. Avoiding is suffering."

The choice is yours.

What will you choose in this moment?

What will you choose in every moment from now on?

The choice is yours.

Anytime you feel pain, tell yourself:

"Pain is not my enemy."

"Pain is my greatest teacher."

"The lessons I learn from pain will transform:

Me,

My family,

And the world."

part two

Identify

CHAPTER TWO

Identify Your Feelings Through the P.E.W.F. Process

APPLYING THE PEWF PROCESS TO YOURSELF, AND WITH YOUR PARTNER AND/OR CHILD

The "I" in the F.I.S.T. Process stands for "identify," as in identify your core negative feelings. In order to **identify** your core negative feelings (i.e. weeds) you will now apply what I call the P.E.W.F. process. (You can think of the sound "POOF!" to help you remember.) Before we proceed, if you are applying the PEWF process with your partner or child, the following are some important things to consider:

APPLYING THE PEWF PROCESS WITH YOUR PARTNER

If you are applying the PEWF process with your partner and you want to better your relationship and get to the root of your issues, do each step within the process together.

WHAT IF MY PARTNER IS NOT WILLING TO PARTICIPATE?

If your partner is unwilling to participate because, for example, they don't want help or you two have separated, it is still beneficial to apply the FIST process onto them to get an understanding of the relationship. In this scenario, it is recommended that you apply the FIST process onto your partner after you have completed it onto yourself because after having applied it onto yourself, you can effectively apply it onto others.

APPLYING THE PEWF PROCESS WITH YOUR CHILD

You are going to want to have your child apply the PEWF process onto themselves and then have them apply the PEWF process onto their parents. This will be interesting to see what your children already intuitively sense in you. Obviously, you still want to apply the PEWF process onto yourself, as it will help your child tremendously in receiving additional information to where their feelings could be coming from.

I want to remind you, as much as you are concerned about the issues and the well-being of your child, stay adamant in continuing to apply the FIST process (beginning with the PEWF process) onto yourself, the parent. Continually finding out your core negative feelings and intergenerational trauma are vital key links in understanding and resolving your child's emotional well-being.

In fact, it will amaze you how understanding your child's experience will help provide missing key links in your own personal healing journey. Your child's pain and struggles are mirror reflections and extensions of your unresolved feelings and intergenerational trauma.

Remember, in families, the FIST process is best done together as a family unit. To understand any singular puzzle piece (i.e. the child, the marriage, the parent) you need to view and understand the entire puzzle set, the family unit. You will get to see all the seemingly separate puzzle pieces together (the child, the parents, the marriage, the intergenerational trauma from each parent) and how they are all related and deeply mold each other.

WHAT EMOTIONS DO YOU EXPERIENCE?

In reading this book, you are going to work through and get to the underlying root of every problem or issue you want to focus on, but it is important to first ground these problems in an emotion to help understand these problems on a deeper level. Otherwise, you will be forever thinking about a problem like a hamster on a wheel, if you don't ground the mental understanding of a problem with the first level of "feeling" which is an emotion.

Before you proceed with the PEWF Process, I want you to first identify which negative emotions out of the main three do you experience and each one has its own subcategories.

Do you experience anxiety, worry or fear? (If yes, which ones):

_____

_____

Do you experience anger, or frustration? (Note: anger does not have to be a violent emotion, it's just a feeling and frustration is really just repressed anger.)

_____

_____

The last negative emotion has a negative stigma to it and really a misconception. It is the word "depression" which I call "emotional suppression." Emotional suppression is suppressing, numbing, and bottling in how you feel.

If you ever find yourself doing this, ask yourself if you experience worry, fear or frustration because these are all forms of suppression our emotions and write them below:

_____

_____

Important Note on Emotional Suppression:

When a client tells me they experience depression or emotional suppression, I normally counteract it by asking if they feel anxiousness, worry, fear or frustration, which are all forms of suppressing our emotions. Worry or fear are suppressed forms of anxiety because it is a "mental" way of processing "anxiety" as something that is only conceptualized in your headspace in order to avoid the feeling of anxiety. Frustration, as mentioned before, is really just the suppression of anger.

Additionally, one classic way we suppress how we feel is by constantly thinking and doing, intellectualizing everything, and being very logical. Later I will explain why, but even the need to be in control is another classic way to suppress how we feel.

CHAPTER THREE:

Problem and Emotion

P.E.W.F. PROCESS (PROBLEM AND EMOTION)

You are now going to begin to uncover the underlying layer to the problems you want to work through by grounding them with an emotion (anxiety, worry, fear, anger or frustration) because otherwise working through your problems will be a never-ending downward spiral if you only live in your headspace and avoid all feeling and emotion altogether.

You are going to identify your core negative feelings (i.e. the weeds) by using the P.E.W.F. Process. You can think of the sound "POOF!" to help you remember.

P.E.W.F. Process

"P" stands for problem and "E" stands for emotion.

What problems or situations bring up strong feelings of anxiety, worry or fear? (List at least two because there often can be different elements to your anxiety, worry or fear)

_____

_____

_____

_____

Important: *When identifying problems in the PEWF process refrain from identifying problems and negative events from your childhood. We will definitely tie your negative emotions and feelings to its past, but that will happen later on. When applying the PEWF process, it is important to bring up events that happened more recently.*

Interestingly, it is the thinking mind that likes to source our pain to past events as opposed to current or recent events because it is a coping mechanism that helps us avoid feeling our negative feelings in the moment.

What problems or situations bring up strong feelings of anger or frustration in you? (If anger or frustration is your most dominant emotion list two problems that bring up feelings of anger or frustration in you)

_____

_____

_____

_____

Note: It is helpful to think of what about this problem or situation makes you anxious, worried, fearful, or angry and frustrated? This will help you have a deeper understanding of the problem so you can later see what's the underlying root of it all. You will see an example of what I mean shortly with a client example named Monica.

If you noticed, I did not ask you to do this exercise with the emotion of "depression" because depression is an act of emotional suppression. If you experience depression and emotional suppression, focus on thinking of problems that bring up feelings of anxiousness, worry, fear or frustration; which are all forms of suppressing our emotions.

> **MICHAEL'S EXAMPLE WITH THE PEWF PROCESS (PROBLEM AND EMOTION)**
>
> **Problem:** After having my first child was born, I experienced terrible insomnia. Every time I woke up during my sleep (either to go to the bathroom or to help take care of the baby) I immediately felt crippled by the immense fear that I would not be able to go back to sleep. And almost always I did not go back to sleep. This situation made me anxious because I felt my health was going to be ruined.

Now, we move onto a coaching dialogue with me and Monica applying the first stage of the PEWF process.

COACHING DIALOGUE WITH MONICA'S PROBLEMS AND EMOTIONS

While showing you how to apply the FIST process, I will use a client example, whose name is Monica, where I am coaching her through the process. The actual dialogue between me and Monica will be included, which will help you learn not only how to deeply apply the process to yourself through these real-life examples and storytelling, but also how to apply the process to others, if you ever wanted to do this professionally.

Michael: Do you feel any anxiety, anger, or depression?

Monica: Honestly, I feel all of them.

Michael: Okay. It's very common.

Monica: I know I'm frustrated and angry a lot, and then I suppress things because I don't want to pick a fight or make myself "look like the girl."

Michael: Tell me a problem or situation that brings up strong feelings of anxiety, worry or fear in you.

Monica: Social situations. Meeting new people, being in a group. I don't do group therapy, even though it might be amazing for me. I can't. It's crippling at this point.

Michael: Got it. Got it, and before we uncover what's going on underneath this, let's identify the other emotions as well. So tell me a problem or situation that brings up strong feelings of anger or frustration.

Monica: My husband's hoarding.

Michael: What about that frustrates you or angers you?

Monica: Honestly, we have been financially upside down for years and years and years and years and years and years and years, and he has seven or eight storage units full of crap, and he pays on those, but he doesn't pay on our house payment. And so we get evicted every time.

Michael: You said 6 to 7 storage units?

Monica: Oh yeah! He's got a problem . . . and there might be more. He hides them from me. So that doesn't help anything. That makes me frustrated when I see these storages. As he shows me them, he opens the door, and I get an immediate emotion, like a shower over my head of just – it goes from confused and sad to just angry and then I can't deal with that. I can't help him with it. I can't help him process it or empty it or anything because it's overwhelming. It's like suffocating me.

Michael: You mean you're angry because you cannot help him?

Monica: I'm angry because he has all these storage units. He reveals more and more of the storage units to me, and I'm like, "Wait, I thought you had four?" "No, I had six." "No, I have eight." "What? How many do you have?"

I honestly don't know at this point, but it's like he's tried to show them to me and say, "I need help. I need help emptying these." He tries to get me involved with him and like I said, it's like a shower. It starts with shock and sadness, and then it just turns to the anger of, "What on God's creation is wrong with you?!!" And it's, you know," You're paying for this to keep all that stuff here, and you're not paying for our bills."

Michael: I understand that this situation is unacceptable, but I just want to know and clarify what specifically about the situation is angering you?

Monica: Mainly it's because he's paying for these storage units to stay afloat and keep all these storage units, and yet he isn't learning. He has lost storage units. He's had a bill of $8,000 on the storage unit, and they let him just empty his stuff out, and it's like an addiction.

Michael: Got it. Got it. I think there's something underneath this. We'll wait and definitely get to that.

Monica: Well, he's made my house a storage unit at one point where I had nothing but crap from the ceiling to wall... There's also that he's made my house a storage unit for a good five, ten years as well.

CHAPTER FOUR:

Worst Fear and Worst-case Scenario

Ultimately, we will need to identify your core feelings (i.e. the weeds). In order to do so, we need to complete the "W" in the P.E.W.F. process, which stands for "worst fear and worst-case scenario."

IDENTIFYING YOUR WORST FEARS AND WORST-CASE SCENARIOS

With each of your stated problems, stretch them into your worst fear and worst-case scenario, and then describe what they would look like.

GOING DEEPER INTO YOUR ABSOLUTE WORST FEAR

Sometimes the "worst fear" you identify is not your absolute worst fear. In order to identify your true worst fear, ask yourself, "If my worst fear came true, what would I fear would happen because of it?"

For example, when going to bed, I can get anxious because I fear if I will not get good enough sleep, and a possible worst fear would be that I didn't sleep at all that night, but if I go even deeper, and ask myself "What would I fear would happen if I didn't sleep at all not only for that night but for a week straight?" The answer would be that I would continuously not sleep and as a result of that sleeplessness, I would eventually die.

THE LOGICAL MIND SAYS YOUR WORST FEAR IS NOT REALISTIC

The logical mind will tell you that your worst fear is not possible or realistic. Although your worst fear most often will never happen, you need to identify your worst fear because your logical mind actually creates a worst fear in order to prevent it from happening, because if your worst fear were to come true, it would bring up a core negative feeling (the weed) in you, which your logical mind is designed to help you avoid from feeling. These core negative feelings, although existed before the worst fear or problem ever happened, are not true about who you really are, and are subconsciously controlling how you feel and think.

Worst fear and Worst-case scenario #1:

_____

Worst fear and Worst-case scenario #2:

_____

Worst fear and Worst-case scenario #3:

_____

SOME COMMON WORST FEARS

- A very common worst fear is death. You may experience health anxiety, or poor sleep, all of which leads to the worst fear being death.

- Likewise, you can feel immensely responsible for others, and fear something bad happening to the well-being of your loved ones.

- Others not listening, respecting or agreeing with your desires, opinions or thoughts, making you feel your desires and feelings do not matter.

- Being judged and thus looked down upon by all others; making you feel abandoned and alone because of it. This judgement from others can happen in various scenarios.

  - Social anxiety: say something wrong or nothing at all and others judge you for it.

  - Being exposed as a fraud or hypocrite.

- Completely fail and lose your job or all your money. Or, basically lose it all and become homeless.

  - This can be associated with the worst fear of failing to provide for your family.

- Anxiety and panic attacks that consume you to the point that you will lose yourself, and thus make you feel as though you have no sense of self and are completely worthless.

COACHING DIALOGUE WITH MONICA ON HER WORST FEAR

In regard to Monica's social anxiety, and fear of meeting new people, I ask her to stretch it to her first worst fear – her worst-case scenario – and describe what it looks like:

Monica: The worst-case scenario is they ask to speak to me and ask me a question and I simply have no answer. Even if I should have an answer on a general basis, I tend to freeze. And so when they walk up and they talk to me, I don't know what I'm going to say to them. I don't know where to go from there when they talk to me.

Michael: Let's stretch this even further. So let's say they asked you a question, you have no answer whatsoever, and then you not only don't have an answer, you just completely space out and blank out. If that were to happen, what do you fear would happen because of it?

Monica: Well, definitely being judged. They're going to say I'm looking like an idiot or, "What's wrong with her?!" People think I'm rude a lot because I choose, one, to not speak with them, and two, I have nothing... I don't know. I don't know what to say to them, and so I know that they judge. Many people think I'm rude all the time or I'm angry at them... It's looking like an idiot and them being like, "What is wrong with her??!! Geez!"

Michael: So let's go to the second scenario. You said the anger and frustration are brought up by your husband's hoarding. Stretch this scenario to your worst fear, worst-case scenario. I want you to speak from the place of the emotion of the anger and the frustration.

Monica: The worst-case scenario is he ends up like those hoarders on TV. He has turned my house into a storage unit. The fear is that he will turn my house back into a storage unit and then we'll end up living with filth and grunge and garbage and odds and ends, and we'll end up having to, like, be on that hoarder show, and they have to condemn the house and there's no place to live. And you know, we haven't washed in weeks and it's just disgusting, becoming a monster in itself.

Michael: So if that were to happen, what do you fear would happen because of that?... I'm just giving you an example. I'm not saying this is the case for you, so like if you were on TV, then you would be humiliated on TV.

Monica: I'm humiliated either way. My family knows that he's a hoarder, and they make snide comments about it, and I understand that I'm not my husband. I don't have a problem, but I'm hanging on to somebody who does. Especially a serious problem. I mean, it's pretty bad. His problem is pretty bad.

Michael: It's definitely bad. It definitely is unacceptable. But I just want to know your worst fear, worst-case scenario, and why is that so terrifying for you? Of course, his behavior is unacceptable, but why is him and your house being on Hoarders TV, your worst fear, worst-case scenario?

Monica: Well, if we're on Hoarders TV and the state is threatening to condemn our house and kick us out and shut it down or whatever they do, one, I would lose my place to live, again. Two, we're on TV and I have huge social anxiety, so that's just "no."

And I guess three, you know, if they had to – if the state or city is willing to step in, it must be that bad, like worse than I ever had imagined. Because the thing is, I mean, people come to accept new norms. We accept things as new norms. I don't want to end up turning this into my new norm of my house. I can't have people over. I've never been able to have people over, but I can't have people over. I can't have guests over. I can't have family over. The kids used to get hurt on his stuff.

CHAPTER FIVE:

Feeling about the Self (F.W.P.)

"F" in the PEWF process stands for "Feeling about the Self"

You want to imagine, if your worst fear and worst-case scenario came true, how it would make it feel about who you are. There are three common core feelings that you will uncover in which I will explain in a moment. First off, I want to say these core negative feelings are "weeds" and will claim something extremely negative about you, and although they feel real, they are not true about who you truly are. You need to "cut the head off the snake" by identifying these feelings.

CUTTING THE HEAD OFF THE SNAKE

Let us revisit the PEWF process because P.E.W.F. is the core mechanism of the "thinking mind," the ego, or what I like to call the head of the snake.

The "thinking mind," the head of the snake, tells you to:

Fixate on the "problem,"

Fixate the "emotion,"

Fixate on the "worst-fear" in order to prevent it,

All of which is a coping mechanism designed for you to avoid feeling your core negative feelings, the "weed."

But the issue is, you only avoid something if it were real. Just like if a bear were to run after you, you would obviously run, right? Ask yourself, when you feel these uncomfortable feelings, do you "run" and escape into the abyss of constant thinking and constant doing? If you do, then you are subconsciously saying these negative feelings are true about who you are, that you are a failure, that you are worthless, that you are powerless.

Your whole goal in the PEWF process is to "cut the head off the snake" by identifying these feelings that are subconsciously controlling how you feel and think.

Just by facing your feelings, and feeling them, allows these feelings to lose power and control over you. Feel safe in feeling your feelings, because remember, avoiding pain creates all pain.

F.W.P. (FAILURE, WORTHLESS, OR POWERLESS)

Now you are ready to identify these "weeds" and core negative feelings by imagining if your worst fear or worst-case scenario were to come true, how would it make you feel about who you are and why. Now there are three common core negative feelings that come up, which I call, "F.W.P."

Note: These three core feelings are only general guidelines. It is important to be more specific by answering if your worst fear came true, how would it make you feel about who you are (F.W.P.) and WHY.

"F" STANDS FOR "FAILURE" OR "FAILING OTHERS"

For example, feeling "I'm a failure," or "I failed others."

"W" STANDS FOR FEELING "WORTHLESS" WHICH HAS MANY SUBCATEGORIES:

"I'm alone," "I don't exist," "People don't care about me," "I'm unwanted," "I don't matter," "I'm disrespected, "I'm unappreciated," "I'm abandoned," "I'm betrayed," "I'm unaccepted," and very often the fear death as it can be the most extreme version of worthlessness, because if you die, you cease to exist. Additionally, the fear of being "judged" by all others is a very common one that can make you feel alone, isolated and abandoned.

"P" STANDS FOR "POWERLESS"

There are two forms of feeling powerless. The first form is feeling **"powerless as the protector,"** which is when you feel immensely responsible for others. When you feel responsible for others, know that you cannot use your personal key to drive the vehicle of life for another. In this scenario, you are trying to be in control of something that is out of your control and thereby making you feel powerless.

The second form of powerlessness is always needing to be in control. Ask yourself the following: are you a person that needs to be in control? Do you get uncomfortable, anxious or frustrated and angry when you don't feel like you are in control?

If so, know that, above all else, **control is a coping mechanism** in order to prevent something bad from happening, because if that worst fear were to come true, an uncomfortable feeling would come up. Ultimately, control is a coping mechanism to avoid feeling some negative feeling.

If you defined "powerlessness" as your core negative feeling, ask yourself if you were not in control and completely powerless, what do you fear would happen because of it? And if that were to happen how would that make you feel about who you are? Failure or Worthless? And why?

For instance, a very common example I come across with people who need to be in control is that they need to have things done a certain way, because if they are not, then they feel what they want does not matter and therefore who they are, does not matter.

Neither does control have to be about controlling others. You can seek to be in control over yourself, your thoughts, your anxiety or feelings of panic, and feel powerless because of it.

Seeking perfection is another form of needing to be in control, because if you lost control, you would fail and possibly be worthless because of it. Thus, control is a coping mechanism to avoid this feeling.

Ask yourself whether you seek to be in control. And if so, what do you fear would happen if you were not in control and completely powerless? And if that came true how would that make you feel about who you are?

IF YOUR WORST FEAR CAME TRUE HOW WOULD IT MAKE YOU FEEL ABOUT WHO YOU ARE?

Now go back to each of your stated worst fears and worst-case scenarios and imagine if they came true. How would it make you feel the F.W.P. and why (very important to be specific by answering "why?".)

Some things to take note of:

1. Quite often, you can see a connecting theme of the same feeling to all or several of your worst fears and worst-case scenarios.

2. Remember, all these core feelings sound extremely bad, for example, "I'm a failure," or "I'm worthless" but these feelings are not true about who you really are. You just need to cut the head off the snake and identify and pull out these weeds so they no longer control you on a subconscious level.

3. Once again, try your best to be specific in identifying your core feeling by answering why (For example, why would your worst fear coming true make you feel like a failure, make you feel powerless or worthless?)

Worst fear #1 / Feeling about the Self (and why)

_____

Worst fear #2 / Feeling about the Self (and why)

_____

Worst fear #3 / Feeling about the Self (and why)

_____

MICHAEL'S WORST FEAR EXAMPLE:

My worst fear with terrible and constant insomnia, along with the prominent dark circles under my eyes, was the fear of death. If my worst-fear came true, it initially brought up the feeling that "I failed to protect my family." I have later found that the underlying feeling of failing to protect my family was the feeling that if I were to die I would cease to exist which comes from the feeling of "worthlessness."

The dark circles, not only brought up the fear of death, but also the fear of being judged by others as someone who tries to help others but can't even help himself. I would inevitably look like a hypocrite. More importantly, if I were to be judged by all others, I would be abandoned.

THE DIFFICULTY IN IDENTIFYING THE FEELING OF WORTHLESSNESS

ATTACHING SELF-WORTH TO FAILURE

As was the case in my example, identifying the feeling of "worthlessness" can be challenging because it is a deep-seated feeling that is more painful and thereby hidden to our consciousness. We tend to first identify with the feeling of failure, but underlying this feeling of failure is often worthlessness. You can find yourself attaching your sense of self-worth to your performance, productivity, success, and money. Ultimately, feeling if you fail, then you are worthless. If you are not productive, if you make a mistake, if you lose your money, then again, you are worthless.

CONTROL AND WORTHLESSNESS

As discussed before, the feeling of worthlessness can also be the underbelly feeling of "powerlessness" as well. Very often the need to be in control is tied to needing things to be a certain way and having other people do things the way you want them to be done and if they are not, you can feel not only what you want does not matter but also who you are does not matter.

You may also feel "invisible" or "unappreciated" if your desires are not being seen, heard or respected.

Or maybe you don't like to be told what to do, and what then happens, you get angry because it makes you feel like you don't matter.

ATTACHING SELF-WORTH TO POSSESSIONS

People can often attach their self-worth to their possessions. I am not talking about being flashy with your possessions. For example, if people don't respect your possessions by not putting your possessions where they belong or using them without asking you, it can bother you, because it feels like not only are your possessions being disrespected but who you are is being disrespected. It can be as simple as "who touched my remote?! Who moved my chair?!"

My wife is very much this way. If I borrow one of her pens, which by the way, she is already reluctant to allow in the first place, she will come to me moments later, anxiously and nervously asking me, "Where's my pen??!!"

One time I ate her bag of chips and when she found out she started frantically yelling out my name from the other room (I say this jokingly) as if a family member just died, "Michael!!! Michael!!! Michael!!! Who ate my chips?????!!!!"

POWERLESS AS THE PROTECTOR:

The protector is always trying to protect others from being neglected, mistreated, or also protects others from feeling emotional pain and suffering. Although on the outside, the protector's core pain seems to be feeling responsible for others, it's actually often a feeling of worthlessness within their own selves.

What do I mean? The protector is actually the one feeling worthless and they want to protect others they care about from feeling the worthless feeling that they themselves actually feel all the time. It's easier for them to fix this internal pain and suffering outside of themselves by projecting it on others, rather than have to face the immense and horrendous pain of the worthlessness and self-hate they have for themselves.

As painful as these feelings may be, remember, "feeling is healing," and these feelings are not true about who you really are. You need to cut the head off the snake by first identifying this feeling of worthlessness. Avoiding the feeling by projecting it onto others and then "protecting" them from these feelings you actually feel about yourself, not only doesn't help anyone but most importantly confirms these feelings of worthlessness are true about yourself since you only avoid what is real.

The person you are trying to "protect" very likely does harbor feelings of worthlessness, but be conscious of how your angst to protect them could be coming from protecting them from the feelings of worthlessness you are avoiding within yourself.

My mother constantly does this as she compulsively and obsessively fixates on the health and safety of others to project her fear of death rooted in worthlessness onto others. I, in turn, do the same thing with my wife, and my other loved ones. I can often find myself fixating on the health of others to prevent their poor health and eventual death, which is really just me projecting my intergenerational pain of worthlessness onto others.

I in turn, do this to my wife and my family. I worry about things they are doing that are not good for their health and when they don't listen to my suggestions, I become very anxious and frustrated, because I worry their poor actions will lead to their poor health and ultimately death. But I must remind myself, this pain of worthlessness I feel within myself that I am projecting onto others comes from an intergenerational trauma of abandonment.

THE IDENTITY OF THE SERVANT

There is another revealing aspect of the protector which is the "identity of the servant." The servant feels they must serve, protect or provide for others, especially their loved ones. If they do not or fail to do so, they don't have a reason to exist and thereby feel worthless. The identity of the servant is ultimately a coping mechanism to suppress, avoid, and numb the feeling of worthlessness they feel inside already (although not true about who they really are). I cannot overemphasize enough how common this phenomenon is within our world. I see it every day within my clients and as well as in me personally.

As I am writing this book, I very often feel the immense pressure and fear of making a mistake that would somehow ruin my entire book. My fixation on failure is that if I fail, I won't be able to provide for my family. Interestingly, when I first had sleep issues upon the birth of my son, my initial fear was that if I die then I will fail to protect my family.

If I happen to somehow make a mistake that ends up "ruining" the messaging of my book, the book will have failed and I won't be able to provide for my family and serve others in the way I had hoped. Being a servant to others is how I falsely identify myself. I'm constantly worried about if I said or did the wrong thing to upset, or disappoint others. Because if I fail to serve others, then others have no reason or purpose to be in my life, thereby making me feel all alone, abandoned and worthless as I have no reason to exist. Remember, abandonment is my intergenerational trauma on both my mother's side and my father's side.

I can especially see how I inherited much of this "identity of the servant" from my mother. In fact, when I used to live with my parents, I remember one time my mother talking and yelling at this crazy lady on the phone that my mother had randomly met recently. My mother had already bought her a hotel room and now this lady was wanting my mother to buy her a plane ticket. My mother kept on talking to her, while my father was yelling in the background to get off the phone.

Here is yet another example of my mother being a servant. My father owns a long-standing pharmacy and is well known within the community because of it. My mother wanted to use these many connections to serve others and started a matchmaking service. She feels so responsible for others that she can often invade another's personal space as she tries to overtake the steering wheel of another person's vehicle of life all because she feels she must serve others to feel she has self-worth.

To share another personal example of myself, I find myself often overreacting to how my wife spends our money, even when it's just a matter of a few dollars. The reason being is that without money, I will have failed to provide and serve my family and thereby feel that I do not exist because I identify my very existence as a servant.

I can also find myself feeling obsessed with not wanting to inconvenience others so I choose to swallow my voice and hide my true desires around others. A servant dedicates their whole existence to serving, protecting and providing for others. To a servant, to inconvenience another is to be a burden to another, which is the servant's worst nightmare because the servant dedicates their whole existence to serving, protecting or providing for others.

Don't get me wrong. You are meant to serve others in a way that is far more powerful than you can ever imagine, because it is why you exist. The final phase of the F.I.S.T. process is "T" which stands for transformation. Transformation is about transforming your pain into your source of light, creating your own movie, and answering your calling. Many of my clients, when we get to this stage, will say that "Helping others is my calling." However, you serving and helping others is the aftereffect of you honoring your true self, life's purpose, and your calling. Serving others cannot be the vehicle through which you use to help others, or else you are just being the servant once again in order to mask the feeling of worthlessness you feel inside. The engine to your vehicle of life in which you use to serve and transform others is your calling, life's purpose, and most importantly, the content of your movie.

Take some time to think and ask yourself:

Do you identify yourself as a servant and feel immensely responsible for others?

Do you sacrifice all your needs for the sake of putting the needs of others first? Are you fearful that if you "mess up" and disappoint others that they will no longer have a reason to be in your life because you have failed to serve them?

Do you fixate on the fear of failure and the fear of not being able to provide or protect others?

If you fail to serve and provide for others, will you be all alone, and worthless, because others no longer have any reason to be in your life?

Finally, is this pain of feeling alone, invisible, abandoned, or worthless, the pain of your intergenerational trauma and you featuring yourself in someone else's movie?

COACHING DIALOGUE WITH MONICA ON HER FEELING ABOUT THE SELF:

The following is a dialogue with Monica in order to identify her core feeling in relation to her worst fear of other people judging her and looking down on her:

Michael: So think about if your worst fear came true: you were judged, and people looked down on you, and probably didn't want to be around you or associate with you because of it. How would that make you feel the F.W.P. and why? Failure. Worthless and Powerless. Remember, these feelings are just general guidelines and you want to answer "why?"

Monica: It's probably worthless.

Michael: Worthless, because you would feel alone?

Monica: I desperately want to be friends with people, and I have no friends, but I desperately want a connection with somebody else, and frequently my first impression is awful. Mainly because I'm too shy to say anymore, and they're like, "Well! Nevermind!" So it's the invisible piece of, "I don't matter."

Michael: It's not because "it's the way I'm interacting with others. I don't give a good first impression, which is giving me this experience of feeling alone." I want you to gently reframe because it's not about this situation per se. It's falsely holding onto this feeling of worthlessness and feeling alone that is creating your experiences.

Monica: Of course it is fear of being judged ... so what occurred to me as you were talking about the root of the feeling, I was kind of pondering the feeling a little bit more, and the origin is actually ... I mean, I've had social anxiety and problems talking to people since I was three years old, four years old. I remember trying to ask for a glass of water. And the fear was that I was going to be told no, which you know, a lot of people are like, "Oh, you know, what's the worst they can say? "No," is not going to kill you. I dunno what was so intense about being told the word "no." So I practiced over and over and over (for an hour) asking for a glass of water before I actually asked for the glass of water.

Now we moved onto identifying Monica's core feeling in relation to her worst fear of her husband's hoarding addiction getting completely out of control and being on the Hoarders TV show, leading the state to condemning and then taking away the house:

Michael: Obviously his behavior is unacceptable, but I just want to identify these feelings because once you identify them, how you handle that situation with him, I think will be easier ... So if all of this came true, if your worst fear, worst-case scenario came true, how would that make you feel the FWP and why? Failure, Worthless or Powerless.

Monica: Powerless. (Michael: Because?) I should have made him stop or it shouldn't have gotten to this extent. I should have been in more control and this is my house. This is the only thing I can control besides like, you know, the simplistic things, like, you know, where I go and what I do. There's a lot of limitations to that. My house is my sanctuary, and it's like "You ruined it!"

Michael: You're powerless because you're not in control?

Monica: I'm powerless because I cannot control him. I cannot make it stop.

Michael: Is it like you feel responsible for him?

Monica: Sometimes ... I feel like I have to clean up his messes a lot. I feel like he gets himself in trouble cause he doesn't pay attention from what I can tell and I'm always having to pick up after him, clean up his messes.

Michael: Got it. Got it. So a part of it is just a feeling of powerlessness, just being completely unable to control his behavior, but also you feel powerless as a fixer because you feel responsible for him and no matter what you do, he never listens.

Monica: I've tried to talk to him a million times about his problem. "You need to see a therapist. You have a problem. This is not normal." And it's in one ear and out the other.

Michael: Got it. Alright. I think the other part you said being that you have social anxiety and then having to be on Hoarders TV, you would be exposed, causing the world to judge you.

Monica: Oh yeah! The whole world would know. I don't know if they would send comments and questions. You know, people would know us in the neighborhood, and they would be like, "You were on Hoarders!" or "I saw that house" or whatever. And I mean, people will come out of the woodwork. I know that they do.

Michael: Got it. Got it. Alright, so we identified the core negative feelings.

part three

Separate

CHAPTER SIX

The Gift of High Sensitivity and Emotional Antennas

"S" in F.I.S.T. stands for "separation," meaning separating from what doesn't belong to you. Before I explain what this means, I want to ask you an important question:

> **"If somebody around you is feeling anxious, angry, sad, or depressed, are you able to feel it, sense it or pick up on it?"**

If you answered yes to this question, it means you have the gift and the ability of high sensitivity and high empathy, allowing you to strongly feel what other people feel. Everybody is born with some level of sensitivity because sensitivity is a part of being human, but answering yes to this question, means you are the 1 out of 5 people born with the gift of high sensitivity, allowing you to feel what others feel, much like an X-ray.

CLIENT EXAMPLES OF THE GIFT OF HIGH SENSITIVITY AND HIGH EMPATHY

I asked Angie in a podcast coaching session this question and she answered,

"I went up to somebody the other day at work and I said, 'What's wrong? Are you okay? Like you don't seem like yourself?' And she just looked at me and she just looked away. And then the next day she came up to me, she goes, 'How did you know something was wrong with me?' And I said, 'I could tell.' I just can tell. She didn't say anything. She didn't do anything. She just felt low. And she's like, 'Yeah, my friend passed away yesterday and I just couldn't say those words to you because I would have started crying.' I'm like, 'I'm so sorry.' And like just, you know, so I've got confirmation, but it kinda sometimes sucks, so it sucks up my emotions and it ruins my whole day. Sometimes I can't get out of it."

Here is how Stacey answered this question of high sensitivity and high empathy:

Stacey: *"Absolutely. Yeah. I definitely absorb the energy of any room I walk into."*

Other examples of how people can describe their ability and gift of high sensitivity:

- *"I can read a person's body language."*

- *"When my wife is stressed, I feel it, even if she doesn't say anything because I can see it in her face."*

- High sensitivity not bound by space: Best friend going through a divorce, the pain of loneliness she is going through; *"Just thinking about her, I feel her depression and sadness inside of me."*

- *"I don't just pick up on the energy of others, I internalize it ... I'm sad, and bummed out for the rest of the day."*

A deeper way to understand what "separating from what doesn't belong to you" means, is by pulling up your worst fears and core negative feelings about the self that you have previously identified, and then asking yourself the following question:

"WHOSE MOVIE AM I IN?"

When you go to the movies, no matter how scary or dramatic it may be, you know you will always be okay because you know that it's just a movie.

However, when you are highly sensitive, and you don't use your gift of high sensitivity consciously and correctly, you can unconsciously zap yourself into the movies of others, all the while, thinking it is your own movie.

This is a terribly painful, confusing, and even traumatic experience, because no matter what you try to do, nothing ever works, because it is simply not your movie.

You can find yourself featured in the movies of many people, but it's important to first begin with the people you first ever knew: your parents.

Note: The connections made from this part of the process may not be clear in the beginning, but they will be evident when you complete the process.

CHAPTER SEVEN:

Applying the PEWF Process to Your Parents

You are going to apply the PEWF process to both of your parents and begin with the parent that is more emotionally expressive.

Note on deceased parents, non-present biological presents, step-parents and adoptive parents:

Your parents may have already passed, been largely absent from your life, or completely absent from your life (a biological parent that you only met a handful of times or never met at all). Still, try to apply the P.E.W.F. process by picking up the pieces through the stories you heard about them. Also, if you were raised by a step-parent or parents that adopted you, I would like you to apply the P.E.W.F. process to them as well, in addition to your biological parent. If you were raised by a caretaker (who was your family member like a grandparent) apply the PEWF process to them as well.

Note on wanting to improve relationships with your partner:

If you are wanting to improve the well-being of your relationship with your partner, it is extremely beneficial to apply the PEWF process to both sets of your parents together with your partner. This will allow you to see whose pain exactly is causing all the commotion and turmoil within the relationship.

Note on improving the well-being of your child:

If you are wanting to improve the well-being of your child, now you will be applying the PEWF process to yourself; the parent. Afterward, you will be applying the PEWF process to both sets of your child's grandparents (your parents and your spouse's parents.

I will talk about this in greater detail later on, but it is tremendously powerful to apply the PEWF process onto your grandparents which will be your child's great-grandparents. Understanding the 1st through the 4th generations will help you uncover this hidden yet powerful connecting weave through all four generations.

APPLYING THE PEWF PROCESS TO YOUR PARENTS

Begin with the parent that is more emotionally expressive. Now, identify, in that parent which emotions they experience out of anxiety (worry or fear), anger (or frustration), and depression (or emotional suppression).

_____

_____

P.E.: Identify a problem or situation that brings up strong feelings of anxiety, worry or fear (skip if this doesn't apply and list two if it applies)

_____

_____

_____

W: Stretch that problem into your parent's worst fear and worst-case scenario and describe what that would look like. (At this point there are people who can second guess themselves and feel they can't really say what their parent's worst fear is because they have not explicitly expressed it, but remember you have the gift of high sensitivity and high empathy, so use your intuition to apply the PEWF process onto your parents).

_____

_____

_____

_____

F: If your parent's worst fear(s) came true, how would it make them feel the F.W.P. (Failure / Worthless / Powerless) and why:

_____

_____

_____

_____

P.E.: Identify a problem or situation that bothers your parent which brings up strong feelings of anger or frustration (skip if this doesn't apply and list two if more than one problem applies).

_____

_____

_____

_____

W: Stretch that problem into your parent's worst fear and worst-case scenario and describe what that would look like:

_____

_____

_____

_____

F: If your parent's worst fear came true, how would it make them feel the F.W.P. (Failure / Worthless / Powerless) and why:

_____

_____

_____

_____

Note: When applying the PEWF process onto someone you believe is narcissistic, remember that a narcissistic person has to make everything about themself, and they need to keep doing so because they need to fill up the void and bottomless pit they feel within themselves, which is rooted in a feeling of worthlessness.

Now, we will move onto the coaching dialogue between myself and Monica, during which I am applying the PEWF process onto her parents and beginning with her more emotionally expressive parent.

COACHING DIALOGUE WITH MONICA ABOUT HER PARENTS:

MONICA'S FATHER (THE MORE EMOTIONALLY EXPRESSIVE PARENT)

Michael: So with your father, what emotion does he experience out of anxiety, anger, and depression?

Michael: I think it's all three. I think anxiety is number one, and depression is next.

Michael: So what problem or situation brings up strong feelings of anxiety, worry, or fear in him?

Monica: I think his lack of control. He raised my brother and I, and we're not doing what he thinks that we should be doing.

Our lives are not fitting in the pattern that they're supposed to. And I think he feels powerless in the sense that he cannot move mountains and make us do X, Y, and Z to have the ideal life. We don't have ideal lives. My brother's never been married ... I have five kids. I had five kids by the time I was 22 and married.

I've been married 21 years with a lot of ups and a lot of downs, and I was supposed to go to college, and I was supposed to get a degree. I was supposed to buy a house. I was supposed to get a picket fence and a dog and have two kids. I was supposed to be a millionaire by now or financially set. I wasn't supposed to be having all the struggles.

I've had a lot of struggles, A LOT, and my brother, you know, "he's a failure to launch." He's been living with my father for probably 18 years. He's got no kids. He's an alcoholic. My father's an alcoholic. He got a high school diploma finally in the last five years. He doesn't have a college degree. He doesn't have a house. He doesn't have children, a wife. We're just not the ideal family in his eyes.

MONICA'S FATHER'S WORST FEAR AND FEELING ABOUT THE SELF:

Monica: I think his worst fear is that we will financially become so screwed. I only have one child left at home. But we'll become financially so screwed we'll be living under a bridge, we'll be begging for money, we'll be flat broke, we'll be, you know, walking around everywhere, homeless. Just living under the bridge and being the bum, the one that stands on the side of the road and begs for money. That type of low. Not just homeless, but like lower.

Michael: If your father's worst fear came true, how would it make him feel the F.W.P. and why?

Monica: Failure. He would feel like a failure as a parent. We didn't get the message. He did something wrong.

Michael: Got it. And probably feel powerless too because he feels immensely responsible for your well-being.

Monica: Oh yeah! He still does. And I'm 39 years old and I'm like, "Really???"

THE MORE EMOTIONALLY SUPPRESSIVE PARENT

Remember, the emotionally suppressive parent may seem emotionless, but really dig deep and identify in that parent which emotions they experience out of anxiety (worry or fear), anger (or frustration), and emotional suppression/depression. Really emphasize and uncover problems or situations which bring up strong feelings of worry, fear and frustration in your emotionally suppressive parent, as these are all forms of suppressing our emotions.

_____

_____

P.E.: Identify a problem or situation that brings up strong feelings of anxiety, worry, or fear in your parent.

_____

_____

_____

_____

W: Stretch that problem into your parent's worst fear and worst-case scenario and describe what that would look like.

_____

_____

_____

_____

F: If your parent's worst fear came true, how would it make them feel the F.W.P. and why (Failure / Worthless / Powerless)

P.E.: Identify a problem or situation that brings up strong feelings of anger or frustration in your parent.

W: Stretch that problem into your parent's worst fear and worst-case scenario and describe what that would look like.

F: If your parent's worst fear came true, how would it make them feel the F.W.P. and why (Failure / Worthless / Powerless)

_____

_____

_____

_____

Note: *the parent that is more emotionally suppressive possibly may have a deeper or more secretive impact on you. Because that parent consciously suppresses how they feel, the impact they have on you is an unconscious one, making it hard for you to make a conscious connection.*

MONICA'S MOTHER: THE EMOTIONALLY SUPPRESSIVE PARENT

Michael: With your mother, what emotion does she experience out of anxiety, anger, and depression?

Monica: Probably anger. My mother is non-expressive besides criticism.

Michael: What problem or situation brings up strong feelings of anger or frustration in her?

Monica: Control. She wants to control everything and everybody. She wants absolute control. She did it to me as a child. She's does it to me still ... My mother is, "I want to control what you say, what you do, where you're at, where you've been, what you do with your life, what choices you make. I want to control it all."

Michael: You painted a really good picture, but I always like hearing specific examples. Can you give me a specific example?

Monica: If I don't pick the right clothes, she gives me other clothes to go try on. If it's Easter and I'm not dressed up, she tells me I need to go get dressed up. She's heavily religious. If I don't do something with my kids, she'd be like, "Monica!!! Why don't they have shoes on?!" Or "How come they didn't do this?" Or "How come you didn't put a backpack on them or a jacket on them? It's 59 degrees out here!" Just these goofy specifics that you're like, "Who cares?!"

In coaching Monica we came to identify her mother's worst fear as nobody ever listening to her.

Monica: She needs somebody to listen to her. She wouldn't feel important. She wouldn't feel valued, I think is one of her big needs in life. If she doesn't have it, it's the end of the world. She needs to be heard, have somebody listen to her, for her to tell somebody what to do. And if she still has nobody to control, she has my daughter. She controls her.

Michael: So if her worst fear, worst-case scenario were to come true, and nobody were to listen to her ... If nobody listened to what she told other people to do, and if they just didn't listen to her in general, or talk to her, or give her time and attention. And if her worst fear came true, how would that make her feel the F.W.P. and why? Failure, worthless or powerless?

Monica: She would definitely feel powerless, which would be the end of the world for her. She likes to feel in control.

Michael: But something I'd like to explore with you. Normally we like to be in control because we want to prevent our worst fear from happening, something bad happening. So, like, it's a coping mechanism. And if she's not in control and other people are not doing what she wants or they're not listening to her, it sounds like she would feel worthless.

Monica: She would definitely feel out of control. I think ultimately, maybe, she would feel worthless. She would feel abandoned. She would feel like nobody's listening to her and she's lost her importance. My mother's a schoolteacher. She's used to having that control over people and places. I mean, if she's not controlling somebody, it's the end of the world.

Michael: Yes, that sense of powerlessness. But underneath that, it sounds like worthlessness because she needs to be listened to. And if she's not, then she feels like she's not valued. And not valued means that she would feel worthless. Obviously this is not true about who she really is, but that's the feeling that she's probably harboring and using control as an obsessive coping mechanism so she doesn't have to feel that underlying feeling.

Monica: She's pretty detached from her emotions, so yeah I would say that...

APPLYING THE PEWF PROCESS TO YOUR NON-PRESENT BIOLOGICAL PARENT, OR STEP-PARENT, OR ADOPTIVE PARENTS

Remember, if you have a biological parent that was virtually absent from your life, step-parents, or parents who adopted you, or maybe your parent(s) passed away when you were young, you will want to apply the PEWF process onto them.

You may question, how could your biological parent that was virtually or completely absent in your life affect you? This speaks to how powerful your emotional antennas can be, as well as how dark family secrets can bleed through the generations.

You will see detailed powerful examples of this later in the book. (If you would like to read ahead, to a particularly powerful example, you can go and read page 188.

You may not be able to apply the PEWF process onto a biological parent because you never knew of them, but you very likely knew stories about them which will be key missing links in uncovering your intergenerational trauma. You will learn how to uncover intergenerational trauma in the second half of the "separation" phase in the FIST process.

Note: This is a very important part of the process for those of you who have step-parents or adoptive parents. Very often, I see that my clients can be living primarily in the movie of their step-parents or adoptive parents.

Now identify in that parent which emotions they experience out of anxiety (worry or fear), anger (or frustration), and depression (or emotional suppression).

_____

_____

P.E.: Identify a problem or situation that brings up strong feelings of anxiety, worry, or fear (List two if applies and skip if doesn't).

_____

_____

_____

_____

W: Stretch that problem into your parent's worst fear and worst-case scenario and describe what that would look like.

_____

_____

_____

_____

F: If your parent's worst fear(s) came true, how would it make them feel the F.W.P. (Failure / Worthless / Powerless) and why:

_____

_____

_____

_____

P.E.: Identify a problem or situation that bothers your parent which brings up strong feelings of anger or frustration (skip if this doesn't apply and list two if more than one problem applies).

_____

_____

_____

_____

W: Stretch that problem into your parent's worst fear and worst-case scenario and describe what that would look like:

_____

_____

_____

_____

F: If your parent's worst fear came true, how would it make them feel the F.W.P. (Failure / Worthless / Powerless) and why:

_____

_____

_____

_____

THE EMOTIONAL ANTENNAS EXERCISE

Now that you have identified your core negative feelings and that of your parents, begin to notice the similarities between your feelings and your parents' feelings.

Find an object with significant weight and place it on your lap (preferably not a cell phone) where at the same time you do not have to hold it with your hands.

Remember when I asked if you can sense the negative emotions of others? This was me really asking if you possess the gift of high sensitivity. In fact, this gift and ability of high sensitivity and high empathy is what I call "emotional antennas."

Just for fun, take your two index fingers, your emotional antennas, and put them on both sides of your head, as depicted in the picture below, for a few seconds, and then place them down.

Your emotional antennas allow you to feel what other people feel. Even though when you put your hands down, your emotional antennas are always there because you were born with them.

Now, I want you to take a moment to close your eyes (Read each paragraph first and then close your eyes and apply what you read).

Your true emotional antenna is your body because your body is the channel through which you feel the feelings of others, internalize them, and store them. Now, I want you to feel all the negative emotions, worst fears, and core negative feelings (recall the specific ones you identified through the PEWF process) within your body and then transfer it all into this weight and object on your lap. Transfer every last drop of it. After you have transferred it all:

I want you to reframe all these negative emotions, worst fears, and core negative feelings as the "emotional signals" you picked through your emotional antennas from your parents since you were a child.

Allow this newfound awareness to settle and sink in within your body.

IMPORTANT: It's important to keep your eyes closed and go back to each of your originally stated negative emotions, worst fears, and core negative feelings and see how they are your parents' feelings and how you are casted in their movies.

Pull up each and every one of your worst fears and core negative feelings and then ask yourself "Whose movie are you in?" Are you in your mother's movie? Father's movie? Step-parent's movie?

Worst Fear and Core Negative Feeling #1: Whose movie are you in?

_____

Worst Fear and Core Negative Feeling #2: Whose movie are you in?

_____

Worst Fear and Core Negative Feeling #3: Whose movie are you in?

_____

You can also accomplish this by matching all the feelings up together to see if you and your parents share the same feelings.

To give you an example, I was working with a teenager (the identifying markers have been changed to preserve the client's anonymity) who feared social situations because he was worried he would be judged for saying the wrong thing. When applying the PEWF process to his parents, this fear of being judged did not naturally come up, but when I asked the client if any of his parents had the fear of being judged, he said yes. His father had a fear of being judged at work. He felt like he didn't connect with his co-workers and worried if he was being judged and that there was something wrong with him.

On the other hand, the child's mother owned her own hair salon and would get very frustrated when her employees did not listen to her because it made her feel like she did not matter. This phenomenon of not being listened to and not mattering because of it, did not come up for the child initially when I was applying the PEWF process onto him. I then asked the child if he ever felt this way and he revealed yes. When he would ask friends for favors and if others did not say yes or if they did not do the favor in the specific way he wanted to, then he would get frustrated because it made him feel like he did not matter.

MONICA'S EMOTIONAL ANTENNAS EXERCISE

Below is the dialogue I had with Monica with her eyes still closed after the emotional antennas exercise.

Michael: So what does this all mean? That social anxiety of "What if I'm judged and if I am judged, I would be alone. Nobody would want to be around me... If I am on Hoarders TV, I'd be humiliated in front of the world, judged by the world. Nobody would want to be around me. I'd be worthless because I'm alone." That is you feeling your mother's feelings. That's you being in your mother's movie because she needs to be in control. She needs for other people to listen to her, and if you don't in any single way, it brings up, and it triggers feelings of worthlessness.

But she just masks it, and copes with it all through the obsessive need to be in control.

Monica: Wait, so you are saying that I feel her emotion of worthlessness and within myself?

Michael: Yes. You're living in her movie, when you're thinking and fixating on a social situation. The social anxiety of "What if I'm judged? If I'm judged, I would be an outcast. I would be abandoned. I would be alone. I would be worthless." This is her feeling. The core feeling is worthlessness, feeling alone, and not feeling loved. That's her core feeling. But because when we internalize other people's feelings, pains, fears, and trauma, we internalize it into our life.

That's not our stuff, but we can't fix what doesn't belong to us. So we have to create a fear in our life to make sense of it. Because what you're experiencing with this social anxiety. This stuff is not yours, but you have to create something to make sense of it. Right? (Monica: Right) You know, like, my mother has health anxiety and she fixates on health and safety because she fears death because of the wartime trauma and the intergenerational pain of being abandoned. And then I've internalized that, and I fixate on the fear of not getting good enough sleep, so when I don't sleep well, I fear I will die, and I'll be worthless because I cease to exist. But it's not my stuff, so I have to create this fear of not sleeping well.

Monica: I see, that makes sense.

Michael: Okay, so with your husband and feeling powerless, thinking like "Oh my God!" once he shows you another container, another container, and another container, and all this anger immediately shoots up in you thinking, "Oh my God!" You try to talk to him, you try to clean up after him. You feel all of this because you feel responsible for him.

Monica: I do.

Michael: But you're using your personal key to drive his vehicle of life. And that's you being in your father's movie. Because his worst fear is for his children to become homeless and if that were the case, he would feel like he failed his children, he failed as a parent and he feels powerless as a fixer.

I'm not saying that his (Monica's husband) behavior is acceptable in any way.

Of course, it's not. But when you can identify these core negative feelings, know that you're in your father's movie, then how you handle that situation, will be that much different.

Monica: Okay. That makes sense. I never really thought about it in that way. Yeah. Especially with hoarding and my reaction to it.

WHOSE MOVIE ARE YOU IN EXERCISE

Take a moment to close your eyes once again and visualize a miniature movie screen in front of your eyes. From the place in your body that your felt your pain (throat, heart, stomach), project that energy onto the miniature movie screen in front of your eyes and first visualize the scene of you in it, feeling the negative emotions, core negative feelings and worst fears you identified through the PEWF process, and then change the scene and see your parents feeling the same feelings and you will truly see whose movie are you in.

Enjoy this healthy separation as you are using your incredible gift of emotional antennas consciously and correctly by watching the movie and not subconsciously zapping yourself into someone else's movie as your own.

YOU MUST SEPARATE FROM THIS PAIN TO TRULY HELP OTHERS

You must first separate from this emotional pain that doesn't belong to you, in order to help others in the most powerful way and regain the peace, joy and power of who you are because ...... (and I want you to say this out loud right now):

"I am not an emotional sponge, but a source of light."

You have to separate from this pain that does not belong to you in order to shine the light of your true self to truly help others in the most powerful way.

However, when you misuse your gift of high sensitivity and high empathy and internalize the feelings of others as your own, these feelings seep into your personal space (that weight and object on your lap) and become your **emotional kryptonite that breaks you down physically, emotionally and mentally. It turns your life into the living nightmare it feels like right now.**

Note: If you don't know what kryptonite is, kryptonite is a certain stone that came from the planet that Superman was originally from. When Superman is around this stone, he loses all his power, becomes extremely weak, and will eventually die if he is around the kryptonite long enough. You have a similar effect when you misuse your emotional antennas and internalize the feelings of others as your own. Your physical self won't die, but your spiritual soul experiences a sense of death, until you awaken and separate yourself from this movie that does not belong to you.

"HOW DO I KNOW WHAT FEELINGS ARE MINE?"

Sometimes my clients who although clearly see how they carry the same feelings as their parents, ask me how do they know when the feelings they feel are theirs or someone else's? They wonder if they are assuming the victim mentality by just saying their negative feelings are helplessly "caused by another" but to take them on as their own through their gift of emotional antennas.

First of all, you want to respect the tremendous magnitude of your emotional antennas and see how can you not, as a child, take on the unresolved feelings of your parents as your own.

How you best find out what belongs to you, is found in the last phase of the F.I.S.T. Process, which is "T" standing for "true self" and "transformation." This final phase is about answering your calling and fulfilling your life's purpose. When you ask yourself, "What belongs to me and what belongs to others?", you can undoubtedly claim your calling as yours because it is the very reason why you exist.

S.A.M.

You are probably noticing that the object is still sitting on your lap.

The question is . . . .

How do you separate from this pain that has become your false identity and has consumed your life to the point that it feels like a part of your left arm?

We will do an exercise now that will help with that, but before you proceed I want to forewarn that this exercise will include a little playful cussing. This exercise is called S.A.M.

"S.A.M."
STANDS FOR
"SHIT AIN'T MINE"

What does that mean? That means that these negative emotions, worst fears, and core negative feelings do not belong to you. They belong to your parents.

It is important to note that when you say "S.A.M," you are not saying it to your parents, but rather, to yourself.

When you are ready, place this object off of your lap and across an imaginary health line of separation separating your personal space and personal space of your parents, and as you do so, say out loud **"Shit ain't mine"** (You can say "stuff ain't mine" instead, if you are a child doing this exercise or if you are not comfortable with playful cussing).

As you are placing this object across the healthy line of separation, feel your body, your true emotional antenna, separating from all these negative emotions, worst fears, and core negative feelings that do not belong to you.

Once again, you are not an emotional sponge. Don't misuse your gift of emotional antennas and live in the nightmare of other people's movies as your own. You absolutely don't help anybody that way, and you only make your life the living nightmare that it feels like right now.

It's time to use your incredible gift consciously and correctly, not as an emotional sponge but a source of light, because that's who you are: light. That's who we all are. By releasing the pain that does not belong to you and separating from the movies of others, your light is activated. Your light is your reason for existence. Do not deny the infinite power and beauty of why you were created, because doing so only denies others of the impact you were meant to give them.

Say it now:
"Shit ain't mine. Shit ain't mine"

and let this be your national anthem and your daily mantra, because the pain of others is so much embedded in you that you need this constant daily practice of reminding you that this shit ain't yours.

In no way does "shit ain't mine" mean you don't care about others and you are kicking them out of your life. "Shit ain't mine" means the release of ownership of what does not belong to you. Releasing what does not belong to you activates your greatest power to help others because your light shines brightly once you release what is not yours from your body, your true emotional antenna.

Tell yourself once again "Shit ain't mine" and feel the immediate release of this emotional kryptonite of the pain of others from your body and personal space and feel the activation of your light expanding limitlessly and feel the infinite power of it all.

Close your eyes now, and physically stretch your arms out wide as if you were spreading your wings like an eagle and allowing your soul to elevate and to soar to the heavens. In this state, nothing is impossible. In this state, the impossible becomes completely possible.

Activate your light, by simply releasing ownership of what does not belong to you. That is what "shit ain't mine" is all about, activating your light. Now, truly feel the limitless expansion of the beacon of light that you are and were created to be.

TAKE A MOMENT TO DIGEST IT ALL

You are doing some amazing work here! But we have only just begun. You have now completed the first half of "separation" in the F.I.S.T. Process. Before you continue on to the next section, I want you to take some time, at the very least a few moments, or a day or two if you need it, to process, digest, and feel everything that you have gained and healed thus far. You are doing some major deep healing and you need time to digest it all and very importantly apply it before proceeding.

TWO LEVELS OF PAIN

"How is this pain not mine and not caused by the abuse of others?"

You may question this phenomenon of living in your parents' movie because you feel that it was the abuse, neglect or mistreatment that you received from your parents, that has caused your pain. This is not, in any way, meant to invalidate what has happened to you. To give you a personal example, my wife has a terrible concept of time. On our second date she was 40 minutes late. Additionally, although she is very loving to me, she can have the strong tendency to be very focused and fixated on herself. Therefore, when she is late, or exhibits self-centered behavior, it makes me angry because I feel like I don't matter. Although this feeling is not true about who I really am, it was there before I ever met her.

Should her behavior change? Yes, but it's not the primary cause of my feelings of not mattering as her behavior is only bringing these feelings to the surface so I can have the opportunity to be free of it.

When you are focused on your parents' mistreatment or abuse of you as the primary source of your pain, I want to remind you that there are two levels of pain. The first level of pain is how a parent mistreats a child. The second level of pain which is the core level of pain, is the pain that the child subconsciously internalizes from their parents as their own. This pain is often greater because it not only is completely subconscious but you cannot fix this pain that you falsely think is yours because it does not belong to you.

Although your parents may have been abusive, controlling, or even narcissistic, their toxic and narcissistic behaviors were rooted in a pain of feeling worthless. When they are abusive, they are secretly abusive to themselves. When they are controlling you, it is because if what they want does not matter, then who they are does not matter. Lastly, when they are narcissistic, they make everything about themselves because they feel a never-ending void within themselves. It is this feeling of worthlessness that is being inherited and passed down through the generations.

A POWERFUL EXAMPLE OF THIS IS SCOTTIE:

Scottie's mother committed suicide less than a year ago, which was her 14th and obviously final attempt. Scottie is terrified that her loved ones will die. Her husband has sleep apnea and she will wake him up in the middle of the night to see if he is still alive or check to see if he is still breathing.

Scottie says she experiences angry feelings towards her mother for taking her life. Scottie was there for her mother her whole life as her personal therapist and she felt angry for her mother leaving her like that despite all that she had sacrificed for her since she was a child. Interestingly, these feelings of abandonment by her mother's suicide was actually Scottie internalizing her mother's feelings as her own.

Scottie's mother was sexually, physically, and verbally abused by her step-father, and her own mother (Scottie's grandmother) knew about it all. However, she told Scottie's mother "not to make trouble for the family" because she had been through many marriages and this was her last shot and didn't want to be alone.

Although a big part of Scottie's mother feeling alone was due to her mother not protecting her in this most critical time of her life, the more hidden and possibly more impactful aspect was that Scottie's grandmother felt so alone that she chose not to protect her daughter due to her deathly fear of being alone; and it is this fear of being alone and abandoned that is being inherited throughout the generations.

The reason why Scottie's grandmother felt so alone and abandoned was because her father died when he was 8-9 years old from Lou Gherig's disease; which explains why Scottie is so fearful of her loved ones dying, explaining why she wakes up her husband in the middle of the night to see he is still alive.

Due to Scottie's mother's mental illness, Scottie lived with her grandmother, thus probably setting up the circumstances for Scottie to internalize her grandmother's pain that much more.

As horrifying as it was for Scottie's grandmother to choose not to protect her daughter from the sexual abuse, the greatest pain that Scottie's mother and Scottie herself experienced was the core pain of loneliness they subconsciously internalized from Scottie's grandmother who lost her father as a child to Lou Gherig's disease.

CHAPTER EIGHT:

Intergenerational Trauma Healing

REDEFINING "TRAUMA"

You have now reached the second half of separation, which is about intergenerational trauma healing. When we hear the word "trauma" we normally think of sexual, physical and verbal abuse, but the word "trauma" encapsulates a very wide spectrum. On top of that, these well-known forms of traumas, when they happen, we eventually know that it was wrong. Additionally, the trauma of living in the movies of others as your own is traumatic because no matter what you do in this movie, nothing changes, because it does not belong to you. Your pain becomes that hologram that no matter what you do to fix it, your hands go right through it time and time again.

INTERGENERATIONAL TRAUMA HEALING

Now that you have identified your parents' core feelings, it is important to know that your parents' feelings were there even before you were born. The question I want to ask you is what past family trauma or societal trauma (i.e. War, The Great Depression, Communism) that happened either in your parents' childhood or more so to their own parents (your grandparents) or even possibly great grandparents, that could have planted the seed to your parents' feelings. Remember, it could also be a trauma that happened to an aunt, uncle, or sibling.

Something to take note of is that intergenerational trauma doesn't have to be a singular event. It can be a few traumatic events and subsequent feelings that you are unknowingly harboring within yourself.

YOU CAN FEEL INTERGENERATIONAL TRAUMA IN YOUR GUT

When you identify the true intergenerational trauma, the trauma of just talking about the event should hit you in your gut where you can feel it. For example, some clients will tell me their parent's pain of feeling worthless and neglected comes from being the youngest child in a very big family. Negative events are not necessarily traumas. When you identify the intergenerational trauma you should be able to feel it in your gut because you can feel its pain.

As you begin uncovering your intergenerational trauma, know that the connection that will be made in this part of the process will not happen immediately as it will take a lot of digging.

COMMON EXAMPLES OF INTERGENERATIONAL TRAUMA

Below are some examples of different experiences of trauma that your past family members could have experienced. Remember when connecting the dots, not only think of your parents' childhoods but think of your grandparents, even great-grandparents, as well as aunts or uncles. Neither do you want to exclude biological parents that were not a part of your life, step-parents, or parents who adopted you.

- The trauma of losing parents to death at an early age and feeling alone because of it. Or, the trauma of a child being entirely severed from their family due to war or communism.

- The trauma of communism. This trauma is a very common one, because communism creates the trauma of losing all your wealth and assets, family separation, tragic murders at the hands of communism. This includes the trauma of:

- The trauma of losing the entire family's wealth making one feel like an absolute worthless failure. (as mentioned, can often be tied to the trauma of communism)

- The trauma of the Great Depression. This trauma is a very common one. During the Great Depression, people lost it all and all they had left was their image. Their image was only the thing they had left through which to create a sense of self-worth.

- Wartime trauma: witnessing, fleeing and escaping death, murder, or starvation. Additionally, the trauma of fighting in war and seeing your colleagues die and not being able to protect them but also having to kill people from the other side because it was a kill or be killed situation.

- Societal trauma creating a world of death, violence, murder, and/or starvation.

  - The trauma of the Great Chinese Famine during 1959-1962 where there was a complete shortage of food across the entire country since agriculture was made illegal. This led to 36 million deaths just from starvation, 40 million deaths for failed births. People were even forced to resort to cannibalism just to survive.[3]

  - The Partition of India in 1947 leading to the violent deaths of 1-2 million people.

- The trauma of family secrets. I will speak more about this later, but family secrets bleeds through the family and in turn, bleed through the generations. By making a trauma more secretive, the trauma becomes more impactful.

- The trauma of certain religions, where if you did anything "wrong" in the eyes of the church, you would be permanently and publicly excluded. This trauma is an extremely common one.

- The trauma of a child being sexually abused by another family member, and the parent(s) not protecting their child because of their own insecurities (i.e. fear of being judged or the fear of being alone if it was their partner who molested their child)

- The trauma of a tragic family death or having a close family member murdered. (i.e. In the beginning of the book, we talked about Tia's aunt being murdered by her husband who was also a serial killer)

- The trauma of a spouse having an affair and even secretly having another family as a result of that affair.

- The trauma of a child being given away (i.e. orphaned) by their parents due to lack of finances and already having too many children.

> • The trauma of a child being entirely severed from their family due to the conditions of war.

USING THE PEWF PROCESS TO UNCOVER THE INTERGENERATIONAL TRAUMA

To uncover your intergenerational trauma, it takes a lot of digging and excavating and doesn't happen immediately. If you can already begin to uncover the intergenerational trauma, that is great. However, at first, we normally are not able to identify the intergenerational trauma. In this case, it is extremely helpful to first identify the core negative feelings in, for example, your grandparents, by applying the PEWF process onto them.

After you have identified your grandparents' core negative feelings, you can then ask yourself what past family or societal trauma could have planted the seed to these feelings. Remember, you will want to uncover a traumatic event and experience that hits you in your gut.

Note for young families: if you are a young family completing the FIST process, you can continue to apply the PEWF process to yourself, the parent, and then you will be able to see where your child's feelings may be coming from, and then ultimately tying that back to the intergenerational trauma of your parents or even grandparents (which would your child's great-grandparents). As discussed before, doing this is a very powerful process, because by understanding all four generations, you can see a powerful connecting thread throughout the generations.

Take some time to try to uncover your intergenerational trauma, but as you do so, reflect on the following many stories of people I coached for my podcast and this book in doing this intergenerational trauma healing work. Reading these stories will give you powerful insights and examples which will help you uncover what may be lurking in your family's past. The first story I will begin with, is by continuing where we left off with Monica's example.

WHOSE MOVIE ARE YOU IN ?

COACHING DIALOGUE WITH MONICA ABOUT INTERGENERATIONAL TRAUMA HEALING

In my second session with Monica, right before we dove deep into her intergenerational trauma healing and the origin of her parents' feelings, she brings up how she is completely at a loss about whether to complete her nursing studies or not and has no idea why. I included this part of the dialogue because it is intimately related to Monica's intergenerational trauma.

Monica: What I did want to focus on is that I am literally split down the middle, fifty fifty, on a decision to become a nurse. I'm already an EMT. I've been one for 15 years, and the next natural step seems to be nursing, but I can't quite seem to pull the trigger, and I've actually got all my nursing classes done, prerequisite-wise. I just need to get into a program, which I technically have done, but it's more of I can't commit, and I don't know why. It's literally fifty fifty. I mean, everything is ... is split all the way down the middle in terms of why I should and should not stay or continue.

And I do wonder if I'm doing it for the wrong reasons, and why I'm doing it. Why am I, you know, why am I truly pursuing this career? I'm literally split down fifty fifty on whether I should continue pursuing it. I know I'm tired of school. I've been at this for a long seven years. I think, from the very bottom to where I'm at now, which is an educated idiot. A lot of education, no degree.

Michael: Got it, and this lack of decision...?

Monica: It's ruining my marriage. It's dragged me cross country. I've moved to different places out of my hometown just to pursue it, and I still can't pull the trigger.

It has a huge impact. My husband wants me to finish. He wants me to complete it. It's just definitely taken a toll. Last semester, I took five classes and I almost literally lost my sanity in the process. And I mean, they were intense, and I couldn't work because I took on too much schoolwork.

And so it's the push-pull of "you need to work," "but I can't, I'm in school." And "you know we're financially struggling." "I know, but I can't, I'm in school." It just messes with my marriage. It messes with, you know, where I'm headed, what I'm doing, and I really need to nail down what is my driving force against and what is my driving force for.

Michael: Got it, got it. So this situation or the lack of decision is bringing up what emotion in you, out of anxiety, anger, or depression?

Monica: There's definitely anxiety. I'm not strong on my math skills and it scares me to death. I mean, it scares me beyond anything that I will kill a patient because I can't ... I mean. It's not that I don't try my math. It's not that I don't want to. It's that it literally evades me and it scares me to death that I'm going to kill a patient because I didn't shift a zero. I didn't add a thousand. I didn't change it from point A to point B, microgram to milligram, and on and on and on.

Michael: Let's say you – and this is hypothetically speaking and for the sake of identifying your core negative feelings – let's say if you did kill somebody, what do you fear would happen because of it?

Monica: I think it depends on what happened. I mean, I could definitely go to jail, lose my license, be sued by the family, be hated by the family. I mean, I would feel immense, immense guilt. Like maybe I would take my life. Immense guilt. It would be that intense.

I mean, I'm not a suicidal person, but I think it would reach that level, if I didn't get it in check, by taking my own life. That the guilt would be that much. There would be that much responsibility on my head.

After explaining to Monica what intergenerational trauma is, I ask her what intergenerational trauma all her feelings of immense and horrifying guilt for others could be coming from. Monica first mentions that her father was a baby boomer born in the era of responsibility, during which responsibility to family and God was of supreme importance. However, this experience is not a true trauma. Like I tell other clients, when you uncover intergenerational trauma, you should feel an "oomph!" feeling in your gut because you can just feel its pain. This following dialogue is where we begin to uncover the intergenerational trauma for Monica's grandfather.

Monica: I guess, you know, my father's father was actually a full-blown alcoholic and my father is as well. But he quit drinking cold turkey because I think he either did or nearly killed a pregnant woman driving drunk.

I don't remember if he actually killed her. I don't think he did. I think he harmed her or something along those lines.

He quit drinking. Absolutely. Next day. He never touched it again.

You can see already how this incident is tying back to the failed responsibility that Monica's father feels towards his children. However, despite that, there seems to be much more underlying this, since Monica's grandfather was already a full-blown alcoholic prior to this incident, and his alcoholism is the act of numbing a pain you will soon find out. I then continue to ask Monica why her own father drinks and why is he is an alcoholic, and she says it's because of his two failed marriages and that both of his wives left him due to his alcoholism. But I offer the question to Monica about whether her father's alcoholism is still numbing some kind of pain, and I wondered if it was due to the trauma of her grandfather harming and almost killing the pregnant lady while driving drunk.

Monica: I don't think it's simply because of the trauma of the grandfather. I'm sure it doesn't help. I'm sure it's in there somewhere, but I think the more pressing issue with my dad is the two failed marriages to two failed kids.

Both wives left him because he's a full-blown – he's a functioning alcoholic. The idea of him being a functioning alcoholic is when he was working. He's now retired.

He would get up at 7:00 AM. He'd go to work till 5:00pm, 5:30pm, and then he'd get blitzed and go to bed and get up and do it all over again.

Michael: The alcoholism is just a coping mechanism to avoid feeling (Monica: correct.) some type of negative feeling.

Monica: He seems sad when he gets good and blitzed, and he goes out of his mind, and he just kind of starts zoning off in space. He seems very sad. Super sad ... His alcoholism has affected me tenfold for all these reasons. Because I can't fix them, and I can't change him, and I can't cure him. I want to ... desperately ... I still think I can fix him and cure him, and I am accepting that I cannot. (Monica gets emotional and teary.)

Michael: Let's explore this. I know he feels the sadness, but does he have any anxiety, worry, fear, anger, or frustration?

Monica: I think anxiety, worry and fear.

Michael: Okay. Not the anger and frustration, right?

Monica: He just seems very sad.

Michael: Okay. This sadness is more like giving up and suppressing and numbing what we're feeling ... What problem or situation brings up strong feelings of anxiety, worry, or fear in him?

Monica: Anxiety is about the safety and the well-being of me and my brother ... He worries about – and especially since COVID hit – he worries about my safety tenfold. On a general basis, he worries about how our decisions are going to turn out, and if we are going to be okay, if we are going to be okay when he's gone. (Monica gets emotional.)

Michael: Got it. Got it. So his main pain right now – because his anxiety and his worst fear is like something bad happening to his children ... so he has this immense responsibility and that guilt. (Monica: Right.) That's his main pain. The alcoholism seems to be just the numbing coping mechanism for this feeling, for this feeling of guilt and failing others and failing his family.

Monica: Yeah. He definitely uses it to hide behind.

Michael: So I'm wondering where does this feeling of guilt and failing others come from?

Monica: Well, as I said, you know, he was a baby boomer, so men were breadwinners. Men had a tremendous responsibility, and they were the rock of the family.

Michael: And so why was his father an alcoholic?

Monica: His father was an alcoholic because he came back from World War II broken. Before we named it a thing, it was PTSD. It had to have been. He would talk about the war and odds and ends. He would talk about, you know, the Japanese and Vietnam, and I mean, on and on and on.

Michael: What would he say?

Monica: About killing them and about the death. Then you know about what happened over there...It is ugly, violent, and dangerous to say the least.

Michael: What was his main pain about that experience that he would share with you?

Monica: It would be death – death of fellow soldiers and the native people. Wherever he was at the time, cause he talked about the Japanese, and he also talked about Vietnam.

Michael: Oh, so the people that he had to kill in wartime on the other side?

Monica: People that he knew that died and the people that he had to kill. Because it was kill or be killed.

Michael: Got it. Got it. So close your eyes for a moment. Connect with your body, your true emotional antenna. So that feeling of guilt that you feel, like with nursing – "What if you become a nurse? What if you kill somebody?" – this is stemming from you being in your grandfather's movie, not only with him harming or almost killing that pregnant lady, but also the guilt that he carried in the PTSD of World War II, of not protecting his fellow soldiers and also the guilt of killing native people because it was a kill or be killed situation. And the tremendous guilt and trauma of that, he had to numb it through alcoholism. And your father also lives in that movie and carries that tremendously.

That's why he drinks to cope with the guilt and constantly feeling like he's failing his children, but really, it's just the guilt of his father remembering and experiencing the PTSD of World War II in that kill or be killed situation. (Monica: okay)

Michael: I want you to keep your eyes closed and repeat that mantra that we talked about before. I want you to say it out loud. Connect with all these feelings in your body, but then tell yourself, "I'm not an emotional sponge..." (Monica: I'm not an emotional sponge...) Michael: "but a source of light" (Monica: but a source of light).

This is how powerful your gift is. How incredibly powerful that, through the generations, you are picking it up as if it's happening to you. That thing when you're talking about, "If I become a nurse and make a math miscalculation, and what if I kill somebody?" And if that were to come true, even though you don't have suicidal thoughts, that could push you to the edge, if you didn't manage it.

So you are experiencing your grandfather's trauma in this very moment, and I want you to visualize a miniature movie screen in front of your eyes, and then, when you feel and experience that thought of, "What if I kill somebody?", I want you to visualize your grandfather on that movie screen, in that kill or be killed situation, in that situation where he almost killed a pregnant lady, which probably triggered that trauma of that kill or be killed experience.

Separate from all that doesn't belong to you, outside of your body, outside of your personal space. Tell yourself, "I'm not an emotional sponge but a source of light" and imagine you shining your light onto your father and onto your grandfather saying whatever words that they need to heal. Meaning, "It wasn't your fault, it wasn't your responsibility. You are infinitely loved."

Is there anything you want to say to your father as you're shining your light onto him? You have separated from his pain, and you know it's not yours and it doesn't belong to you. You can now use your gift correctly and consciously by shining your light. Is there anything you want to say to him?

Monica: I'm sorry.

Michael: Sorry for what?

Monica: How he feels about himself, about how he carries on the guilt and the pain day in and day out.

Michael: Well, when you say, "I'm sorry," do you feel bad for him?

Monica: I do.

Michael: Yeah, so you don't want to repeat the cycle by feeling bad because when we feel bad, we feel responsible for others, and that is his core pain, that he felt guilty and responsible for others. And so you don't want to feel sorry for him. You just want to shine your light, but not out of responsibility, just as an expression of who you are as a source of light.

(Michael checking back in with Monica): Any questions? I want to check in with you. Any questions, thoughts, or feelings thus far? (Monica: No.) Okay. Not just about what we discussed, but anything else? Or do you feel good? Do you feel complete for today?

Monica: I feel like I still don't quite have an emotional decision on nursing.

Remember, initially, Monica didn't want to pursue nursing because she was fearful she would kill a patient due to a miscalculation. Monica begins to get lost in her thoughts and overthinking. She shares how she is worrying that if she is doing nursing for the wrong reasons – meaning for reputation, self-worth or money – and questions if she really wants to do nursing in the first place, then she is saying she's actually not very fond of nursing.

Monica: Maybe I'm doing all of this for the wrong reasons?

Michael: It's not about the wrong reasons per se. Okay, let's explore this. Okay, you want that respect. You want to be known and not looked at as a failure. Let's flip the script, by finding out what is your worst fear, worst-case scenario?

Monica: That I don't finish nursing school. I don't finish what I started, and I'm treated by my family and friends ... I mean, they may not say it, but you can feel that look (from them), and what they don't say, their nonverbal communication ... I guess it goes back to being a failure, "She didn't finish what she started."

Michael: So if you failed and you didn't complete your studies, then you won't be accepted by your family members or your inner circle?

Monica: I will be looked down upon by my family. They don't say it, but you can tell ... It's either my fear, or it's what they don't say. Their nonverbal communication. It's a "she didn't finish what she started. I told you she never would get through nursing school."

Michael: But they have never said this? It's their nonverbal communication?

Monica: Right. And it's either that or it's all in my head. I honestly am not sure. My family is very judgmental. (It's like) I cannot do anything ... I don't do anything right. They criticize me.

My mother has always been judgmental and critical. When I was a girl, when I was growing up as a kid, and I was in high school and I was struggling ... you know, we all struggled with what's hot and what's not. And especially as girls, we're trying to do makeup and we're trying to fit in.

We're trying to look cool. And I tried to do makeup and my mother didn't want me wearing makeup. I think I was already 16, and I was experimenting with makeup, and I was playing with it. And I was trying to put it on and ... I had no idea what I was doing! My mother had never helped me. Never, never, never, never, never. We never had any of those talks. She just let me stumble through life. She told me that I looked like a clown because I had messed up my makeup. "It looks awful" or whatever, I don't really know at this point. It's irrelevant. She always put me down.

Michael: How else did she put you down?

Monica: My mother always criticized the way I raised my kids. "They need a jacket. How come you didn't do their hair? Where are their matching socks? How come they're not wearing pants right now?" My mother always was criticizing me instead of speaking from love. It was speaking from embarrassment and bitterness.

Michael: What is her worst fear? Worst-case scenario? If you were to stretch this all the way. I mean, cause obviously, she's critical and judgmental of others because that's how she subconsciously and unknowingly feels about herself. So from that space, what is her worst fear? Worst-case scenario?

Monica: I'm not 100% sure.

Michael: Because it sounds like her criticism and judgment is that you're incompetent. Is that true?

Monica: I would imagine it comes from her mother. Her mother was very – my grandmother was very disconnected. My mother is very disconnected, as far as feelings, and love, and family. I never got love from my mother.

I don't even tell my mother I love her. I don't have any physical affection from her. Never have. So my mother and grandmother are very disconnected. She (Monica's grandmother) was very critical of her children.

Michael: You said your grandmother was very critical of her children?

Monica: Oh yeah. She was critical of me. I couldn't understand her (because Monica's grandmother only spoke Spanish and Monica could not), but you could understand her tone, and she was angry with me all the time. All the time. For my grandmother, looks were everything. Your children had to be clean, their hair done, and in church every Sunday. And they were church-going people.

Michael: So you said looks but also your reputation?

Monica: Oh yeah! It was everything. All that stuff meant the world. It wasn't a matter of your last name. It was a matter of how you looked and how you went out and presented yourself to the world. And if you, let's say that you had four or five children – you know, out of the ten or whatever it is that you had – come back with skinned knees and messed-up hair and dirty clothes. The whole block talked about it, and we were the embarrassment of the world.

So I think my grandmother was very, very hard on her children to be perfect and look good and present their best foot forward in public at all times. They were not allowed to speak English at home because my grandmother couldn't understand them.

Michael: What would be your grandmother's worst fear, worst-case scenario?

Monica: Embarrassment. Looking like a fool, coming back looking like the dog dragged you in, you know, the cat dragged you in ... or whatever you want to consider it. To look bad.

Michael: Look bad or look ugly?

Monica: I think it's to look bad. I think you bring shame to your family's name if you are looking disheveled, as I think that's how even my mother thinks. I think my grandmother thought that way, and I think she portrayed that to my mother.

Michael: So her worst fear is everybody looking down her?

Monica: I would imagine her worst fear is that she raised a hooligan of a child. You know, whether it's me, her grandchildren, looking like a little hellion running around, whether it's being dirty or acting bad, or cussing, swearing or whatever the situation.

Michael: And if that came true, it would bring shame upon her?

Monica: That's how my mother thinks as well. But it was definitely how my grandmother felt.

Michael: So based on how other people would perceive her, both your mother and your grandmother, if her children or grandchildren weren't looking the part, then these people would look down on the whole family and look down on her. (Monica: Yes.) So if they were to look down on her, this would bring up a feeling of being alone, right?

Monica: She would feel rejected.

Michael: Because I'm wondering ... cause in the very first session, you talked about social anxiety. I remember you said you were fearful of even asking for a glass of water as a child.

Monica: Probably practiced that over and over and over again for an hour. Dying of thirst in the process. Just because I didn't want to make a fool out of myself and sound retarded. And they might say no, like it was the end of the world.

Michael: Got it. Got it, so there's this phenomenon, this intergenerational phenomenon of like, "If I'm looked down upon, if I mess up, then I'll be rejected. I'll be abandoned. I'll be judged."

Monica: I'll be judged.

Michael: So with social anxiety, and considering what you just said about nursing, like "If I fail, then my family members will look down on me, I won't be accepted, I'll be judged, I'll be abandoned."

Monica: Yeah, I would look like a failure.

Michael: But if you are a failure, then people would judge you, and then it would create feelings of worthlessness and isolation.

Monica: Ultimately.

Michael: Yeah. So in that experience, you're in your mother's movie, and primarily your grandmother's movie, cause that's the mode that she operated in.

Monica: I do that with my kids.

Michael: What do you mean?

Monica: It's definitely intergenerational as you are saying. I am critical of my kids. I'm critical of how we look. If they have a meltdown because, you know, they didn't get something at the grocery store. I will leave instead of looking embarrassed.

Michael: If they do what at the grocery store?

Monica: If they have a meltdown at the grocery store because they can't have candy ... because "he hit me" ... because, I mean, I, you have to understand, I had five kids ... So at one point, it was like herding cats and it was easier to leave, but I do have, "How do we look?" generational issues from grandma. Definitely carried that trait.

Michael: Got it, got it, got it. So catch yourself when you're in that experience and know that you're in your grandmother's movie. If we're not able to uncover this, it is fine because I feel like this is good enough for now, but do you happen to know any past family trauma, any experience that could contribute to and set off your grandmother's feeling of and fear of being judged, looked down on, and abandoned and her obsession with the way she looks and presents herself.

Monica: I don't know that it's as much fear as it was generational. It was the time, the ages. Back in the early 1900s (during the Great Depression) all you had was your looks and your name. If you didn't have money, you married for money. And I'm sure there's something in there that, you know, it was imperative that you look like a lady, a princess, a perfect role model as a woman, or you didn't get a husband, or you would end up being an old spinster.

Michael: What's a spinster?

Monica: An unmarried woman that will always be alone. She's a forever bachelor.

Michael: Basically, an old lady with cats in our current day?

Monica: An old lady with cats is what we ultimately would consider it now.

Michael: I'm curious, why was it like that during that time?

Monica: It was the early 1900s. Everybody was broke. If you had money, you were listened to. I mean, think about it. If you had money or you had glasses on, you're considered educated. Just like, if you're fat, you're considered rich.

It was the times. It was the era.

Michael: Oh, because everybody was broke because of the Great Depression?

Monica: Everybody was broke, and you wanted to look like a perfect lady. God forbid you shame the family and don't marry off to a rich butcher that's 50 years old.

Michael: Why was there so much judgment around this, if everybody was experiencing the financial struggle of the Great Depression?

Monica: Because they wanted to come back. They wanted to survive and have a family name and be known for centuries. I don't know exactly why...

Michael: Because the Great Depression made them lose it all and...

Monica: Because of the Great Depression, that's all they had left, was their name and their looks.

Michael: Got it. Got it, got it. It was the trauma of the Great Depression.

Monica: I'm sure it took quite a toll on everybody.

Michael: And I think we're about to enter it right now, again. (Michael speaking about the economic recession happening alongside COVID-19)

Monica: Oh yeah! I, you know, I think that's how people were riding. And I think that's how, you know, people were desperate. If you had a coupon book and you had ... the understanding I have from my mother and my grandmother and stuff, you know, what I could get is that you had a coupon book, and it was, let's say, 20 bucks – you know, obviously back in the 1900s, 20 bucks is like $100 or $400 – then you could use those coupons to pay for your chickens and your rice and your grain and whatever else, your meat.

And once that money was gone, IT WAS GONE! So if you ate like a king for the first week and used the whole thing, you didn't eat again until the first of the next month.

So my grandmother, you know, I would imagine that would be hard on her. That would stress me out hardcore, to be down to, like, my pennies. I mean, we're that way now, but ... (laughs)

Michael: And the trauma of having a normal and sustainable life and having all of that completely taken away ... And then all she can do is hold onto the only thing that she has left, which is her image.

Monica: Yep. That's all that she had left was her image. Back in the day, the pretty face won you the butcher who was super rich, and they're like, "Yea! He's only 75 years old but marry him anyways!" And then when he died, women we're not allowed to have property and they couldn't have money, so they had to remarry and lose it all to the next man. There was a lot of trauma and chaos and a lot of it was based on reputation and how you looked. Women weren't given a right to vote and we didn't have a voice then. The only way that you were allowed to be rich and keep your money was marrying into it or something. You know? He had to leave it to you. I mean, it had to be awful.

Michael: Got it, got it, got it. All right. I think we're about coming to a close for today, but I just want you to practice, and flex this gift of high sensitivity, high empathy, as a muscle. Practice and flex the muscle of the emotional strength F I S T process, and as you know, "Feeling is healing." Don't let your overthinking consume you but balance your thoughts with feeling. And identify your core negative feelings and see how you are in both your grandfather's movie and your grandmother's movie on your mother's side. (Monica: Okay.) And visualize that movie screen in front of you and say, "I'm not an emotional sponge, but a source of light."

You don't want to use your gift, your incredible gift, the wrong way so that it becomes a double-edged sword and creates emotional harm for yourself and for your children. You want to say, "S.A.M., shit ain't mine." You're not saying this to your past family members. You are saying this to yourself so you can truly shine the light that you are.

Monica: Yeah. I need to learn to practice that at work.

Michael: Yeah. Because with what's happening at work, it brings up very eerily similar feelings and energies that your grandmother was around.

Monica: Yeah! Panic.

Michael: Because this is like another Great Depression that's happening along with COVID-19.

Monica: Yeah ... the emotion at work is – it's like walking onto a battlefield. Especially for me.

Michel: What do you mean?

Monica: People are scared. People are panicking, and then we're angry because we can't do our job, and people's emotions reflect... I can feel their emotions, so I can feel when they're angry and pissed off because we can't give them what they're looking for.

And then they come in irate because there's no toilet paper, and it's every day. It's... wow... I haven't quite learned to manage it, like learning how to wash away and desensitize myself to some of it, get my shield up and keep it from penetrating me.

Michael: But also know that this was a part of the world. A lot of this energy is very similar to the energy that your grandmother was around and had to survive in.

And so it's like, it's going to hit you a little bit deeper. So separate from this pain that doesn't belong to you. It doesn't mean that you don't care about the other person or your past family members. You just separate from it because you're not an emotional sponge, you're a source of light. That's when you can actually begin to use your gift correctly, consciously, and help others in the most powerful way.

THE HEALING POWER OF KNOWING ALL FOUR GENERATIONS IN RELATION TO THE FAMILY UNIT

Everyone is typically knowledgeable about the narratives of their grandparents, but not of their great-grandparents. The blessing I have in working with young families is that when I speak to the parents, I am able to uncover information about their grandparents, which are their child's great-grandparents. It truly amazes me, each and every time, as I uncover the seamless, yet hidden thread of intergenerational trauma inherited throughout the four generations. I often see the child mimicking the same exact intergenerational traumatic event of the great-grandparent as if the child was experiencing it themselves in real-time.

Making these connections from the 1st to 4th generation sends a transformative shock wave of healing throughout all living and future generations. To understand the power of knowing all four generations, as well as, healing together as a family unit, I want to provide you with a powerful personal example.

I have this relentless and daunting pain of feeling ugly and experience the recurring thought that I won't be accepted and loved by others because of it. What exacerbates this fear is my sleep issues because the poorer the quality of sleep I get, the more worn out, aged, and "ugly" I feel I become. I fear if I lose my appearance and become ugly due to the wear and tear of poor sleep, then I will somehow lose it all by losing my friends and family and my practice as I would no longer be accepted by loved by others.

As I mentioned before, I began to have sleep issues after I started dating my wife. She experienced a tremendous amount of trauma in her childhood much like prior generations of her family. In fact, my wife's horrifying family trauma bled into every facet of our relationship, in turn contributing to my sleep issues. This is namely because my wife's intergenerational trauma and my mother's intergenerational trauma share in common the same pain of abandonment.

The thing I physically notice the most from not sleeping well is the dark circles I develop underneath my eyes. On a night that I experience particularly bad sleep, I become obsessively consumed with my dark circles, as they become even more pronounced. When I look into the mirror, I immediately fixate on my dark circles and nothing else. If I see that they are more pronounced, I end up ruminating about it and then hurriedly busy myself with anything to distract myself from this pain. I can find myself distracting myself by mindlessly browsing social media, being productive just to be productive, and very often, turn to overeating in an attempt to numb and suppress my feelings.

This feeling of ugliness also comes up when I have to get my picture taken. The ugliness I experience is so deeply embedded within me, that as my picture is being taken, I can forcibly feel the painful feeling of ugliness being exposed for all to see. My ugliness being exposed to others leads to my fear of being unaccepted and basically abandoned by others.

Another pain around my appearance came about at the start of my wife's pregnancy with our son. I don't know why, but at that time, I started experiencing dramatic hair loss. Although to this day, it's not that noticeable, I obsess and panic when I can visibly see my scalp in the mirror. I am especially sensitive to elevators because there are mirrors and bright lights all around where I can glaringly see my visible scalp and hair loss staring right back at me.

When I wash my hair, I wash it ever so gently because I am terrified of my hair falling out. After rubbing my hair and scalp with shampoo, I look at my hands out of sheer terror, anxiously counting the hair strands on my hands. Moreover, my wife likes to run her hand through my hair as an expression of love and I will usually swipe her hand away because I am worried she will make my scalp oily with her hands, leading to more hair loss, and in turn, more feelings of ugliness.

Where does this nightmarish fear of ugliness come from? It comes partly from my great-grandmother on my mom's side. My great-grandmother was divorced and abandoned by her husband for a "prettier wife." My great-grandmother was forced to leave her first child, my grandmother when she was only five and never was able to see her again. Eventually, my grandmother fled China to escape the rise of communism to Taiwan, thereby making it forever impossible for my great-grandmother to ever see her firstborn child.

A couple years ago, I had a relative from China visit my family for the first time here in the states. She told me she had gone looking for my great-grandmother and was able to find and meet her once. When my relative met my great-grandmother, she was already bed-ridden from having had a stroke. My great-grandmother lost it all when her husband divorced her due to her " lesser appearance." She lived a life of extreme poverty, having to work in the fields, and developing a severe hunchback because of it. She basically lived alone with only her son (from a latter marriage) living with her. My great-grandmother in her later years would sit on her front doorstep staring hopelessly into the stars wondering when she will ever get to meet her firstborn child; my grandmother. My great-grandmother tirelessly tried to contact my grandmother but was never able to find her number, and yet, all of the pain she endured was because of the negative feelings about herself that her abandonment fueled.

My grandmother assumed this burden of ugliness and took it out on my mother when she was a child. When my mother would smile, my grandmother laughed at her, saying that she looked like a cut-up watermelon with seeds. Note: I must say that my grandmother, who I love dearly, is no longer that person and has a loving and healed relationship with my mother.

In thinking of this story, I fear the same thing will happen if I become "ugly" and I will lose it all. My worst fear is that I would lose all my hair and look old, wrinkly, and ugly like the troll Smeagol from Lord of the Rings. If that were the case, I would just lock myself in a room and not want to meet anyone, shunning myself from the world because I feel I won't be accepted by others for my troll-like ugliness.

This feeling of ugliness is something I, very unfortunately, project onto my own family. Although my wife is an incredibly gorgeous woman, my ego will tell me things on how she is not as pretty as she was before; things like, "She needs to lose weight. She needs to flatten her post-pregnancy belly."

Another thing I fixate on about my wife's appearance is how she tends to not dress up or take care of her appearance. What is worse is that I even find myself looking at the other women, not because I want to be unfaithful, but simply out of wishing that my wife would take care of her appearance and physique as other women do. However, all of this is really just me projecting my pain of ugliness onto my own wife.

What is perhaps the most tragic aspect of all is that, as embarrassing it is to admit it, is that I wonder whether I even projected this pain onto my son the moment he was born. When my son was just about to come out of his mother's womb, Although I naturally worried about ensuring that he was healthy, I had thoughts of "I hope he is not ugly." Obviously, this thought and fear have nothing to do with my son and much to do with my great-grandmother's movie, the very movie that I was living in as my own.

This intergenerational pain of ugliness not only existed on my mother's side of the family, but also, on my father's side just as much. My paternal grandmother placed a lot of importance and self-worth on appearance and status. My father was the eldest child out of six children and my grandmother heavily favored her second child over all her other children because she thought he was better looking and he went to a better school.

When my mother visited my father's home for the first time when they were dating, she was surprised to see that the only pictures my grandmother had of her children in her home were of her favorite child and no other children. Finally, one of the most shocking stories I heard was that when my parents got married, the first thing my grandmother said to my mother was that she will never be as pretty and as smart as her other son's wife.

Not surprisingly, my father uses success and productivity as a coping mechanism to suppress these feelings of worthlessness tied to image and status. For example, three years ago he had stage one kidney cancer, and two months after his surgery, he went back to work full time. Also, when we returned back to the states from our family trip to Taiwan last year, he prided himself on the fact that he went back to work on the very same day because he had slept throughout the plane ride.

I notice how I, too, use productivity, money, and success as a coping mechanism to establish self-worth. I always feel the pressure to provide worth to others, because otherwise, others would have no reason to be in my life. For instance, every time I am writing my book, I constantly fear thinking what if I make a mistake and the book becomes a complete failure due to any one small mistake. I know it sounds ridiculous and even irrational, but that is the feeling I carry as I am writing this very book you are reading. I believe my feelings are rooted in the pain of feeling worthless because if I am not contributing any worth, leading me to conclude that I have no worth. Again, if I am not contributing any worth or if I have no worth, then others have no reason to be in my life, making me endure and experience the same intergenerational pain of feeling unaccepted by others, worthless and abandoned.

Additionally, I have a tremendous fear that I will lose my practice and platform to share my message if others were to find out about my ongoing sleep and image issues. Others would then not accept me or my message because I am an ugly and arguably, hypocritical, fraud who can't even take care of himself.

In my previous book, I featured a lot of pictures of me holding signs in it. While in this current book I used the same pictures as I did in the last book but I still had to create one more photo of me holding a sign containing the main message of this book which is "Pain is your greatest teacher. The lessons you learn from pain will transform you, your family and the world." However, for the longest time, I didn't want to take the photo because I feel I have really aged and look uglier since my last book was published a couple years ago; mainly due to all the emotional and physical toll that normally takes place in being a first time parent. I tried to wait for the right time to take the photo, hoping for an opportune moment when my appearance looks good enough and I have slept well the night before. I am terrified of being exposed to the world as an ugly fraud who can't even help himself, thereby making me feel unaccepted and abandoned by the world.

It's very interesting to note that my father's brother, the favored one, also pursued a life of image and status. For example, he lives in Minnesota where there are a lot of lakes and he unnecessarily bought two boats for image. Later, he ended up losing his high profile job due to the 2008 crash and having to work as a gardener to get by. He lost a lot of his face and severed himself from the world, including his very own family, which not only led to his divorce but caused him to sacrifice his relationship with his own two sons to whom he no longer even speaks. Neither does he really talk to any of his siblings. However, when he does visit Taiwan, he is given spending money by one of his siblings because of his financial situation. Although I have never personally met my uncle, I can only imagine his painful loss of image and status that he must feel and how that loss has undermined his sense of self-worth, in turn, destroying everything he once had. My uncle feels if he doesn't present an image of worth then you won't be loved by others. This pain of exclusion is a concept that my grandmother passed down to her children by favoring one child over her others due to looks and status and it is a pain that was almost effortlessly internalized by the next generation.

I hold onto the same feeling of worthlessness by concluding that, if I am not providing worth for others, others have no reason to be in my life and thus excluded. My father is always trying to serve others. He serves my mother throughout all her struggles with compulsive anxiety, panic, worry, and fear. He serves his family, as well as his community, by tirelessly working his entire life. Keep in mind he is 74 years old and still working full time. I also find myself always needing to serve others and feel responsible for others. It comes to the point where I am not exactly sure who I am if I could no longer be busily and worriedly serving and providing for others. I try to remind myself that my worth is not defined by what I do for others, but for who I inherently am and who I was created to be.

Not only do I suffer from the fear of not being able to provide worth for others, painful feelings of ugliness, but I also have a tremendous and paralyzing fear of death. The fear of death is rooted in the feeling of "I don't exist," because if I die I cease to exist. This fear of death and feeling of non-existence is something I inherited from my mother.

My mother would have panic attacks in the middle of the night when I was a child. It would be 1 or 2 in the morning and she would be crying, screaming and hyperventilating and then wake me up so I could comfort her. She would lie on her stomach in bed and have me soothe her by running my hand down her back. My father would stand in the corner helpless because at the time he did not know how to connect with his emotions and handle my mother so distraught by her emotional pain and suffering.

I vividly recall a memory I had as a teenager, when my friends and I were spending time with my dog on my parents' front lawn as he was living out his last days. Although my parents live in a very nice and completely safe neighborhood, my mother told me and my friends to get back in the house, anxiously warning that there could be a drive-by shooting.

Inside the house, my mother keeps all the blinds closed at all times. Therefore, even during the day, it's dark inside the house. She is scared that other people will be able to peep into the house and try to harm her, although the house is surrounded all around by a big wall.

My mother's fear of death does contain an element of violent deaths that were due to war, communist uprising, and Japanese invasion happening in China at the time. When my grandmother was a teenager, communists had invaded her family's home. My grandmother was hiding in the barn and she saw communists line her family up, brutally killing them execution-style. When my mother was only two years old, my grandmother was fleeing with her on a train. There was no more space on the train, so my grandmother had to sit holding my mother on top of a moving train while it was raining. On the train ride, they had barely escaped death as there was a moment when the train passed a bridge, that it was bombed by communists.

My mother has not deprogrammed herself and continues to live to this day in this world of death and violence she was born into, the only reality she has never known. Although she has no conscious recollection of these experiences because she was so young, she could still subconsciously feel it all. The fear of death cripples and consumes my mother. That is the only mother I know. I, in turn, am crippled and consumed with this fear of death. Just as my mother, I fixate on health by being a hypochondriac to avoid this pain and fear of death rooted in the feeling of worthlessness, abandonment, and war-time trauma.

I am very scared to look at myself in the mirror, not because I feel ugly, but in many ways, because I fear seeing how much I have aged due to not sleeping well. The more aged I look, or the more worn out I look, the more the fear of death comes to haunt me. It does give me a sense of emotional release to fixate less on my fear of my appearance being deteriorated and more on the core pain which is the fear of death rooted in my family's war-time trauma.

If I feel something is risking and harming my health I can feel my gut reaction swirling with panic and terror as if I'm going to die. Obviously nobody wants to put their health in harm's way but I can easily go to the deep end by thinking and feeling as if I am going to die. When I feel this feeling, and finally can calm and center myself, I remind myself of how I am living in the movie of my past family members and that, as painful it is to admit it, I am committing the very same emotional crime that my mother has inflicted onto me.

All my life, my mother has micromanaged my seemingly every move for the purpose of projecting her fear of death onto me by obsessively fixating on my health and safety. In turn, I also project this fear of death onto my wife and child by micromanaging their lifestyle choices and behavior. I micromanage my child's health indirectly because whatever my wife eats is what he eats, as she is still breastfeeding. I do have an extensive background in holistic health, and yet, I misuse it by overreacting to my wife's actions in regards to her health. She has a major sweet tooth and eats large amounts of carbs, which makes me feel upset, panicky, and powerless. Although it is true her actions in regards to her health can sometimes reflect poor choices, but I overreact as though it's the end of the world because this fear of death comes to the surface. As I said before, this fear of death that I am projecting onto my wife is ultimately rooted in my family's intergenerational pain of exclusion, abandonment, and war-time trauma.

It helps to remind myself how I am living in my mother's movie, my father's movie, both of my grandmothers' movies, my great-grandmother's movie, and even my uncle's movie, who was the favorite of the family. He cut himself off from the world because he lost his image and status. I, too, would want to cut myself off from the world if I lose my appearance and lost my status by appearing as a fraud who can't help himself. As a matter of fact, I already am doing this to some extent. For example, I tend to not want to share photos and videos of myself, even for the purpose of sharing my message, because I am afraid I will appear as an ugly fraud who can't take care of himself.

I have to admit, for the longest time, I was reluctant to share my deepest personal struggles here in this book. I feared it would make me look like a hypocrite and a fraud, thereby rendering me unacceptable and abandoned by the world. In the end, I committed to sharing my deepest struggles with you because in being transparent with my most painful emotional wounds, it naturally heals them by shedding light on them. This commitment to self-transparency is saying that I accept myself just the way I am, which begins to cut my intergenerational umbilical cord of feeling worthless, unaccepted, and abandoned by others. I accept myself. God (The Creator) accepts me. Thereby, my sense of self-worth is independent of anyone else's acceptance of me and I can begin to restore the identity and higher purpose I was meant to live up to.

This transparent, raw, and public acknowledgment of my deepest pain and struggles greatly mends, heals, and transforms all the broken pieces within myself, so that I don't pass down this intergenerational pain for the next generation to my son. It is very important that I always continue to do the work from within, and that I am cognizant not to project this intergenerational movie onto my family unit with my wife and child.

I share my transparent and raw story with you of me putting together all the pieces of my family's past and how it affects both myself and my family unit so you can do the same. I work with countless families and it is such a beautiful experience to tie everything throughout the generations so that every individual within the family unit can finally be free of the movies that do not belong to them.

Through this seamless thread of intergenerational pain and trauma that has been intricately woven throughout the generations and your family unit, you can unveil how truly powerful your gift of emotional antennas and high sensitivity can be. You can see how you and your children are living in the movies of people you have never met, and traumatic events you or your children had no prior knowledge of. However, you may wonder how is it possible that you, or your children, are picking up pain and trauma from past family members you have never met and events that you had no prior knowledge of until now? The following study will shed a lot of light on this.

STUDY: THE CHERRY BLOSSOM SCENT CONNECTION

As you are identifying the past family trauma that is sending ripples down your family line, you may feel doubtful or resistant to the process, because you wonder, "How could something that did not happen to you personally, could affect you so strongly, as if you happened to you?"

Many of your answers can be found in an important study revealed in the book "It Didn't Start With You," written by Mark Wolynn.[4] Although this study is eye-opening and groundbreaking, try not to comprehend it literally from a purely scientific standpoint.

This study was taken place 2013 at the Emory School of Medicine in Atlanta. In this study, researchers took a group of male mice and exposed them to a cherry blossom scent, and right after gave them an electric shock. They did this repeatedly, to the point that once the male mice smelled the cherry blossom scent, they immediately began to panic, even without the administration of the electric shock.

The researchers then took the sperm of these male mice and impregnated female mice who never themselves were administered an electric shock. Afterward, when the offspring were exposed to a cherry blossom scent, they too began to panic, even though they were not given any electric shock. The amazing thing is that, when the offspring of these offspring (the third generation) were exposed to a cherry blossom scent, they panicked as well.[5]

What the author is suggesting through this study is that intergenerational pain can be transferred through the expression of your genes, meaning this "curse" is not set in stone and can, in fact, be undone and healed.

Having said this, science is very often understood through the mind, and I want you to also understand this study through the heart. When you are highly sensitive and highly empathic, through your incredible gift of high sensitivity and not purely from a genetic standpoint, you are going to feel and internalize the intergenerational trauma of your past family members. I have countless clients who are living in the movie of their step-parents' parents, thus reinforcing that it doesn't have to be a direct genetic influence. Yet again, a child can subconsciously feel the energies of those who raised them and the families they come from.

Now, we will move onto other eye-opening and fascinating examples of people and their unique journeys towards intergenerational trauma healing. Learning these real-life examples will give you a powerful window through which to uncover your own intergenerational trauma.

CHAPTER NINE:

Powerful Stories of Intergenerational Trauma Healing

THE TRAUMA OF COMMUNISM TAKING EVERYTHING YOU BUILT AWAY FROM YOU

TOMMY BUI

Tommy got into a car accident recently with his partner in the passenger seat and fortunately enough, both sustained no physical harm. However, after the car accident, Tommy was without a car and thus was completely dependent on others for car rides. Being completely dependent on others in this way really bothered Tommy because for one he is used to supporting others. When I asked Tommy to stretch this all to his worst fear, he said it would be being paralyzed because he would be completely and utterly dependent on others.

Additionally, Tommy struggles with creating a work-life balance and worries that if he invests more of himself into friendships, the relationships will fail and that somebody will betray him, making it all just a "wasted effort."

Moreover, even spending time with his partner, although as much as he enjoys it, he worries about how much time it will take away from his work. But then, I turn to Tommy and ask him what would happen, not only, if he had unlimited time with friends, family and his partner, but also unlimited time to spend towards work, yet he still failed in his professional life. Tommy responded by admitting that he would feel "ashamed."

As you can see, this whole work-life balance issue is clearly not about others wasting his time and efforts or taking time away from his work, but these are all really excuses for Tommy to avoid feeling "ashamed" as a failure.

TOMMY'S MOTHER

Tommy's mother is a person who worries a lot. She recently has had to temporarily close down her business due to COVID-19 policies and she feels very bad for all her employees as she often feels responsible for others. Interestingly, her worst fear and nightmare is to lose her cash flow and, and just like her son Tommy, to be completely dependent on others.

Before COVID-19 hit, she had a couple of investments that went bad, and had lost quite a bit of cash flow because of it, which took a lot away from her ability to provide for others. Her loss of cash flow triggers not only this need to only provide for others but also the even greater fear of being dependent on others. It's almost as if the identity to help and serve others that Tommy's mother holds onto is to mask the fear of being dependent on others, including Tommy.

TOMMY'S INTERGENERATIONAL TRAUMA

Tommy's maternal grandfather was constantly angry. He was very controlling and everybody had to act in accordance with his rules and expectations. To give you an example, when Tommy was just a child, Tommy's grandfather mandated him to take a shower every day before coming to dinner, and if Tommy had not, he would become infuriated and even scream at Tommy.

Where does this anger all come from? Tommy's grandfather had lost it all due to the Vietnam war and the rise of communism in Vietnam. His children first fled to Australia and he and his wife were left to stay in war-torn Vietnam and had to depend on their children to be able to come to Australia.

After coming to Australia, it was a complete "180 change" for Tommy's grandfather. In Vietnam, he was the sole provider for his family. However, in Australia, he did not speak the language and had to be completely dependent on all of his five children for the remainder of his life.

Thus, controlling Tommy in this extreme way, was what his sense of self-worth and ability to provide for others by controlling others, was sadly reduced to.

You can now see how Tommy's fear of others taking away valuable time from his work, was really about the fear of failure, which would then lead him needing to be dependent on others, which was him living in his grandfather's movie. As we connect the thoughts, it becomes clear that this intergenerational trauma was really brought to the surface by the car accident because he had to be completely dependent on others for car rides.

Tommy's mother is also worth mentioning. In fact, she was living in her father's movie by holding onto money and her false identity to provide for others financially, which was all masking her fear of being dependent on others.

THE TRAUMA OF RELIGIOUS EXCLUSION

BRIAN

Brian has stress-related acid reflux and the doctors cannot find anything wrong with his health other than this issue. Still, Brian obsessively worries that maybe there is something that the doctors have missed in their evaluation of him and then one day when it's already too late, the doctors will have found that he has something gravely ill like cancer. His worst fear is not death but the process of dying, because he feels powerless that he could not control a terminal illness by stopping it.

What is causing Brian this stress, to begin with is that he wants to quit his comfortable salary job to pursue being a full-time entrepreneur as a counselor, coach, and podcaster, but just doesn't know what's stopping him from doing so although he truly hates his job.

Brian is frustrated over the fact he is 49 years old and he is not where he wants to be in life. He is only now trying this solo venture which he feels he should have started already years ago.

In identifying Brian's worst fear, his thinking mind came up very strongly by creating lesser degree worst-case scenarios that were "not that bad" in order to help prevent Brian from feeling a certain negative feeling.

At first, he stated that his worst fear was "not so bad" because it was to be stuck in this salary job and not fulfilling his passion. I then asked him, what if he were to be let go from his salary job and then he goes on to say that he has clients from his private practice to fall back on.

Brian then proceeds to say that his worst fear is to not be able to provide the lifestyle his family deserves, but remember, as we discussed before, the role of the protector, aims to protect others from feeling worthless to avoid what, in actuality, the protector secretly feels all the time.

In the end, Brian admitted that his worst fear is to live a meaningless life, doing something he hates just to make money because he "failed" at following his passions. Brian, at first, consistently stated that failure would not bring up feelings of worthlessness. However, after discussing how the feeling of worthlessness is very often the underbelly feeling of failure and acknowledging that it is much harder to connect with since it is more painful; Brian was able to begin to sense this feeling of worthlessness within himself.

BRIAN'S MOTHER

Two years before Brian's mother passed away, she finally revealed to Brian that his father was not his biological father. (His step-father was largely absent from his life). Brian tried to make contact with his biological father recently, only to discover that he had already passed away 6 months ago.

In order to see how this could be a part of Brian's intergenerational trauma, we first applied the PEWF process onto Brian's mother. Brian's mother experienced a lot of anxiety and anger. In fact, she had a lot of anxiety about not having enough money. Her worst fear was to be homeless or on welfare because it would make her appear as a worthless "loser." Brian's mother would get very angry if she didn't feel like she was in control. For example, after she had cleaned the house, if Brian or his sister didn't put something back to its original place. Brian's mother attached her self-worth to things being her way, as well as her possessions being "respected", so if she wasn't listened to, or if her property and possessions were mishandled, then she would feel that she wasn't being respected and valued, bringing up the feeling of worthlessness in her.

Interestingly, you can already see the connection of Brian's fear around putting himself out there into the world with his podcast and as an entrepreneur, because of his fear of being exposed as a loser, just like his mother's fear of being seen by the world as a "loser" who is homeless or on welfare.

A week passed, and in the next session with Brian, he told me that he was actually furloughed due to the COVID-19 situation. Although he stated in the previous session that this was what he always wanted so he could focus on his dream, being furloughed created a lot of anxiety for him.,

Even despite having the safety net of his company telling him that it was only for 90 days, while being able to receive regular unemployment checks, he was still fearful and paralyzed with inaction by not devoting any time and energy towards his dreams; even though he had all the time in the world to do so.

BRIAN'S INTERGENERATIONAL TRAUMA

Brian tells me that his mother was pregnant with him at the age of 19 in 1970. His mother's parents actually wanted to give Brian up for adoption, because having a baby at this young age and out of wedlock, was greatly looked down on in the eyes of the Catholic church.

To better understand Brian's maternal grandparents, I applied the PEWF process onto them. His grandfather would get very angry if his children dabbled in more or less harmless illegal activity such as underage drinking at a house party because it would be considered "immoral" according to the standards of the Catholic church.

Brian found out recently through his biological father's sister that his mother and his biological father were high school sweethearts. After the two found out about the pregnancy, they happily wanted to stay together and make it work, but not only did Brian's maternal grandparents wanted them to give Brian up for adoption, Brian's grandparents on his biological father's side, especially the grandmother, forbade them from being together. Brian's paternal grandparents were also devout Catholics and were worried that this would bring shame to the family because it was taboo in the eyes of the Catholic church.

FAMILY SECRETS BLEED

The complete secrecy over Brian's biological father's existence was all due to the fear of being judged by the world, or more specifically, the Catholic world.

This shows how family secrets can be more impactful and traumatizing because these family secrets are purposely not made conscious, even though you still feel the trauma of the family secret wholeheartedly. You may have the good intentions to keep family secrets hidden from your children in order to "protect" them, but ironically enough, it has the very opposite effect because children can still feel it all. In other words, until you make these dark family secrets consciously known to your children, they will feel and experience this secret family trauma as if it was their own.

You may personally question how you (or your children) could be holding onto the intergenerational trauma of someone you have never met. However, Brian's story shows how incredible the gift of high sensitivity can truly be, as you can see how Brian is holding onto his grandparent's pain of his biological father's side although he never met them or knew of their existence only until a couple of years ago.

THE TRAUMA OF DEATH BY BETRAYAL AND THE TRAUMA OF SLAVERY

ELAINA JONES

Elaina has social anxiety disorder. She is a single mother and is trying out dating apps, but doesn't know why it's been hard to really put herself out there.

Elaina did find someone she likes through one of the dating sites, but she is constantly analyzing and questioning his motives and intentions. She has already decided that she probably will not meet him in the future (since they can't meet due to the "stay at home" order).

This difficulty to trust others is not just the case with this guy, but with all others, as Elaina explains, *"I over-analyze every single thing that someone may say to me or do, like, I ruminate. It's a constant thought."*

Elaina admits that she also experiences frustration over social media, dating apps, or just in general:

"When people represent themselves to be something other than who they actually are, that really gets under my skin because then at that point I feel like I can't trust you or I feel like you think that I'm stupid, in regards to social media, dating apps, or just in general...

When you think about dating apps and how people present their lives on social media, it's like those that know you, know the truth, and this is not who you are. You know, dating apps, you can be whoever you want to be. You can live a fabulous life and none of it can be true. Like you can, give a fake picture and name and to me, it is like, what's the point of that?

Even when I think about one of the reasons why I backed away from Facebook and Instagram, cause everyone posts a lot of the great things that are happening as, 'Hey, look at me! This is awesome! I'm living the best life!' But in reality, you're miserable. And it's like, just be honest and be truthful, and you will have those around you that support you. I just think that the lack of authenticity that we sometimes represent causes me to feel like, you know, what's the point if we can't be real with each other."

Elaina's worst fear is dealing with people who don't present themselves as who they truly are.

"Worst fear, worst-case scenario would be that I fall hook, line, and sinker into someone's trap, and you know, and I put myself in danger somehow."

INTERGENERATIONAL TRAUMA ON FATHER'S SIDE

Elaina's father passed away when she was 8 years old. Elaina's uncle was a leader of a prominent gang, and he was with his friend one time inside a house, and his friend asked him to go outside the house, to where he shot and killed him. Being that Elaina's uncle was a leader of a prominent gang this was about a power struggle.

Elaina: "My other uncle David, he was with people that, you know, one of his closest friends who had called him outside, and when he came outside, they shot him.

Michael: Why did they do that?

Elaina: My uncle was, I don't really know why, but he was a leader of a prominent gang in the suburb that he lived in at the time."

Another trauma of the ultimate betrayal happened to Elaina's aunt. In fact, Elaina's aunt was doing drugs with friends at a home, and her aunt overdosed but her friends, who could have saved her life by calling for help, just left her there to die.

"Even one of my aunts, the one that died of an overdose, she was in a home with people she thought were her friends and they left her. So there's always that question, 'have they had called for help? Could she had lived?' "

Elaina's frustration over people not portraying themselves as who they really are on social media and dating apps is rooted in this intergenerational trauma of the ultimate betrayal leading to one's death, by those you are supposed to trust the most. To Elaina, it's more than just others not presenting themselves as who they really are, because when that happens, to Elaina's subconscious, it means death by betrayal.

Elaina relays this intergenerational trauma of betrayal with her fear of letting people close to her in:

"I mean, there's definitely this trend of like, I do have a fear of letting people in close and it's like, those are the ones that can hurt you." (begins to get very emotional as she is saying this)

Michael: *The social anxiety and putting yourself out there and you're worried that if your daughter does the same, it's like if you put yourself out there, you make yourself vulnerable and people betray you.*

Elaina: *Yes. I can see that. Because that is, you know, that's a fear that I've carried with me for a long time. And I think that's why I keep my guard up with a lot of people... like it takes a lot for me to let you get close to me. Like we gotta go through some stuff for me to be like, okay, you in the circle, I can be me around you.*

ELAINA'S FEAR OF JUDGMENT

Elaina not only has the fear of being betrayed or fooled by others, but she also carries the fear of judgment. Elaina is scared to put herself out there with her love for writing and also podcasting in which she recently started:

"I've always wanted to write novels. I write stories all the time, but I don't share that because I don't know how people are gonna respond to it. So things like that. Even with the podcast, one of my really good friends, I kind of jumped on the bandwagon. It was like, 'Yeah, let's do it.' You know? And I don't know if she wouldn't have cosigned that if I would have actually done it. I'd probably would've just talked about it for the next 10 years."

Elaina also worries about whether she is doing a good enough job parenting her daughter, who is turning 15 at the age of beginning to come into her own. More importantly, Elaina's worst fear is that her daughter turns out to be a person, like herself, who doesn't really go after what she wants in life, and doesn't "shoot for the stars."

"My worst fear is that she wouldn't have a fulfilling, joyful life. Like, I don't want her to go through life and struggle and not try and things of that nature. Like I want her to

feel comfortable enough to put herself out there and shoot for the stars. . . I don't want her to feel like I do with being afraid to go after the things that she wants in life. Like I want her to feel comfortable enough and confident enough to take those risks and be okay if it doesn't turn out well or celebrate those successes."

But as you can see, Elaina is really projecting her own feelings onto her daughter.

Elaina's fear of judgment also affects her work in the sense that she normally doesn't say what she really wants to say in her work meetings because of the fear of judgment although some people at her work can be really nitpicky at times or even if she really disagrees with others.

Elaina's mother also experiences this fear of judgment. For example, she is the primary caregiver for her 96-year-old mother. Despite her being frustrated that her siblings don't help out more and have her do 85% of the workload, she worries a lot about not providing good enough care for her mother, because her worst fear is something were to happen to her mother, her siblings would blame her for it.

Elaina's aunt (her mother's sister) often puts on a mask and works hard to make others like her, because how she is perceived is everything to her otherwise she would feel worthless:

"My aunt is a person that likes to, she's one of those fraudulent people who likes to put on this perception that she's caring and loving and giving, and so she wears this mask."

INTERGENERATIONAL TRAUMA ON MOTHER'S SIDE

During the '30s and '40s, Elaina's maternal grandfather worked in the cotton fields in the South and was chased out of Mississippi by his boss who threatened to kill him and his family for complaining about being severely underpaid.

Elaina describes,

"He knew that as a black man in America, he was not going to be respected by his white counterparts. No matter how hard he worked, no matter what he did, no matter how he presented himself, no matter. Cause he was a good dresser, he was a sharp dresser...and so I think he did all that to somewhat be respected, and I think it was just the harsh reality that no matter what he did, he was still just going to be a black man."

Michael ties this back to Elaina's aunt:

"Everything is about jealousy. She's not good enough. Everything's about her, her perception, her perception to others. That's everything she cares about because if people don't perceive her the way she wants to, she feels worthless, but this is all rooted in their father. Your grandfather's feelings of no matter what he did, nothing was ever good enough. No matter, he tried to dress the part, but he was never good enough and they even tried to kill him for trying to be good enough. for trying to be equal."

Here is Elaina's response:

I think there's been some ill feelings that I've had towards my aunt. But when you said it, kind of resonated with me, when you said that she was in my grandfather's story. I was like, well, that makes sense. You know, looking at it from that perspective.

Elaina's fear of judgment is her being in more so her aunt's movie than her mother's and ultimately Elaina and her aunt are in the movie of Elaina's grandfather, who tried with all his might to be accepted but never was and others even tried to kill him for his desire to accepted and treated fairly and equally.

THE TRAUMA OF SOCIETAL POVERTY

ANGIE MALOVINI

Angie feels emotionally drained because she feels like nothing good happens to her despite all the good work and positivity she is sharing with others and the world. She dedicated herself to 30-minute meditations on manifestation for a whole month straight yet nothing good has happened.

Because nothing is manifesting and nothing good is happening, it makes Angie question her self-worth thinking, "My biggest fear right now is, am I really that great like I think I am?"

If Angie's worst fear came true it would make her feel that there is something wrong with her and that's why she cannot be loved and accepted by others.

Angie ultimately feels emotionally drained because she is always needing to prove her self-worth to others, especially her parents, and in particular, her mother who is clearly not accepting of her. What makes things worse is that being that Angie is a very naturally unfiltered and outspoken person, as she has her own podcast called "My Ugly Truth Podcast," her parents tell her things like to not be so outspoken on her podcast:

"I'm like, my life, my podcast is about my life stories. 'Don't embarrass your kids' is what they said. I'm like, 'if that's embarrassing, then you're telling me my life is embarrassing.' Like I just have to always prove, like just show everybody my worth and I am tired of doing that."

Angie is also bothered because of a court issue that has taken away her drivers license for the next 90 days, on top of the "stay at home" order. I ask her what is her worst-case scenario for this scenario and she says:

Angie: Alone. I'm alone and like just all the stress. It would be nice to have a companion, you know, to go through that stuff. I just feel alone. So like my biggest worry I guess would be, the fact that I can't get in a car and take my kids anywhere, especially with what's going on now. I feel trapped. I feel stuck. I feel like I'm in prison in my own home, even though everybody now, everyone feels that. But I just feel like it's just even more on my situation."

(This situation is bringing up two feelings in Angie, which is a feeling of being alone and a feeling of powerlessness because she feels "trapped.")

ANGIE'S FATHER

Angie's father cheated on her mother a lot in the past. Obviously it does not excuse his behavior but he did this mainly because he suffers from a lot of feelings of loneliness.

ANGIE'S MOTHER

Angie describes her mother as someone who has to be in control of everything and everyone, with everyone having to follow her specific order, schedule, rules, and expectations:

"I used to have a job, where I was just waitressing. So she has an order (to everything). She doesn't work (so she has this strict order about the house). Like on Monday, she cleans and she does this and this...So on Monday was my only day off around that time. So we would always argue cause I would want to sleep in. And she's like, 'Well, I have to vacuum at eight in the morning!' And I'm like, 'You can just vacuum at noon, mom. It's just one day.'

Like the control and the anxiety. And like yesterday, when she didn't have dinner ready when the kids walked in and she was just freaking out. My dad's like, 'Calm down, calm down,' and like, Jesus, this woman is driving me crazy. So yeah, anxiety for sure. And she just has to have control of everything."

Currently, Angie is working three jobs. The times when she comes home from work feeling very tired and if she does not give her mother the utmost attention, Angie's mother will usurp all control of the situation by criticizing and targeting Angie where it hurts Angie the most just so she can grab all of Angie's attention.

"I got off work one day and I was just like, tired, and not in a good mood. I didn't really want to talk. She's home alone all day, every day by herself. So she always just needs (attention), and if you act like you don't listen to her, you're not caring what she says, she'll be like, 'Why? Why are you coming in with a bad mood?'

You know, like, you shouldn't. She'll just start criticizing you and then she'll start digging into something that really hits you to a core that she knows. It's like she just wants to take control of the fact that you're not giving her attention so she could take all your attention by targeting something at you."

You can clearly see how if Angie's mother feels she is not in total and complete control and not listened to in the slightest way, she immediately feels she does not matter. Interestingly, the reason why Angie is especially bothered by feeling stuck without her driver's license and being stuck at home due to the quarantine is because

Angie is in her mother's movie. Angie's mother always needs to be in control to make herself feel like she matters. Angie, just as well, in feeling powerless due to her circumstances, brings up feelings of loneliness and not mattering. The feeling of not mattering is a reflection of her being cast in her mother's movie, but the feeling of loneliness is her being in her father's movie.

Surprisingly, Angie and her mother actually had a very good relationship growing up but what changed it all was when Angie divorced her husband and it bothered Angie's mother tremendously. Angie described the situation:

"Because that was the image that we had to have. No divorces. You stick with the father of your children, and that's it. Now, step-parenting, what is that? You know, that's not part of our law, our family. Very traditional, very in control and order."

Since the divorce, Angie and her mother's relationship took a sudden and dramatic downturn and Angie's mother would say very toxic remarks to her like:

"Sometimes I wonder why did I get pregnant with you? I should just stopped with your brothers." And then my dad was like, "You can't say that. She is your daughter!" My mom's like, "Well, I'm not sorry, but I was told that by my mom" and my dad's like, "You need to stop because I was there when she did that and you were broken over it. Don't act like it doesn't matter to you now."

You can see that Angie's mother had a strong attachment to image which is why when Angie got a divorce, it bothered Angie's mother so much because it tarnished their family's reputation. Now the question is, where does this attachment of self-worth to image come from?

ANGIE'S MATERNAL GRANDMOTHER

Angie talked about how her grandmother had obsessive attachment and fixation to image:

"She (Angie's grandmother) wanted my mom to get married to a doctor, to a lawyer and anyone below that was low class for her. So, that's just how my grandma was. She was like that with us too. We had to call her Elsa, not actually like her role, grandma.

She wanted everything good on paper like my grandma was more worried about what the ladies around the neighborhood would say, more than the value of a person, and she wanted anything that looked good on paper, like a resume, like everything was good on paper, but you don't know if they're really that good. She wanted everything perfect."

ANGIE'S INTERGENERATIONAL TRAUMA

In coaching Angie through the FIST process, I initially had difficulty finding the core intergenerational trauma as Angie didn't know that much of what trauma could have planted the seed to her grandmother's toxic behavior.

I then shared with Angie the story about Monica's grandmother and the Great Depression, and it helped shed light on Angie's grandmother to where her behavior and emotions were coming from. Angie's grandmother came from extreme poverty in Argentina, where at the time there was no middle class, only the poor class and the rich class.

(To give you an idea of the poverty and economic situation in Argentina here are some statistics; between 1975-1991, inflation rose on an average of 300% per year. In 2002, 44.2% of Argentinians were living on $5 or less a day.[6] Argentina throughout the 20th century was riddled with military coups, exorbitant and continuous inflation, leading to protests and riots.)[7]

In times where poverty within a country spikes, as you saw with Monica's example and the Great Depression and with Angie's family, all that you have left is your image. It explains the source of why the relationship between Angie and her mother went sour after Angie had her divorce because in Angie's mother's eyes it tarnished the image of the family.

Additionally, in extreme poverty, you are very powerless because there is not much you can do to change your situation, which explains why Angie's mother and grandmother are ultra controlling, and how Angie felt powerless without a car and having to stay home due to the quarantine.

But even more so, control is a coping mechanism to avoid feeling some negative pain. When Angie's mother and grandmother are not in control and are not listened to, they feel like they don't matter, which is the same reason behind why they are so attached to their image because if everyone looks down upon you, you are worthless.

All of which ties back to what Angie said at the beginning of the session, that she is always feeling the need to prove her self-worth to others and be accepted by others.

Towards the end of the session, Angie asked how she could set up better boundaries and not be affected by her mother's toxic ways which made her feel she is unaccepted and unloved by her own mother. Yes, it is true that Angie's mother's treatment towards Angie does make Angie feel unaccepted by her, but Angie is actually more picking up on her mother's feeling of being unaccepted but mistakenly feeling it as her own.

THE HIDDEN IMPACT OF THE EMOTIONALLY EXPRESSIVE PARENT

STACEY GROSS

Within the 24 hour period before Stacey releases a podcast, which she started four months prior, or the column she used to write for in the local newspaper, she would go in this spin cycle of thoughts saying that "this is horrible."

Stacey: "Every time I would put out a column and every time that I put out an episode for the podcast, I go through this like usually 24-hour thing where I'm like, Oh, this is horrible. And you know, imposter syndrome, I guess."

Even after she releases an episode she "picks it apart."

Her worst fear is somebody saying her work "is a joke." If her worst fear came true, it would make her feel worthless because she has no value to provide.

Stacey also feels frustrated with herself over if she is parenting her kids the right way. She has two girls who are fraternal twins but who have complete opposite personalities. Her worst fear is that she won't have a good relationship with her kids when they get older and that she might become a barrier to their success, above all, creating a severed relationship that would make her feel alone.

Stacy even tries to control her interactions with her children so they like her more.

"I try to have control with our interactions. Everything that I do is sort of strategic with them, trying to either reinforce our relationship, or develop a little bit more rapport. And so if I weren't able to do that, then, you know, I would feel both out of control and like a failure."

Stacey experiences a lot of social anxiety, and her worst fear is to be rejected by others and thereby feel alone.

"Everything that I do. When I was writing my column and with the podcast, it's in an effort to make connections, or to have mutual understanding with someone else." And thus if a connection is not made, Stacey would feel utterly alone.

STACEY'S MOTHER

Stacey's mother is more emotionally expressive and she experiences anxiety and constantly replays her childhood interactions by ruminating over how she could have better presented herself so she would not be judged and perceived as a "weirdo."

Stacey's maternal grandmother came from severe generational poverty and Stacey's maternal grandfather's family would look down upon Stacey's grandmother because of it. Stacey's mother, in turn, took on this pain of being looked down upon as her own:

"I think that my mom grew up with this really strict, 'we need to make a good impression.' We need to be socially acceptable and not reflect what my grandmother had come from."

When asking Stacey to identify her father's negative emotions of anxiety (worry or fear), anger (or frustration) and depression, she says: *"I have never seen any of those in him, but I think out of those three, mainly frustration, but I really just don't see a lot. He's not super expressive."*

Stacey's father would get frustrated when for example he is helping her change the oil for her car and he cannot get the bolt loose. He also gets frustrated when he is stuck in traffic because it impedes him and his overall progress in life.

I then ask Stacey to stretch this to her father's worst fear and worst-case scenario and remind her that it will be harder to identify this in her father because he is so masterful in suppressing his emotions and feelings. Using her intuition and gift of high sensitivity, Stacey identifies her father's worst fear as not being able to accomplish what he wants to achieve which would make him feel like a failure.

Where does Stacey's father's feeling of failure come from? Stacey's grandparents passed away when she was still quite young but as a child, she did overhear a lot of family stories about them and her father's childhood.

Stacey's father is much younger than his siblings because he was the accident child, and his parents, although they did love him, didn't really want to have him.

"My father is quite a bit younger than his two siblings. He has a sister and a brother who are quite a bit older than him. He was, um, a surprise, and he kind of was left to his own devices. Emotionally he sort of did his own thing within the family, (as opposed to) the other two siblings. It seems almost like a fractured sort of situation within that family. And he just, I think, felt emotionally on his own."

"He spent a lot of time in his room. He played guitar. He kind of escaped into music and his favorite records. And I think that he, the sense that I get when I hear, or when I had heard that story told is that he almost felt more attached to the music or the world within his favorite albums than he did to his relationship with his parents."

After making this realization I tell Stacey these feelings of feeling alone and using performance to prove one's self-worth is actually her father's feeling and her being in her father's movie,

Michael: The secret hidden one, which can be more impactful because it's secret and hidden is the one with your father.

Stacey: Yeah. I never really thought about that, but it does, it almost resonates more. It's a really interesting thing too. I never really think of myself and my father's impact on my personality or my temperament or my issues because he was always such a quiet, like a still pond as opposed to a river, you know, in my life."

After speaking with Stacey, it really helped me realize how my father, too, suppresses his emotions very well while keeping his family's past a secret. This session planted a seed in me to really see what may be going on underlying it all since so much was hidden from me.

I will discuss the details of this later on, but I wanted to first make the mental note of this realization.

You may have a parent that shows very little emotion, but that doesn't mean they don't carry negative feelings. Being emotionless is really a coping mechanism to avoid feeling your core negative feelings. Your emotionally suppressive parent may consciously suppress their feelings, but you have been subconsciously feeling all their unresolved feelings since the day you were born. If you have an emotionally suppressive parent, really use your intuition and gift of high sensitivity as you are applying the FIST process onto them to uncover the hidden details to your intergenerational trauma.

THE TRAUMA OF COMMUNISM TAKING YOUR FAMILY AND EVERYTHING YOU BUILT AWAY FROM YOU

TIBOR NAGY

At the beginning of the session, Tibor presented the image that "everything is fine," but it was Tibor's thinking mind that was working hard to help him avoid feeling a certain negative feeling. After sifting through all of Tibor's "logic" and overthinking, we were able to uncover his fear of being alone.

Tibor is so focused on growing his podcast that he fears he will lose all connection with others. He hasn't socialized with anyone in-person, other than his immediate family, for the past year. His worst fear is that years and years will go by and that he will still be this alone.

Tibor also worries about whether his podcast will succeed or not. He feels this is what he has been called to do and that it's the reason for his existence, thus if he fails at it, he will be worthless and cease to exist. As Tibor describes it:

"Worthless because I couldn't fulfill who I was sent to become."

TIBOR'S FATHER

Since Tibor's parents' divorce (Tibor was 11 at the time), Tibor's father has not gotten married since and has basically cut himself off from the world. He fears that if he makes himself vulnerable by getting into another relationship, he will be left again. He ultimately feels alone and further solidifies this feeling of loneliness by living this life of fear-based solitude.

TIBOR'S MOTHER

Tibor's mother feels immensely responsible for her children, and when she is unable to help them, she gets consumed with worry. For example, when Tibor's brother was moving out to another apartment, and she could not help out because of conflicting schedules, she became distraught with worry and frustration from her inability to help.

TIBOR'S INTERGENERATIONAL TRAUMA ON HIS MOTHER'S SIDE

Till this day, Tibor's mother holds a grudge against her own mother because she felt somewhat abandoned by her. After Tibor's grandparents' divorce, Tibor's mother ended up being raised by her grandparents, since Tibor's mother's stepfather didn't want her around. Interestingly, Tibor also felt abandoned after his parents' divorce, and was, in essence, living in his mother's movie.

Although it may seem that Tibor's feelings of loneliness and Tibor's mother's feelings of abandonment can be partly attributed to Tibor's grandmother choosing her lover over her child, it goes deeper than this, as Tibor's grandmother also feels alone most of the time. For instance, she was very sad when Tibor went to Germany to work as an architect, because it brought up feelings of loneliness.

The question is, where do Tibor's grandmother's feelings of being alone all come from?

When she was 10 years old, her brother, who was 20, was taken away by Russians to the USSR and detained there as a prisoner of war. After he was "free" to leave the USSR, he went to live in Austria, then Sweden, and finally immigrated to the US where he still lives to this day. He couldn't move back to Hungary because it was under the communist regime of the USSR.

It was ultimately Tibor's grandmother's brother who truly felt alone because he had to live a life of solitude, completely severed from his family. He couldn't call or send letters to his family in Hungary because of the USSR's communistic control, and he was worried that the USSR would find him or punish his family for trying to make contact with them. Consequently, his family had no news of him whatsoever, as if he had completely disappeared from the face of the earth. They didn't even know if he was alive or not.

He was taken away in 1956, and it was only after 1989, when communism was lifted in Hungary, that he came back home for the first time in 1994. *Imagine that.* Severed from his family for almost 40 years. His mother (Tibor's great-grandmother) had already passed away when he was finally able to come back. Since the time of his disappearance until her death, she was always worried about the whereabouts and well-being of her son.

Now you can see why Tibor's mother worries about the well-being of her children so much – for instance, being unable to help with Tibor's brother's move. Just the same, Tibor's grandmother excessively worries about the well-being and safety of her family – for example, every time Tibor or his brother drives to another country in Europe.

Tibor's mother and grandmother are all reliving the movie of Tibor's great-grandmother as they remain unconsciously consumed by the intergenerational trauma that has lingered in the family: the kidnapping and disappearance of Tibor's grandmother's brother.

TIBOR'S INTERGENERATIONAL TRAUMA ON HIS FATHER'S SIDE

Tibor's father's mother passed away at the age of 62, in large part due to her husband's strict and controlling ways, which had caused a lot of depression in her. When Tibor's grandfather could not control others, he would get very angry. He would try to control Tibor's father's love life by trying to set him up after his divorce, and they would get into very heated arguments because Tibor's father did not want to be set up. Another issue was that Tibor's grandfather could not accept Tibor's uncle wanting to be a musician.

Tibor's grandfather's worst fear was that if his family didn't listen to him then he would somehow lose everything he had worked for and built up in his business, assets, and ultimately, all respect.

The intergenerational trauma lies in Tibor's grandfather's land being forcefully taken away by communists as it was "divided for all." He had always been a businessman and an entrepreneur and this devastated him. This is one reason why Tibor's grandfather always needed to be in control – because everything he had ever worked for and prided himself on was taken away from him just like that.

To him, his business was his identity and when his business was taken away, his sense of identity was robbed along with it, making him feel worthless. This has also been the case Tibor, who said if he failed at his podcast, he would fail at his reason for existence, and thus feel worthless.

Another reason why Tibor's grandfather needed to control others was to make him feel like he mattered because that was the only remaining sense of self-worth he could hold onto. Tibor's grandfather would feel he did not matter and would be unhappy with Tibor's father because he wanted his son to call him more often. As for Tibor's father, his struggles with feelings of loneliness are in many ways him feeling his own father's feelings of having no self-worth and no identity.

WHAT IF YOU CANNOT IDENTIFY YOUR INTERGENERATIONAL TRAUMA?

Ask your parents or other family members for missing stories and information. Use the FIST process and in particular the PEWF process to get the information and missing links you need to make sense of where your feelings could be coming from. I had to do that with my father because he and the family he comes from naturally suppress their feelings and emotions.

Keep asking questions, and piece together the puzzle of your intergenerational trauma. There are still many more examples ahead that you can learn from. If all else fails, you can go on my website (healfromthegroundup.com) to view my availability.

True Self & Transform

CHAPTER TEN:

The True Self

The "T" in the F.I.S.T. process stands for two things. First, the "True Self" and secondly, "Transformation." The "true self" is about honoring your true self and shining your light onto the world. "Transformation" is about after having separated yourself from the movies of others, creating and directing your own movie which stems from transforming your darkness into your light, and then sharing your movie with the world.

We will first begin by discussing the "true self." The first step to honoring the true self is defining your true self through two separate words.

DEFINING YOUR TRUE SELF

Your true self is your source of light, peace, power, wisdom, and love.

Define the essence of your true self through two separate words. These two halves of your true self are like yin and yang and are supportive of each other.

Before you begin to define your true self, I want to first give you a hint, in that:

You cannot define your true self as "compassionate," "kind" or "caring."

The reason being, if you do so, and you are alone in a room, you will feel like you are not good enough because you have to do something for someone else to feel good enough. But, the power and beauty of your true self is who you are, just as you are.

I will now give you two personal examples of how I define my true self. I call myself "The Calm Goofball" or "The Laughing Buddha." An example of how I exemplify my true self is in the title of my first book which is "You are the F*cking Sh*t: Heal your anxiety, anger and depression from the ground up!" As you can see, this title exemplifies my goofy self and my calm intuitive self.

In calming my baby son, it is really when I am being goofy that makes him calm down. Even my wife noticed this and told me that me being goofy gives off a very calming energy, not only for the baby, but for her, too, from simply noticing me. For example, when my baby would cry as a newborn, I would hold him while dancing and singing, "It's my party, and I'll cry if I want to! Cry if I want to! Cry if I want to!" (from the famous 60's song "It's My Party" by Lesley Gore.)

Another example of my goofy self is this picture below, with me and my then 7-month-old baby boy, holding a sign saying "Success is impossible without play." On top of my head is my underwear and on top of my son's head is my mother's bra.

DEFINING THE FIRST HALF OF YOUR TRUE SELF:

The first half of your true self is alive, free, and powerful. Definitive words for the first half of the true self can be:

• Creative: (likes to create new ideas and solutions)

• Explorer: (loves to learn new things and seek out new experiences)

• Warrior: (for that inner strength within you, the feeling that nothing can stop you)

• Goofy/Silly/Clown: (your humor is your source of power)

• Adventurer (loves new challenges)

Note: if you have another word that better resonates with you, feel free to choose that:

_____

ARE YOU STILL HAVING DIFFICULTY IN DEFINING YOUR TRUE SELF, NOT IN RELATION TO OTHERS?

Don't worry because this is extremely common. Use it as both a wake-up call and a gentle reminder to not deny your true self in service to others, because your true self is your greatest gift to others.

CLIENT EXAMPLES OF DEFINING THEIR TRUE SELF IN RELATION TO OTHERS:

Purely defining your true self in relation to others can be deeply ingrained in you, in that you don't know how else to define yourself. For example, many of my clients define their true selves as a "problem solver," but when I ask what problems they are solving and if they are solving the problems of others, they all stop in their tracks and see once again that they are defining their true self in relation to others.

I had one client who first identified herself as a "problem solver" and after the realization that it was really about solving other people's problems, she then went onto identifying herself as "respectful." But, again, one must be respectful to others.

Many clients of mine can't help but define themselves only in terms of the roles they perform in service to others. For example, when I asked a client to define her true self, after repeated failed attempts, she had no other answer but saying she just saw herself as a "mother, friend, daughter, and employee," all of which are roles through which we serve others.

To give you yet another example, several clients have told me, "I don't focus on me. I focus on everything around me."

EMPOWERING WORDS TO DEFINE YOUR TRUE SELF:

A word like "determined" is not as empowering as the word "warrior."

A word like "curious" is better defined as "explorer."

LOGICAL DEFINITIONS OF THE TRUE SELF:

I have also heard clients use the word "thinker" to define the essence of their true selves, which shows that a person thinks too much and doesn't feel enough. Remember, your most powerful self is something you can feel. Living in your headspace is when you are connected with your small self.

DEFINE THE SECOND HALF OF YOUR TRUE SELF:

The second half of your true self is grounding. Definitive words for the second half of your true self can be:

• Peaceful

• Grounded

• Calm

• Quiet

• Rooted

Choose a word that resonates with you to define the second half of your true self (Note: if you have another word that better resonates with you, feel free to choose that):

_____

Now I like to combine the two words into a single identity. Below are some examples. Find a combined single identity that best resonates with you.

• The Peaceful Warrior

• The Grounded Warrior

• Creative Peace

• The Peaceful Explorer

Combine the two halves of your true self into a single identity here:

_____

COACHING DIALOGUE WITH ADRIENNE MACLAIN ABOUT HER TRUE SELF

Adrienne defines the first half of her true self as "playful" and the second half of her true self as "intuitive" and I ask her to give me an example of what she means by "intuitive":

Michael: *Give me an example, like in your life, where this comes up.*

Adrienne: *Hmm. Mmm. Well, whenever I'm helping other people find the core of their story. That I have that ability to kind of cut through all the noise and the details and just get to the heart of the meaning and the message and what you're trying to get out there.*

Michael: *Can you give me an example that is not in relation to others? Obviously, it's going to be the greatest impact that you can have on others. But if you can feel it within yourself at all times, even if you're alone, then the beauty and the power of your true self is who you are just as you are.*

Adrienne: *"Connected" is the word that's coming up now. For me when I go for like walks in nature, for example, I just feel really connected to everything, you know, like not just like a tree or the ground. I get this connected feeling of like, I am part of all of this. I am, we are all one.*

And I get that really strong sense of like connection to everything.

Michael: *Okay. So remember the greatest gift to the "me" is the greatest gift to the "we." Just who you are, your true self, your reason for existence is an unbelievable gift to others beyond your imagination, but it's your true self that is the gift.*

That's the gift. (Adrienne: Yeah.) When you say "Connected, I feel connected to everything. We're all one," then where's your sense of self, right?

And just to be conscious of what you said, because that's your sensitivity on overrun almost cause it's going to be a huge weight. (Adrienne: Right. Yeah.) "I feel connected to everything...We're all one" and if that's how you define your true self as that, then it's all gonna seep through.

Adrienne: Yeah, of course.

Michael: I want to help others and yeah and I know you want to help others. But also it's my message, my voice, who I am, that's what's going to be the gift to others.

So it's not cutting other people off. We want to know who we are just as we are. Where we can even feel the power of who we are when we're alone in a room.

Cause imagine if you're so connected to everything and you're alone in a room, you're not going to feel that connection as much. You're gonna feel like, "Uh-oh, I need to do something. Your mind is going to be racing with the thought, "I'm not going to be good enough."

Adrienne: And that's what happens. You've just described my life.

So, I mean, I think underneath that or beyond that ("connected to everything"), like what...what am I?

Michael: But the playfulness is a good one. Does peaceful, grounded, rooted – or is there any other word that comes up for you – calm, quiet – that counterbalances the playfulness?

Adrienne: Well, to me, it's more like, you know, it's the wisdom, it's the recognition. I've listened to all these other people's stories, and I've listened to my own stories, and I keep learning and growing and recognizing that it is a journey, and we're all kind of on this journey.

Michael: Cause you love to learn new things?

Adrienne: Yeah, but I'm more like a "psychonaut," you know, like I explore the kinds of internal worlds and the stories that we tell ourselves and the stories that we tell each other about our identity and ...

Michael: Okay. Okay. I don't mean to be nitpicky, but I just wonder... so when you say "wisdom," that's like of the mind?

Adrienne: Yeah.

Michael: Because when we live too much in our headspaces, then we don't connect with our hearts, our feelings.

Adrienne: Yeah. Mmhmm.

Yeah. I mean, okay. So that's really what it is. Like I feel things very deeply. I'm a very emotional person and I feel my feelings. I feel other people's shit. Like I have a lot of feelings.

I'm a cool person and I'm a playful person, but I can also be a very melancholy person.

Michael: What do you mean by melancholy?

Adrienne: It's not sadness. It's more like a recognition of grief and of emptiness and of like the cycles of life and things ending.

And, I just feel like everything's a part of everything. And so there's that, like I said, that balance of that. You have to enjoy that joyful experience to feel joy. You have to also know what the opposite of that feels like. You have to experience the absence of joy to recognize joy. Otherwise, it would just be a constant state, you know, we'd have no differentiation.

Michael: So how would you define your true self in one word? The calm grounded one (half of your true self). (Adrienne lets out a big sigh of playful frustration)

I mean, what emotions, what is coming up just right now?

Adrienne: It's hard because I'm like, you know, I want to be peaceful. I want to be serene. You know, I want to have comfort, but like, I recognize it, everything's part of a cycle, you know? And so it's hard for me to see myself, like my true self, as peaceful, because it isn't always.

Michael: I mean, things are happening in your life that are not always peaceful. Our emotions are not going to always be peaceful. That's just the ebb and flow of our feelings, but who we are is not chaotic. We may feel depression, but that's not who we are. (Adrienne: Yeah.) We need to come back to some type of anchor.

Adrienne: Yeah. And I've always had a hard time with that. That's why I seek out people who are very grounded in my life because I have not been a very grounded person, in and of myself. Like I seek out chaotic situations and like I thrive on them, you know, I'm very adaptable. And that's one of my sorts of superpowers that I can get thrown into any situation and like figure out what's going on and figure out how to, you know, have fun here. And so that's where the playfulness aspect comes from, where it's like, wherever I land, I'm going to find it fun and I'm going to bring the fun and I'm going to make it into a game.

But at the same time, like what is there beyond that for me? That's been a real struggle for me to kind of put my finger on my whole life.

Michael: When you say you seek out grounded people. What do you mean? Can you give me an example?

Adrienne: Oh, like my husband, for example. Virgos! My sister is a Virgo and my husband's a Virgo and like, I seek out these people that are very like, "No, this is like this, and this is like this." Everything's, you know, black and white.

And this works like this. And where I am everything's a shade of gray and we could debate endlessly. And you know what I mean? Like it's hard for me to even settle on, like, "This is reality." Like, "Oh, I don't know. How am I supposed to know what reality is?"

I see every aspect of every problem. Do you know what I mean? Like, I can see it from everybody's perspective. And so it's hard for me to like, take a stand and be like, "No, this is like this." And – but I guess the core is just love. Like I always come back to like, love is always the answer and that's always been my anchor, is just love.

And for a long time, that was, you know, I felt like I had to have a partner, like to love. And if I didn't, then I felt like, who am I? Like, what even is my purpose in the world? And it's only been in the last few years that I realized that like, "Oh, I can love myself."

And just coming back to that feeling of like, just being "love" and radiating love and loving myself.

Michael: I want to explore something. Yeah. Cause you said you seek grounded people because you feel everything, you're connected with everything, and there's so much that you're thinking about, and you're connected to. Because when I hear you (speak), I hear you thinking a lot. (Adrienne: Yeah.)

Like, the thoughts are racing and looking for an answer: "It's this and it's that, it's this or that." And the thoughts keep racing. So when your thoughts are racing, you're not grounded.

Adrienne: Yeah! The monkey mind.

Michael: If you connect with your feelings and just to the act of feeling, knowing that feeling is healing. Connect with your gift of high sensitivity, high empathy, and then you will feel grounded.

Adrienne: Yeah. Yeah.

Michael: So I think that's the thing. I think you seek what you already have. You seek who you already are. (Adrienne: Yeah.)

I would define your true self as, let's see if this resonates with you, as "Grounded Playfulness."

Adrienne: Yeah.

Michael: Does that resonate with you?

Adrienne: Yeah. Yeah. Yeah. Playfulness from the heart.

Note: If you were not able to accurately define your true self but reading Adrienne's example gave you a lot of clarity, you can return to the previous sections and define your true self again.

CHAPTER ELEVEN:

Healthy Boundaries Protect Your Source of Light

A major aspect to honoring the true self is setting healthy boundaries with others because boundaries protect your true self, which is your ultimate source of power, light, peace, wisdom, love, and your greatest gift to humanity. Among the people you may need to set healthy boundaries with are romantic partners, family, colleagues, or friends.

HONORING YOUR VOICE IS HONORING YOUR BOUNDARY

The initial step towards honoring your true self is expressing how you truly feel with others. Ask yourself, "Do you express how you truly feel with others? Or do you withhold your voice?" If you don't honor how you truly feel with others, you will have no sense of self and no sense of boundaries. You end up being a chameleon completely infused with others. Honoring your self-expression is a critical boundary, because without a sense of self, you have nothing to protect, and consequently sever yourself from your source of power, peace, wisdom, and love.

FEELING RESPONSIBLE FOR OTHERS DENIES YOUR VOICE

It may be difficult for you to find your voice and set boundaries with others because for one, as a highly sensitive person and an empath you can be so in tune with the feelings and energies of others that you don't know the divide between you and the other person.

Because of the fact that you are so in tune with others, you can naturally find yourself feeling immensely responsible for others. Others can take advantage of this by putting their unresolved feelings into your personal space so they can avoid feeling them, thereby making you responsible for their unresolved feelings. If you don't honor how you truly feel, and very importantly, if you continue to feel responsible for others, you will then allow all the energy of their unresolved feelings and emotions to seep into your personal space and settle within your being.

On the other hand, what may prevent you from setting boundaries with others is actually a subconscious desire to fix your reflection in others in order to avoid the pain you constantly feel inside yourself. This is the role of the "protector" that we talked about before.

THE THREE COMMON WAYS WE EXPRESS OUR VOICE

There are three common ways in which we express our boundaries to others:

We don't say anything at all.

We put up aggressive walls and barriers or fight the other person.

We entangle ourselves in the venomous web of others by trying to reason with their fear-based logic.

In all three scenarios, you don't have a healthy boundary between you and the other person and thereby become an emotional sponge for the pain of others.

SAYING NOTHING AT ALL

When you don't say anything, you are telling your subconscious that you are complicit in what is happening, thus making it a part of your reality and sense of self. Before, when my mother would constantly nag me, I would numb my ears, because I knew if I were to say how I truly felt about her obsessive fears over health and safety, then she would most likely explode into one of her rants. At this time, I was struggling with a lot of anxiety because I was in her movie - because I was complicit in her putting her energies and unresolved feelings into my personal space.

THE AGGRESSIVE WALL

I have clients who have almost systematically cut their parents out of their lives. Their parents may not be emotionally abusive but just overbearing and overwhelming with their worries. My clients can avoid them, or get into heated arguments with them, but with both ways of setting barriers, they still freely take on the pain of their parents.

Aggression and anger are superficial acts of strength, which only serve to mask the powerlessness underneath them.

ENTANGLING YOURSELF IN THE FEAR-BASED LOGIC OF OTHERS

Do not entangle yourself in surface arguments and the fear-based logic of others. For instance, if someone were to tell you, "You are stupid," an inappropriate response would be, "No, I am not stupid!" This other person is clearly putting their unresolved feelings and pain of incompetence into your space. Instead of proving what they are saying is wrong, and thereby entangling yourself with their pain, you need to call them out on projecting their own pain onto you.

Another example is if someone feels neglected by you, but these feelings stem from within themselves. Don't make an effort to convince them that they do matter to you. You are not responsible for the pain that belongs to them. They must do the work to heal, and don't let them use you as an outlet to avoid working through their pain.

SETTING A HEALTHY BOUNDARY BY SAYING A "LOVING NO"

You want to lay the law down but in a loving way. You want to speak to the absolute core of the issue. When you say a "loving no" or create a healthy boundary between yourself and others, it is very important that you speak to the core.

After you have laid down the healthy boundary and said your "loving no," ultimately how they respond to it is not your problem or responsibility. Also, neither are you the other person's therapist. After you have laid down the healthy boundary, it's not your job to therapize them, because you are not and cannot be responsible for their well-being.

A PERSONAL EXAMPLE OF BOUNDARIES WITH MICHAEL'S PARENTS:

When I was living in the Czech Republic with my wife and newborn child, I would often send photos of my child to my parents. There was one time when we were at a restaurant, and we only had a car seat for the baby, and since it's not good for a baby to sit in a car seat for too long, my wife and I placed some blankets in the center of the restaurant table and placed the baby on there. As a joke, I took a fork and made it seem like I was going to eat my baby boy. I sent this photo to my father, and his response was that this photo was inappropriate. My dad has a history of wanting me to suppress my humor because he thought it was inappropriate. I normally would not say anything back and just keep quiet, but I knew then I had to say something, or else I would be doing a dishonor to my soul. Here is how I responded to my father:

"Dad, sometimes you can be too serious. Humor and goofiness are an important part of who I am and it's one of the gifts that God gave to me to share with others and to teach my son. It's not good for me if you suppress it. The photo is a playful joke of me eating him as part of lunch."

Before we left the Czech Republic to move into my parents' home, I had set a boundary with my mother who excessively worries about the health and safety of her loved ones. I set up a video call with her where I told her:

"Just as you and dad were parents to me, it is important that you let me be a parent to my own child."

She totally understood what I was talking about, but of course, asked if it was okay to give messages of caution here and there. I was completely fine with this because I had set the tone and laid a healthy boundary for my nuclear family.

INTERNAL SEPARATION:

When you take on the pain of your parents or your partner as your own, and they still act out of the same pain you took on, it can infuriate you, because you have already sacrificed your soul by taking on the burden of their pain and trauma, and yet they still act out of the same pain.

This shows that you not only do you have to externally separate yourself from the pain of others by setting healthy boundaries, but that it's just as, if not more, important to separate from it internally.

In essence, people can only trigger you when there is something within you to be triggered. Release your intergenerational trauma, and you will become an immovable foundation of peace and calm that can never be shaken or rattled by others.

A very common situation where boundaries are severely violated both ways is within the relationship between what I call "the Hulk" and "the Pacifier."

THE HULK AND THE PACIFIER

The relationship between the hulk and the pacifier can apply to relationships with your partner, but can also apply in other relationships as well, like your relationship with your parents. The hulk is someone who gets either very angry or panicky if someone doesn't do what they specifically want them to do because they need to be in control. The hulk doesn't necessarily have to be someone who is emotionally volatile but rather emotionally suffocates others through this need to be in control. The pacifier is someone who sacrifices their sense of self in order to pacify the hulk to prevent another hulk episode.

Note: In no way am I trying to demonize anyone by calling them "the Hulk." The term "the hulk" only speaks about the pain that a certain person is holding onto, yet this pain is not a part of who they truly are.

Very importantly, the hulk and the pacifier are not roles that are set in stone. In fact, a person can act like a hulk in certain situations and a pacifier in others.

To explain the relationship between the hulk and the pacifier, I will use my relationship as a personal example. A month before my wife and I were supposed to buy a house, she put all of our savings into stocks without even me knowing. Two weeks later, coronavirus hits its peak and the stock market crashed, and we lost half of our savings. Not only did she make a unilateral decision but at the time she initially wasn't even sorry about what she had done and thought I was just overreacting.

Yes, it's true that this experience did teach me the invaluable lesson of honoring my voice and my personal desires because I am a person who too often swallows my voice and desires for the sake of others, just so they don't get upset or triggered. I am what I call the "pacifier" in the relationship. My wife, on the other hand, is the "hulk" in the relationship, a name chosen by our intuitive coach during our couples sessions together to give a name to the times when my wife's anger set ablaze.

We were living in my parents' addition, and due to our dramatic financial losses, it would not have made sense to move out at the time, which triggered a lot of emotions and unforeseen trauma for my wife.

She desperately wanted to move out of my parents' house, as family has always been a major trigger for my wife. My mother, in particular, was a major trigger for my wife since my mother can be overbearing with her obsessive fear about health and safety to avoid death. This would trigger memories of traumatic experiences that my wife had as a child growing up with her mother, to the point where she would react to my mother as if it were her own mother in her tumultuous childhood.

I eventually agreed to go to the Czech Republic within two months where we have residency and the cost of living was more affordable. One day, something had set something off in my wife, just by my grandma wanting to spend time with our grandchild, and she told me that we would have to move out immediately and that in a few days she was going to move to Central California with our child with or without me. I even had called the police, but they told me this was not a matter that they could help with.

To give you another example of my wife's emotional explosions: when the coronavirus was hitting its first peak, my wife would just consume herself with the news about the virus and completely lose it and fly off the handle. One time I couldn't take it anymore, so I turned off the wifi router and locked myself in my office. My wife didn't know how to switch it back on and so she kept banging on my door, and I ignored her for a while.

I eventually opened the door, and while she was holding our then 6-month-old child, she relentlessly punched and kicked me while yelling at me. I ran away from her, and she chased after me all around the house trying to punch and kick me.

We went into couples therapy and our intuitive coach told us that when my wife would go into these emotional explosions to say the keyword "the incredible hulk" as a cue for her to calm and center herself. Although the sessions were critically helpful for our relationship, the hulk still would come out.

There was one time when we were leaving the house and I wanted my mother to see her grandchild and just to say hello. My wife decided to mock me and my mother by sarcastically saying to us, "Hellooo, helloooo, helloooo." *(Note: My wife did this because she wanted me all to herself and having too strong of a connection with my parents made her feel more alone.)*

When we got into the car, I knew I had to honor my feelings and tell her how I didn't like what she did, despite knowing that she could possibly explode again. Because otherwise, I would just be swallowing my voice and feelings once again. After I told her how I felt, soon enough she had another emotional explosion, and we were forced to return home.

When she would have these explosions, there was very little I could do. I would just have to wait until she calmed down but that wait would feel like an eternity because it could be hours or days. Moreover, the "calm" after the storm would just be a waiting period for the next episode of the hulk, especially since, during that time, these fights and explosions were happening every 2-3 days.

After that last incident, I finally had had enough of everything, and I decided for the first time in our 6-year relationship to set a true boundary by laying out what the true consequences would be. Consequences are not threats or ultimatums. Consequences are boundaries when others don't initially listen. It's very important to understand that consequences are also lenient enough to allow enough space and time that gives the other person an opportunity to understand and change their behavior.

The potential consequence I gave to my wife, and I wrote it down on a big piece of paper for her to see, was that with each of her emotional explosions, she had two hours to calm and center herself. If she did not, that would count as one strike. If she accumulated three strikes before the time we were supposed to leave for the Czech Republic, then I would not go with her to the Czech Republic.

On the same paper, I referred to the current emotional explosion she was having, and said if she did not calm down within the next two hours, it would count as a strike, leaving her only two strikes.

When I showed her the paper, you know what she did? She immediately threw it into the trash. Despite what she did, in my heart, I still stayed committed to the consequence of her hulkish behavior because I made the conscious decision from here on out to not tolerate this toxic behavior and energy any longer. It was not only unacceptable to myself but for my son to be around. Usually, during these times of contention and just waiting for the hulk to calm down, my son would just be around her all the time with the toxic fumes of my wife's hulk.

To my pleasant surprise, an hour and a half later, she came to my office and just stood there looking at me and said, "I'm here...I took your paper out of the trash, read it, and I agree to it."

Setting this consequence was not a threat or an ultimatum, but a firm decision on my part that I would in no way accept these emotional explosions as part of my marriage and family, and from then on, it radically transformed our relationship forever. Neither did I have to actually give out strikes because this conscious decision changed the foundation of our entire marriage and family.

There are many relationships (most commonly romantic relationships, or between parent and child, and sometimes with friends or even with people in the workspace) just like mine, where one party is the "pacifier" in the relationship and the other party is the "hulk" who goes into emotional explosions – either through anger or anxiety and panic – if one of their emotional landmines gets stepped on. The pacifier in the relationship has to carefully tiptoe to not step on the landmines of the hulk.

When the hulk explodes, the pacifier will play the waiting game and just wait and see until the explosion settles, but in truth, even when it does "settle," it never really does. Furthermore, if you, the pacifier, play this waiting game, you will wait for an eternity that feels like hell on earth. Your partner, the hulk, will never change, because you allow the hulk to be the hulk. You helped create the monster you are so desperately trying to tame. Taming the beast has become what your whole life has been reduced to.

(Remember, when I say "monster," "beast" or "hulk," I truly mean this as a metaphor for the pain that gets activated in your partner but in no way am I saying that your partner is any of those. The term "the hulk" is really a name for the pain that gets activated in your partner or the other person but doesn't define who they truly are.)

In this kind of relationship, the only way for things to change is by setting what I call "loving boundaries."

ENTANGLING YOURSELF WITH THE HULK BY TRYING TO DIFFUSE THE SITUATION

Before I explain what loving boundaries are, I want to ask you a question. When the hulk gets angry at you, how do typically respond? Do you try to explain yourself and diffuse the situation? If you do so, you are entangling yourself with the hulk's web of pain. By trying to diffuse the situation you are not helping the hulk in any way. The hulk is projecting their pain onto you so they can avoid feeling their pain. However, we only avoid what is real, so by allowing the hulk to project their pain onto you, you are thereby validating that their negative core feelings are true about who they really are.

If the hulk is spewing out emotional venom and toxicity at you (i.e. telling you that they don't feel heard by you when that's their own venom to deal with), while you, the pacifier, try to put the hulk at ease by explaining ad nauseam why it's not so, you are thereby entangling yourself to their web and its venom. Let's say your partner accuses you of cheating due to their fear of abandonment and you explain away on how that is not the case. You are thereby entangling yourself with your partner's web of pain and validating the painful feelings of your partner that they are worthless and abandoned.

SPEAK TO THE CORE

Instead of attempting to diffuse the situation with the hulk, speak to the core of what's truly going on. Tell the hulk to simply stop projecting their pain and negative emotions onto you. The hulk is obviously allowed to voice what they want to say but they cannot unload their unhealed fury, pain and trauma onto you.

To give you an example, when my son was 6 months old while living with my parents, my mother was spending time with my son on the couch. My mother took her eyes off of my son to reach for the TV remote to change the channel, and my son rolled off the couch and fell onto the tile floor with his face. Luckily my son had his hands out in front of him which softened the blow and he turned out to be fine. I chose not to share what happened with my wife because she was in the midst of a lot of emotional instability and trauma and I felt she would very likely stop my mother from spending time alone with my son altogether.

Six months later, after we had already moved out, I finally did share this story of what happened with my wife as we were eating at a restaurant. Upon hearing this, my wife became uncontrollably furious with me asking me how could I not tell her as if it just had happened. Although it was wrong for me to not tell her when it had happened, it is unacceptable for my wife to project her pain onto me. I told her at that very moment that she had to stop. She had to stop putting her anger and pain onto me. There is no discussion that can be had if one person is projecting pain onto another. I did not entangle myself in her web of pain by trying to diffuse the situation and explain myself to her on the reasons why I chose not to tell her at the time it happened. I had to first clear the air of this projection of pain before any true communication could be possible.

My wife soon enough saw what she was doing and calmed down. Afterward, we talked about in detail what had happened and what I should and should not have done. She did admit to the fact that knowing her emotional state back then, she would have acted very drastically.

This is the loving boundary and consequence I set with my wife, telling her I will not engage in a conversation with her until she stops projecting her anger, pain and fury onto me.

REFLECTING THE HULK BACK AT THE HULK

When the hulk is yelling at you to the point where you simply can't take it anymore and you get into a yelling match with them, you are being the pacifier once again and taking on their pain and reflecting it back at them. You may do this because you love them deeply and want to end their pain so badly that you will subconsciously take it on as your own.

Very importantly, do not get sucked into the energy of the hulk to the point that this energy becomes your energy. Stay calm and centered with the hulk and be conscious of not entangling and infusing yourself with their unhealed energies being thrown at your way. Likewise, you want to demand that the hulk calms and centers themself before you two can have any form of conversation.

An example of reflecting the hulk's pain back at the hulk, with regards to a relationship, is you worrying if this relationship does not work out, then you will not only have failed once again but you will ultimately be alone. But it's possible you could very well be feeling your partner's feelings of loneliness as your own, meaning you are living in the movie of your partner.

Ask yourself, are you, as the pacifier, feeling the pain of your loved ones (i.e. your partner, your parent) as if it were your own movie? Are you feeling their pain as your own, and then thinking they are the ones causing you to feel this pain? It is true that they are causing you to feel this pain and hopelessness, but mainly because you have taken on their pain as your own and yet they still don't change.

MICHAEL'S EXAMPLE OF REFLECTING THE HULK

There was a time when my wife and I were living in Taiwan. I had to make sure to wake up early for my video call sessions with my clients. My wife had a bad habit of going to bed late while getting lost in busy work or internet browsing on her computer. I would tell her to go to bed on time, but consistently she would lose herself on the internet. There was one week where she went to bed late for one week straight, and on the seventh day I went into a furious tirade, as my wife yet again was reluctant to go to bed. I was so furious with my wife because I felt my needs did not matter to her.

During a couples session, the therapist revealed the possibility that I could be feeling my wife's feelings of not mattering as my own and then reflecting it back at her. The reason why my wife would drown herself into the computer was to mask and numb her feelings of not mattering. The fact that I feel so heavily responsible for my wife, makes matters much worse because it sets me up to be an emotional sponge for her unresolved pain and trauma.

FEELING RESPONSIBLE FOR THE HULK

What's stopping you from voicing how you really feel in the relationship and setting loving boundaries and consequences? Are you constantly trying to change yourself and adapt yourself to the hulk so they don't get activated? Do you feel so responsible for the hulk and know that the hulk will get activated if you do voice your personal feelings and desires, making you choose instead to continue to swallow your voice and needs and deny your very existence?

Know that when you feel responsible for others, you are trying to use your personal key to drive the vehicle of life f or another. But your personal key will never ever work in the vehicle of others, so you will feel like a powerless and hopeless failure. If you truly want to help others and help your partner, you must stay in your sacred lane. Your sacred lane is your true self, source of light, and reason for existence, and your greatest gift to others.

Do not sacrifice and "adapt" yourself to the hulk and ultimately deny your existence just so the hulk doesn't get activated. You may be so used to "adapting" yourself to not set the hulk off that you end up camouflaging your soul to the point where this camouflage becomes who you are.

God created you. When you swallow your voice, you are denying your existence. When you abandon your sacred lane to pacify the hulk because you feel responsible for them, you are throwing away the reason why God created you down the drain.

Camouflaging yourself is a disgrace to the beautiful light that God created you to be for the world.

Most importantly, know that feeling responsible for others turns you into a subconscious emotional sponge for the pain of others. This will make your life and the pain that you mistakenly feel is yours – into a living nightmare because you are trying to fix something that doesn't belong to you as if it did.

Note: If you don't feel comfortable with the word "God" you can use the word "Creator," "Universe," or "Love" in place of it. I personally prefer the word "God" because the word contains a lot of feeling in it. This is important because, as you know, "feeling is healing" as it connects you to love.

Throughout the rest of the book, when I do use the word "God," know that I am referring to our Creator. My use of the word "God" is not tied to any religious affiliation but simply meant to allow you to feel a powerful connection with your Creator. Only the Creator is in control, or as I like to say, only God is in control. It is important to acknowledge our Creator, because when we don't, we seek control and separate ourselves from the only entity in control which is our Creator; thereby making us feel forever incomplete.

REPAIRING YOUR RELATIONSHIP WITH YOUR PARTNER BY SETTING LOVING BOUNDARIES

Loving boundaries and consequences are in no way a punishment or threat. Consequences are the conscious decision and awakening within the fabric of your soul that you will no longer tolerate and accept the poisonous behavior of another.

Setting these kinds of loving boundaries or consequences are not about viewing your partner as some villain, since these boundaries not only help you but they also help your partner. Your partner's hulkish behavior not only poisons you but your partner above all else.

When you find yourself battling or wanting to tame the hulk, remind yourself of the ultimate end game which is to be married with your life partner and above all to have a family and children together. If you don't have children yet, I am assuming that you want to have children with your life partner. Think of the end game and think of the child as if the child is already present in your family.

You, the pacifier, can no longer allow the toxicity of the hulk to control the family, take hostage of the family and yourself, and ultimately be spewed onto your child.

You do want peace, joy, love, and happiness, correct? Then don't attempt to pacify the venomous pain of the hulk, and let it seep into your soul, your relationship, and your current or future family. Set the foundation now! Set the rules now! Or else, everyone will suffer, including your partner, and especially your children.

Mind you, when I speak of loving boundaries and consequences they don't need to be as grave as the ones I set with my wife by telling her she has three strikes. I had to go to that extreme because I experienced 6 years of emotional and physical abuse and so I laid down a strict boundary because I wasn't going to tolerate it any longer for myself and especially for my child . For example, you can set a minor or significant consequence, such as saying you will not engage in any conversation with them when they are in hulk mode. It doesn't matter how anxious, angry, or lost in their pain they can be. You will not engage in any conversation with them until they have emotionally centered themselves.

You must be brave and simply make the choice to set loving boundaries and firmly stand by it. Remember, mere words are not boundaries. In no way does setting boundaries mean, for example, you helplessly voicing to your partner, "You are spewing your toxicity and venom onto me! Don't you see that? Stop it!"

Loving boundaries are actions that are laid out upfront to your partner to set the foundation for your relationship. Boundaries can only be boundaries when you mean it. Loving boundaries and consequences are when you finally awaken to the decision that from here on out you will no longer allow this toxicity and venom to poison yourself, your marriage, and your family.

No means no.

You wouldn't willingly drink poison, right? No way in hell would you allow your child to drink poison, right?

When you choose to entangle yourself in the hulk's venomous web of pain,

when you choose to swallow your voice and true desires to not activate the landmines of the hulk, and ultimately when you choose to be the pacifier, you are willingly drinking the poison for yourself, your marriage and your child.

Loving boundaries and consequences are not a threat, nor are they an ultimatum. When I set consequences in my marriage, it was not a threat. It was an awakening vis-à-vis what I will not allow in my marriage, my family, and my child. If I tolerate this any longer and it becomes, for the lack of a better term, the "new normal," I will kill my soul.

If you truly want to help your partner, you absolutely must set loving boundaries and consequences because that's the only way they can possibly change. They will most likely never change unless you do this. Beware, your partner may scream, shout and holler like they never did before, when you set consequences. That's only because you are hitting them where it hurts the most and forcing them to face their demons, and hopefully they will choose to be free of this hulk.

Stand your ground when you lay out these loving consequences and the hulk goes into full activation mode. Do not, under any circumstances, give in and once again get entangled in their venomous web of pain.

LETTING GO OF THE IDENTITY OF THE PACIFIER CAN BE PAINFUL

Both of you must do the inner healing work to let go of being the pacifier and the hulk. This is not about pointing fingers at the hulk, since it can feel extremely painful for you, as well, to choose to stop being the pacifier, as it is the only identity you know.

You may "feel at home" with the ordered chaos of being the pacifier and would rather not leave the eerie familiarity and comfort of this chaos and pain. Perhaps you fear that letting go of your false identity as the pacifier will pain you even more because it's all you have ever known. Be that as it may, letting go of all that you know as the pacifier will ultimately transform your relationship and your life forever, by allowing you to reclaim your true self, the person God created you to be.

DO NOT GIVE UP

The challenges of your relationship may feel like hell on earth and push you to the edge and have you wanting to call it quits, but do not give up on your relationship. Relationships, especially with your life partner, are meant to detoxify ourselves of our inner demons by bringing them to the surface so we can work through them.

When things do get very heated or even volatile within the relationship, patiently and calmly apply the FIST process together so that you can understand where each other's triggers are truly coming from. With this newfound awareness, you two can stop fighting the hopeless battle of using the movies of your past family members to fight each other. In that scenario, the relationship is not just the two of you as a couple, but a whole entire movie set of your past family members, endlessly fighting each other.

What if things get so bad that you can't find the willpower to be centered and apply the FIST process together? You can use an emergency reset button for the relationship, by stating to each other, what you love about each other and why you are each other's life partner. This will help you see what you are truly fighting for. You are fighting for each other. No matter if you feel like you are walking through a valley of fire with your partner; everything is worth it when you know what you are fighting for.

Let me remind you, if you ever find yourself feeling you want to bail on the relationship, know that you will face your inner demons wherever you go if you don't work through them. One of the main purposes of a relationship is to detoxify your inner demons so they no longer control you and secretly haunt you.

Face the fire and your relationship will transform itself forever. Run away from the fire, and the fire will haunt you for the rest of your life.

WHAT HAPPENS WHEN YOUR PARTNER DOESN'T WANT TO DO THE WORK?

What happens when your partner doesn't respond to the consequences you've laid out and clearly does not want to look within themselves and work through their inner demons? The purpose of any relationship is to bring your inner demons to the surface so you can work through them and be free of them.

Therefore, if anyone in the relationship is not at all willing to work through their feelings and inner demons, then it is best to leave the relationship because relationships are about growth, evolution, and transformation. If a person is not willing to work through the feelings that the relationship is bringing up in them, then it defeats the purpose of the relationship. I believe relationships are meant to detoxify you of all your inner demons by bringing them to the surface so you can set a healthy foundation for your family and children. Without working through your inner demons, it is impossible for you to provide this healthy foundation.

DEAR HULK, YOU CANNOT ESCAPE

This is a memo to the hulk who carelessly throws out the phrase, "Let's end this relationship then!" You may escape this relationship, but your hauntings will follow you wherever you go, until you choose to work through the inner demons of the hulk and let them go. Above all else, you being the hulk is you living in the movies of your past family members, as if they were your own. This whole shit is not even yours to begin with!

Stop misusing your gift of emotional antennas and inserting yourself into the traumatic movies of your past family members. In this kind of life, your pain becomes a hologram. No matter how hard you huff and puff and try to fight this pain and project it onto your partner and make your partner responsible for it all, it does nothing to this hologram of pain that will haunt you for the rest of your life until you awaken from it and separate yourself from this movie that was never yours to begin with.

You can no longer allow the toxicity and venom of your hulkish ways to seep into and poison not only yourself, but your marriage and child. That is completely unacceptable and that is a core violation of the sacred pact of having a family.

You being the hulk by needing to be in total control is a coping mechanism to avoid feeling your pain. But true pain is the avoidance of pain, which will infect not only yourself but your entire family. Remind yourself: Pain is your greatest teacher. The lessons you learn from pain will transform you and your family forever.

Ask yourself: If you were not in control and if others did not listen to your demands, would it make you feel not only that your needs did not matter but also that who you are did not matter? Feel this feeling, and separate yourself from it, and ask yourself "Whose movie are you in?" so this toxic feeling does not infect you and invade your family unit.

BEING THE PACIFIER FOR OTHERS

I catch myself being the pacifier not just with my wife, but with everyone. I pacify my parents and my grandmother by worrying if they are spending enough time with my son. They are not even being hulkish to me, but I'm so attuned to others, making "the pacifier" my mode of being.

I know I could very well call the pacifier "the pacifist" instead, but being that I have a baby, I love the analogy of the pacifier because when a pacifier is in your mouth, you lose all ability to speak your voice. I don't know how true this is, but my wife told me she read in a mother's online forum that babies are not supposed to use pacifiers because they lose their ability to communicate through crying, which they do when they are hungry, tired, or uncomfortable.

When you are being the pacifier for others, imagine yourself sucking on a pacifier like a baby and losing all ability to speak your voice and express your desires. Imagine yourself being the literal pacifier for the mouths of others, so that they don't "cry" by being angry, anxious, or hulkish.

Instead of allowing others to deal with their inner demons so they can work through them and be free of them, you prevent all potential for healing and transformation by ENABLING them – enabling their demons, enabling their hulk.

When you enable others, you sacrifice your soul, you sacrifice God's creation in you which is your reason for existence. You sacrifice your beauty. You sacrifice your power, your joy, your peace. You sacrifice it all.

And for what? Just to be the band-aid to cover up the emotional wounds of others?

You cannot use your personal key to drive the vehicle of life for others. It is hopelessly impossible. You can no longer abandon your sacred lane because that is why you exist. Stay in your sacred lane because that's your source of peace, joy, power, wisdom, love, and ultimately, the source of light.

Stand your ground. Respect yourself. Respect and honor why God created you. Respect the purpose of your relationship, which is to grow. Respect your family and respect your children (future or present). Above all, respect and honor yourself. Being a pacifier is not who you are, and neither is it who you were created to be. You being the pacifier for others is you completely misusing your incredible gift as an emotional sponge to swallow the poison of others, which is only killing your soul and killing the soul of your marriage, family, and children.

Every single moment, I want you to be aware and remind yourself that you are not a pacifier. You are (Insert full name here). You are God's creation. Don't throw away the beauty of God's creation in you by being the pacifier for the world. Stop swallowing your voice and silencing your existence, all of which is just killing your soul.

Your beauty limitlessly expands beyond the horizon and throughout the universe. Feel the infinite beauty of your presence. Feel the infinite beauty of your inner child and make a pact from here on out that you will never desecrate the beauty of your inner child any longer. You will honor their light and let it shine brightly and limitlessly. Your inner child is you in its purest form. Through your inner child, you can vividly and clearly see the beauty and power of why you were created. Honor the reason for your creation every single moment of your life.

SETTING LOVING BOUNDARIES WITH YOUR PARENTS

Loving consequences are not threats. Loving consequences and boundaries are made from a place of empowerment. Threats are made out of a feeling of powerlessness, fear, and desperation to assert control. When setting a loving consequence with the other person, give the other person the opportunity to understand and change.

I'm going to share a personal example of setting loving boundaries – this time, not with a life partner but with your parents.

One night, I forgot to close the garage, and when my parents came home, my mom was absolutely furious with me, lashing out and unleashing her anger and fury onto me. Granted, I did something I shouldn't have done, but her pain, fear, and trauma were coming to the surface, and she was pushing this trauma into my personal space and being.

When I came back to the addition where my family lives, my wife told me she'd overheard the yelling and asked me what happened. Upon listening to what had happened, my wife decided that my mom, dad, and grandmother could not see our son the next day, which was Sunday. Sunday was a time where, during the coronavirus quarantine, my mother, father, and grandmother all met to attend online Sunday service and also where they got to spend precious quality time with my son, which is a time they absolutely cherish.

I spoke with my mother and gave her one last chance to calm down and said if she didn't calm down that she, my father, and my grandmother would not be able to see my son the next day. As you may have guessed, she didn't take it well, and it seemed to have backfired by just creating more animosity.

My wife shortly calmed down and eased her defense system. We both agreed to give my mother the time and the opportunity to learn why we were laying out these consequences. Since it was already getting late into the night, I went back to my mother and not only gave her one hour to calm down and center herself, but also took 40 minutes of my time and explained and discussed with her on why I had decided on this consequence. This was my way of giving my mother the true opportunity to understand where I was coming from by understanding the negative impact her actions had on me.

Shockingly, as I was trying my best to get through to her, she continually and relentlessly kept coming back and being chained to her fear of death – and how this causes her to become panicked when the house is left unsecured. I told her how I had internalized her fear of death with my insomnia, which would very often make my life feel like a living nightmare, but she still could not for just one second comprehend that she was transferring her trauma onto me and thereby hurting and damaging her beloved son.

In that moment of my mother's seemingly hopeless confusion, I understood why I suffered from insomnia and the fear of death so much. The reason for my crippling trauma was standing right in front of me, in how the fear of death crippled and consumed my mother.

It is true that after my son's birth, I did finally get to sleep much better, after seeing how I was living in my mother's movie of fearing death if her newborn were to wake her up and not being able to go back asleep. Despite the improvement, I still wasn't sleeping fully and there were even times I had sleepless nights which would make me extremely panicky. Every night I went to bed, I would get scared, wondering if I will get poor sleep tonight.

No matter how unfair or unreasonable my mother thought I was, and as much as I cherish my son spending time with my parents and grandmother, I knew I had no choice. If I allowed all of this to continue, then I would continue to live in this ongoing nightmare of insomnia. I knew I had to do it for myself, my family, and my son, because if I didn't set this clear boundary, then not only would I continue to internalize this trauma myself, but so would my son.

After 40 minutes of speaking with my mother and father, and as much as my father tried to help and get through to my mother, my mother was still blindly consumed with anger, fear, and trauma. I went back to our side of the house, thinking it was time to move out as soon as we could get the chance. 15 minutes later, I heard my father's voice through the door. I stepped out, and he let me know that mother had calmed down. I went over to ensure it was indeed true, and my mother told me herself that she had calmed down and even gave me a hug.

She had every right to be unhappy about me leaving the garage open, but it was unacceptable for her to be hysterically mad about it and project her trauma onto me. She understood that, and I was proud of and touched by my mother for seeing that and being willing to make the change.

Interestingly, something else very significant happened that very same night between me and my wife. I had suggested something to do that would be beneficial for a health issue she was dealing with, and she became extremely angry. (Although the health issue is nothing serious, to protect her privacy I will not disclose the details of it.)

My wife is a person who doesn't like to be told what to do because it is imperative for her to be in full control. When I tell her something to do that is, for example, good for her health, she can perceive it as an attack because she feels like she is not in full control. My wife uses control as a coping mechanism to avoid the intergenerational trauma of abandonment.

For example, every time I come back from my parents' side of the house, after having my son spend quality time with his grandparents, my wife's first instinct is to anxiously ask, "How is Zen?" (Zen is my son's name) – meaning was he mistreated, or in a sense, "abandoned"?

It is helpful to note that when my wife's mother was born, her father would not hold her and would walk past her crib, although she could be crying her lungs out. He didn't want to acknowledge her, since he had wanted a boy.

One time when I, my wife, and my son were visiting Taiwan, my wife woke up at 4 am to do some work, and it really bothered me because I couldn't sleep, as we were staying in a one-room studio. I was arguing with my wife, wanting her to go back asleep, and it woke up our son. She would not go to console him because she was angry with me for waking him up, while I was, at first, too angry at my wife for waking me up to console him either. When I eventually did go to console him, I first passed by his crib because I wanted to wash my hands before holding him. When I walked past him, my wife went into an immediate fury and started throwing any objects she could find at me and breaking things. She did all of this because me walking past our crying son set off the intergenerational alarm to the trauma of her mother crying as a newborn with her father walking right past her crib because he desperately wanted a boy.

It is traumatic instances like these that have me often feeling I am walking on eggshells with my wife when I sense I am doing something that could possibly upset her, although I could be doing nothing wrong at all. For example, I could be having my son see my parents on the other side of the house, and if I did not get her prior approval (Yes! believe it or not, I need her prior approval for my own son), I worry whether she'll find out and get angry.

I want to now come back to that night of my wife's emotional and volatile reaction to my suggesting something for her to do to protect her physical well-being. Her reaction had really bothered me to my core and made me think of what I realized earlier with my mother.

Although I did mention that my son's birth triggered horrific insomnia for me, the truth is my insomnia began when I first started dating my wife six and a half years ago. The beginning parts of our relationship were tremendously volatile. Something would set off my wife, and she would often be physically abusive to me. One thing she would often do is grab onto my arms and dig her nails into my skin as hard as she could, leaving scars that would last months. In looking back, it was a similar theme of her not being in full control and feeling abandoned because of it.

On that night, when I was met with my wife's anger for suggesting she do something for her personal health, it made me look back at the totality of our relationship together. Before I met my wife, I never had insomnia before. The reason why insomnia became such a daunting issue after meeting my wife was that, if I have chronic sleep deprivation, then my worst fear is I will die, which is rooted in the feeling of worthlessness. (As discussed before, the fear of death is commonly rooted in the feeling of worthlessness because if you die, you cease to exist.)

Both my wife's and my mother's intergenerational trauma of abandonment sits under the umbrella feeling of worthlessness. Additionally, if I have continuous poor sleep, then I would look like a fraud because I offer healing work to the world, and if I am exposed as a fraud then everyone will "abandon" me.

Most importantly, because I wasn't setting clear boundaries with my wife's need to be in full control to spare herself from feeling the pain of abandonment, I thereby took on this pain as my own, especially because my wife's intergenerational pain of abandonment is so similar to that of my mother.

I had a serious talk with my wife the next day after having cleared my mind through a lot of meditation. I told her that her incessant demand to be in full control "or else the hulk comes out," to avoid the pain of abandonment, was unacceptable because her pain became my pain.

This was not about giving a consequence, but really making a firm decision and becoming truly aware of something I would no longer accept and tolerate. My wife received and heard my message, and I thank her for that.

After having drawn this line in the sand of what I would no longer tolerate, between me and my mother and me and my wife, I ended sleeping a lot better because this conscious boundary and awakening of what I would no longer tolerate helped me stop absorbing their trauma of abandonment as my own.

Loving boundaries will change your life. If you don't set these loving boundaries, you will continue to be an emotional sponge and the pacifier for the pain and trauma of others. Loving boundaries and consequences are not threats. They are as much for the well-being of the other person as they are for yours. Loving boundaries are an act of love toward yourself and the other person.

YOU ARE NOT A SERVANT

The pacifier and the lack of boundaries are really about you assuming the identity of the servant. In particular, when a person acts like a hulk with the servant, the servant feels horribly powerless and worthless. The servant devotes their whole existence to serving others. However, when others are angry with them, the servant feels they have failed to serve others and thus have no reason to exist and feel worthless because of it.

This is an extremely common phenomenon with my clients. I have clients who work in customer service and due to COVID-19, customers can get very emotional and angry with my clients who are already doing everything they can to best serve the customers. My clients will then feel horribly worthless because they identify themselves and their existence as the servant and feel they have failed at their reason for existence and have no reason to exist.

This phenomenon is also especially prevalent in my personal life. My wife frequently can get very emotionally volatile with me due to the insurmountable trauma of not only her childhood, but the intergenerational trauma of her past family members. For instance, my wife needs to be in control to feel like she matters. When she doesn't get her way, she can easily get very angry because it makes her feel like she is being disrespected and thus feel she does not matter. As the servant, I in turn try to excessively serve my wife so I can feel that I matter and that I exist. I not only am the only one currently working to provide a living for the family, but I cook most meals, wash the dishes and basically do everything within my power to make time to help take care of our baby throughout the day. It is when my wife turns into the hulk that really triggers feelings of worthlessness within me because no matter all that I am doing, it's not enough. Once again, I'm failing to serve her, which brings up feelings of worthlessness within me that existed before I even met her. Remember, this feeling of worthlessness and abandonment is the movie that I am living in, which belongs to the intergenerational trauma on both my mother's and father's side.

ARE YOU AFRAID TO SET BOUNDARIES?

In working with couples, I often speak to the pacifier in the relationship about the importance of setting loving boundaries. The pacifier almost immediately turns to their partner and ask would this loving boundary work on them? This loving boundary does not depend on what the other person does or does not do. This loving boundary is for you. Only when you love yourself can you truly love, protect and serve others.

You may find it enormously difficult to set boundaries with others out of the fear of upsetting and disappointing others. This in turn, would make you feel worthless, because you need to serve others to feel self-worth. Remember, you must let go of the false identity of the servant because the "me" is the greatest gift to the "we." Don't serve others out of the pain of feeling worthless. Instead, serve others out of the beauty, power and light you were created to be.

WHAT IF CORONAVIRUS NEVER HAPPENED?

My wife and I had to go through a world of pain and struggle that was set off by the events of the coronavirus, forcing us to attend countless hours of therapy where we were at each other's throats. I remember one couples session lasting three hours. Although it feels like we've been to hell and back, we did the critical work to work through our inner demons and become better people out of this and most importantly become better people for our child.

Very importantly, if coronavirus had not happened, you would not be reading this book right now. So much of what I learned transpired because of all the events that were set off by the coronavirus. All the raw client examples I was able to share in this book of how people were being emotionally affected and triggered by the coronavirus was a major teaching point for this book.

It is when we hit rock bottom that we are forced to confront our deepest wounds so that we can heal them, allowing us to transform ourselves into our destined greatness, purpose, and reason for existence.

My wife took her hauntings and channeled them into vivid poetry so she could work through them in a healthy and empowering way, curating a book of poems out of it called "The Haunted House: A First-Time Mother's Journey Through Trauma." I was truly amazed and proud of my wife when she was reading her brilliantly powerful and healing poems to me as she was writing her book.

For myself, when all this chaos started in my marriage, instigated by losing half of our family's finances due to the stock market crashing, I had not then decided to write this book you are reading now. Losing half of our family's finances made me feel insecure and worried that I was not going to be able to provide for my family.

However, through writing this book, which was about answering my calling and sharing my movie with the world, I was able to connect with my true power and source of abundance.

When the chaos began in our world and in my marriage, I had no plans to write this book you are reading now and at the time I was doing podcasting while just starting my YouTube channel.

One week I ended up spending three full days just editing a single episode which I used for both my podcast and my YouTube channel. On top of all this, I was taking classes on how to build an online membership community, as my plan was to build a community in order to create a movement of healing to transform the world. However, it is not the community I build that would ultimately transform the world. Rather, it is my message, and that is my calling and that is my movie I am meant to share with the world to transform it.

As much as I enjoyed all of these different ventures, it was overwhelming and draining because I didn't have an anchor. That anchor is this book that you are reading now. Without an anchor, nothing you do in life will be rooted in a true purpose or foundation.

In writing this book, I feel so much at home, in fine-tuning and mastering my message for the world. Through all the strife, struggle, and pain, I thought I was going to lose my mind, but my calling and my movie were born out of it.

Whatever pain or chaos you are going through right now, know it's going to hurt like hell, but stick through it, because your greatest message and gift to the world come from your greatest pain and struggles. In fact, the world is meant to transform itself, but the only key that unlocks the world's transformation from all its pain, struggle, and darkness is your own transformation, your movie, and your calling.

CHAPTER TWELVE

What Is Your Movie?

Your movie is your dream, your purpose, your message, and your reason for existence.

Your movie is why you were created and placed on this earth.

Your movie is meant to be shared with the world. There never has been a movie produced in human history that was not meant for the consumption of others.

Your movie is your beacon of light which is meant to help and transform yourself, your family, and the world.

Your movie, above all else, is your calling. Ask yourself, have you answered your calling? Better yet, do you know what your calling is? For your calling is the whole purpose of your very existence.

Your movie and your calling are your ultimate source of light, peace, power, joy, healing, and transformation.

Your movie, which will help and transform the world, is not some charity work you do on the side, or considered "impractical" work that doesn't pay the bills or put food on the table.

Your movie is your connection to your infinite abundance because your movie is meant to be consumed by the world.

Your movie is meant to transform the world, otherwise you would not exist.

It's time to stop thinking small. It's time to stop going through the motions of life. Life is so much more than working just to make a living when abundance is at your fingertips if you choose to answer your calling. Above all else, you exist to answer your calling.

YOUR CALLING IS NOT TO SERVE OTHERS

I have many clients whom I ask, "What is your calling?" and they respond with: "My calling is to serve others." You serving and helping others is only the aftereffect and the result of answering your calling. You serving others is not the means and the vehicle through which you transform the lives of others, your calling is. Your calling is the engine that is the driving force enabling you to serve others. If you believe that your calling is to serve others, then you are denying your sense of self. When you honor your true self and the calling you were created to answer, you will be able serve others in a way far greater than anything you ever imagined.

WHAT IS YOUR MOVIE?

Now let's get our hands dirty and work out the vision, the impact, and the vehicle of your movie. Shortly, you will see coaching dialogues where I help clients find out what their movie is. You can first read these initial questions for yourself on how to determine what your movie is. Answer what you can, and then after reading over the coaching dialogues, you can come back to these questions to give a more in-depth answer.

Take some time to think of what your movie is – your dream, your purpose, and ultimately your calling?

WHAT IS YOUR PERSONAL STORY?

A major part of your movie and your calling will be sharing your personal story. Remember how in the beginning of the book I shared my personal story of having suffered from horrific insomnia after the birth of my newborn son? All of this happened for me only to find out later that I was living in my mother's movie. After all, it was my mother who never took care of me throughout the night as a newborn because she was scared that she would not be able to fall back asleep and ultimately die.

Your personal story, like mine, helps others relate to and understand your core message almost instantaneously, like a hot knife through butter. That is the power of storytelling, especially when you use your personal story.

When you craft the messaging of your movie, you want to own your power. I have many clients whose message – when I ask them to describe to me the message of their movie to me – comes off very bashful, indirect, and lacking the power of who they truly are.

Granted, going after your personal dreams and calling will force you to face your deepest wounds head-on and that is why it has always been more comfortable to stay small. Because what if, for example, you were to share your authentic, yet vulnerable message on, let's say, Facebook Live, and everyone were to judge you? Would you have to face the horror of your intergenerational pain in feeling invisible, alone, and worthless?

WHO IS THE AUDIENCE OF YOUR MOVIE?

When you think of your movie, you also want to envision the specific impact your movie has on others. Ask yourself, "How will my movie help and transform others?" In answering this question, you want to envision the specific audience actually watching your movie. Envision your movie as a box office hit that is being featured on an IMAX theatre screen packed with a full audience. Visualize your audience and visualize the specific impact your movie has on your audience.

Who is the audience of your movie?

_____

_____

_____

What is the specific impact your movie has on your audience?

_____

_____

_____

When you find yourself feeling fear, worry, anxiety, anger, loneliness, worthlessness, powerlessness or failure, the audience of your movie is then downsized to only one person and that is you, your insecurities and unresolved pain, as well as your past family members and their trauma. You are no longer directing your movie, but you are hopelessly lost in the movies of others.

When the audience of your movie is your past family members, it does not help them in any way whatsoever, because you are just living in their movies as your own while remaining utterly powerless to change anything.

FOLLOWING YOUR DREAMS FREES YOU OF YOUR PAIN

Following your dreams, being the director of your movie, and sharing it with the world will inevitably unearth your deepest and most hidden pain, specifically intergenerational pain and trauma, so you can finally heal and let go of it, and be free of it, so it no longer subconsciously controls how you feel and think.

As painful as this pain that you have felt throughout your life can feel, it is imperative to know that your pain, and your healing and transformation through it all, is the very vehicle and beacon of light that you are meant to shine onto the world.

CHANNEL YOUR PAIN INTO YOUR MOVIE AND YOUR BEACON OF LIGHT

Channel your pain into your movie that you will share with the world, and you will see the powerful purpose of your pain. Don't avoid the pain as you always have, because it will defeat the purpose of this "pain." Channel your pain into your art, making your pain the paintbrush and you the Picasso, to transform this pain into your beacon of light.

Embrace the pain while learning, growing, and transforming through it for:

> *"Pain is your greatest teacher.*
> *The lessons you learn from pain will transform*
> *you, your family, and the world."*

CHAPTER THIRTEEN:

Transformative Dialogues About Creating Your Own Movie

The following are excerpts from the dialogues I had with others who volunteered to be coached on my podcast and for this book in helping them uncover what their movie is. This will give you powerful insight on how to uncover the movie you are meant to share with the world, by learning from others who are doing it for themselves.

Through these examples, you can also learn how to help others do the same because you can see the actual coaching take place within the coaching dialogues.

COACHING DIALOGUE WITH BRIAN: BREAKING FREE FROM THE CHAINS OF LOGIC

If you need a refresher for Brian's previous session, Brian was the person who found out two years before his mother passed that his father was not his biological father. The reason why this was kept secret from him was because he was born out of wedlock and his grandparents from both sides forbade his parents from being together since it was considered immoral in the eyes of the Catholic Church. You can also refer to page 124 for the entire summary of the previous session.

Brian: *My dream is to have everything that I have with my wife, my kids, where I live, but when I dreamed this dream years ago, I didn't realize I could dream bigger... But now that I have it, I want more, and it kind of sounds selfish, but I want more. Financial and lifestyle freedom.*

I want my message out there as a therapist. I want... in my dream and my movie, I would like to be a thought leader in the area of anxiety.

I've lived my career life working for someone else and counseling and therapy or practicing therapy on clients in a corporate setting.

And I didn't realize that I had the personality. I didn't realize that I had the ability or whatever the right wording is to launch out on my own and be an entrepreneur in the counseling and coaching world. So I've been living, and I've been playing small, working for somebody and thinking that that was the way to go.

You know, work for someone, get a good salary, get a good 401k, but it's left me completely dissatisfied and discontent. I'm not touching the lives that I want to touch. I'm not touching the amount of people and lives that I want to touch.

Michael: *So when you say counseling, coaching, you were doing it in a corporate setting?*

Brian: *I've worked for a hospital the last 17 years, and I've been in outpatient counseling and therapy.*

And so, you know, the local community comes in, or the people at the hospital come in and they get counseling and I help them, and that's great. But I want more. I want to touch more lives.

I want to write a book. I want to create a course. I want to create multiple courses. I want to be a workshop leader. I want to be, you know, essentially wanting to be Tony Robbins.

Michael: *Let's just explore this. I hear you focusing on the end goal.*

But what about the vehicle? The means, which is you and the message, right? And your vision of that dream. So it's like, "I want to do online courses, I want to be a thought leader." But these are all the result of you embracing that specific dream message and vehicle.

So let's clarify. What is the movie you want to share with the world? I'll use a personal example. A couple of weeks ago I released a YouTube episode – along with the podcasting I was already doing. I was spread completely thin, and I was also taking classes on how to build an online community.

Cause I want to create this movement of inner healing that says world peace comes from inner peace and all the things I want to do. Then my relationship was going up and down, and we're supposed to leave for the Czech Republic June 7th.

There was so much going on, and I took three days to edit the YouTube episode and the podcast episode. They're the same episode, but it was just killing me. I was like, "No, I can't do this anymore. I'm producing just to produce. I need to create. I need an anchor. What's that one thing?

Because my wife told me, "You got to aim for fame. People got to know you." So I was like, I just need to focus on and pinpoint one thing, and it's writing the book because it's condensing my whole message into the most condensed version possible and in the easiest way to distribute. Because I've released these podcasts and coaching sessions, but it's me doing a similar process. There's something amazing in each one, but I just take out the amazing thing and put it into the condensed message of the book.

So that's the book. It just gives you the skeleton. And then all these examples give a condensed version of my message. And when I do the podcast, if I want to do an interview and spread my message, I have an anchor. I've honed my message. And if I want to do a YouTube channel, if I want to do a community, that's my anchor, and that's what I want to share with the world.

That's given me some peace. Even when my relationship is tumultuous, I come back to that and it gives me a sense of peace. So I don't know if you have any questions about that?

Brian: That's pretty understandable: "What's that one thing? That one primary vehicle you're using?"

Michael: Yeah, my book is "Whose Movie Are You In?" Once you identify that, then create and direct your own movie, which is for the purpose of others. Ask the question, "Who's the audience of your movie? How are they being affected by your movie?" Because it cannot be for validation. For me, I was like, "Oh, you know, my wife's squandered all our savings," and so I was like, I need to create this book to make money." But then the audience just becomes me, or I need to build my self-worth. Then my audience is limited just to me. (Brian: Right.) Or it could be my past family members: "I feel like I don't exist. I feel like a failure."

And so that's their movie. And then the audience is just them, and it doesn't even help them. (Brian: Right. Yeah.)

So think about that. Who's the audience of your movie? How's it going to impact, help and transform them?

Brian: Okay, so the primary vehicle that I want to use will be a book, but to begin with, it's going to be creating courses and the people that I want to help. The people that I want to serve are people who have suffered from severe, generalized anxiety, OCD, panic disorder, illness, anxiety; people who are tortured by their thoughts; people who are suffering because they have no way of knowing how to change their relationship with their thoughts.

They're completely dominated by living in their mind all day long. They suffer from severe chronic obsessive worry. And that's who I've been helping, you know, however long I've been a therapist, and that's how I've sort of tailored and mastered this approach to help these people cause I was once them.

Michael: Yeah and how will your movie help them get out of this experience? Because I know you said the vehicle is the book and the courses. The vehicle is actually you. The vehicle is your message. The vehicle is your vision.

Brian: I guess I don't understand the question. How will my movie help them?

Michael: Because you said that's your audience: people who are experiencing anxiety and tortured thoughts and being just stuck in this vicious cycle. But when they watch your movie, which is your dream, your vision, your message, it's going to help and get them out of this experience.

Brian: So when I'm living my dream, when I'm living in my movie, I am more active on social media, I am more active on presenting myself and my teachings to people. I have a really nice website under development now, and in my movie, people are able to access me through me intentionally spreading my message through me.

Having the confidence to know that what I have to teach, people need to learn. So when I'm living the best version of myself, people will see me.

Michael: Well, what's the message?

Brian: The message is how to stop suffering from your tortured thoughts.

Michael: I know, but what is it? What is that? How do they stop? What I'm sensing is just the result.

Brian: They'll learn the lifestyle, the cognitive processes. They'll learn the way, the mindful way, the acceptance way. They'll learn the tools that eventually get turned into a total lifestyle to help them be their best selves.

Michael: But what are those (tools)? I understand it (what you are saying), but I just want you to really be imaginative. No inhibitions. Really harness and uncover and embrace "What are these tools?" Because I think you're in the thinking mind, which is like, okay, "Do A, B, C, and D, and then you'll get to the endpoint." But it's deeper than that.

It's not an A,B,C, or D. It's a light that's so powerful but it just needs to be cultivated, uncovered. But what is the tool? What is the message?

Brian: I guess I don't get it. To me, it is an A, B, C, D, and E, you know, to me, that when you follow this protocol...

Michael: Yeah, but then I hear that you have a good website, you're being active on social media, you have a huge following or you have online courses, but these are all like the bells and whistles. It's like a car without an – don't take this the wrong way, okay? You have a beautiful car, you have a beautiful website, but what's the engine?

Brian: It's the core cognitive tools to stop suffering.

Michael: But it's your message, you know? What's the core cognitive? Like this is your movie. You want to really define what that is.

Brian: Okay. So I'll be teaching people mindfulness, acceptance, positive neuroplasticity training. Is that what you mean?

Michael: But you want to be specific cause it's so unique and specific to you, because these are all things that, you know, a lot of people are learning, but you gotta make it specific to you. This is just an example, okay? So for me, like it's this FIST process. Then I created this mantra "Problems bring up feelings in us..." "Feeling is healing," "Identify through the PEWF process," "Whose movie am I in?", and then like directing your own movie and then honing it, like forgetting the noise of the podcast, YouTube, cause that was all the bells and whistles.

Like thinking, "Oh, I need a community." I said, "Forget that. You know? Cause if I don't have an anchor, I ain't going to go anywhere without an anchor. I'm going to sink if I focus on all the bells and whistles. What's my message? What's my message? What's my message? Hone it, hone it, put it all together, all these coaching sessions on the podcast."

Does that resonate?

Brian: Mmhmm. A little bit. I guess I still don't see ...like, so my message is how to stop suffering.

Michael: Yeah, but how do you stop suffering?

Brian: Suffering to me is self-created. So you stop creating the suffering. You learn the inner resources to stop creating suffering. You learn how to work with your thoughts. The thoughts are the basis of suffering. You learn how to work with thoughts so that they're no longer baiting you to sit around and overthink and to worry, and once you know this path, then you're no longer creating the meaningless or unnecessary suffering...So, essentially, you're unlearning.

Michael: Yeah. So what are your thoughts and feelings about just focusing on this part? The engine to the vehicle, and really developing, writing it down, brainstorming around it?

Brian: It sounds interesting. I guess it's difficult for me. I don't know. It seems difficult for me. It seems like I have a difficult time wrapping my head around it. I mean I like the idea .... I guess maybe I'm too thought-oriented or something.

Michael: What do you mean you're too thought-oriented?

Brian: Well, I guess I said that because I think, for you, a lot of it is based in feelings. A lot of what you teach. And so a lot of where I'm coming from is more based in thought.

Michael: You want to combine the two (Brian: right.) And then you'll unlock something powerful because the mind is like this (Michael brings his hands closer together), but the heart sees the whole forest.

Like my wife, she loves to plan. She's unbelievably structured, and when I came into the relationship, I'm more like feeling, feeling, feeling. I learned to combine the two. So then like with her help (of), "structure, structure, structure," I thought of creating this process, F I S T, and it was like that structure in the session. (Brian: Okay)

So let's kind of hone in on what that movie is that you want to share with the world.

Brian: Okay . . . (long pause) I guess, I don't know. I thought I said... in my mind, I've already explained it. So what's lacking from what I explained? What's missing?

Michael: It's a very logical way of understanding. It's like an A, B, C, D. But you want to hone in on your message. Nobody can share it other than you. It's that unique, and it's that powerful that you can feel it...Do you feel your message? Do you feel the power of this message?

Brian: Yes.

Michael: Okay, so let's kind of revisit, so let's see, if you were to create a podcast episode, a book, and here was your message that you want to share with the world for the purpose of healing and transforming the world. In one paragraph or a couple, what would it be? And you have to feel the power in the message, not an A B C. It can have structure to it, but I don't want you to define it so clearly. I want you to incorporate feeling into it as well. I want to feel your message.

Brian: Teaching people suffering from anxiety how to understand who they are. Teaching people how to understand the mechanisms in their mind and their heart and their body that hold them back from living life, that hold them back from being happy.

Michael: So that they can?

Brian: Be who they were meant to be.

Michael: Yea that's more (like it). Yeah. What was your experience of that?

Brian: It was harder. That was more difficult.

Michael: But I could feel your message.

Brian: Yeah. There was something there. Yea there was something there that was more than thought-based.

Michael: Yeah and I know (with) what's going on in our world, and I know you said, you've been furloughed, you have a lot of free time (now). And you want to create your dream. You want to be a podcaster, Tony Robbins, but this is your Tony Robbins right here! (Brian: right.) This is everything right here.

Everything else is gravity. It's a natural aftereffect. You don't need to do anything after that. I mean, it's just easy (afterward). (Brian: Right.) But, all the gravy sauce is right here. (Brian: Right.) So your message is like a Christmas tree, and after that, you're just putting ornaments on it.

Let's define it more, uncover, explore. This is the exploratory phase, okay? I mean, I loved it (your message so far), what I heard was understanding the mechanisms of anxiety, of the ego, so they can be who they're meant to be. Did I get that right?

Brian: Yeah that was pretty much it...Yeah, understanding what drives them, understanding the mechanisms that are potentially hardwired to help them survive, but aren't making them happy. And once a person can understand what's going on and why they've lived in such a way for so long and not found the happiness that they desperately wanted, they can realize that what they've been doing, it hasn't worked because it isn't meant to work.

You can't change your thoughts by trying to control your thoughts. There are more skillful ways, but we've been stuck in cultural media and self-help books that are telling us: just stop thinking. Just control your thoughts. Just do this. Just do that.

Michael: Or just do positive thinking.

Brian: Yeah, exactly! "Just do that and you'll be all better." But if that could have worked, it would've worked by now. So people are just riddled with bullshit messages that they receive from the media. And so I'm trying to unveil how the mind really works.

Michael: I like what you're saying. I like where you're going, and I can feel you, more of you, as you're explaining this. (Brian: Okay! Okay, yeah.)

What are your thoughts and feelings about, you don't need to do it right now, but taking some time within the next week to brainstorm, "How do we understand the mechanism of the ego?" How to get out of it? What are the traps? What are the illusions? What are the myths? And how to get out of it.

What about taking some time and really fleshing that out. (Brian: okay.) Just bit by bit. Just like, okay, that piece and that piece and that piece. And then you learn from your own life. Personal stories are always very powerful, you know? (Brian: Right.) Stories that you know about others, you know, like you just put everything together and you are just putting piece by piece together and then eventually creating what will be your masterpiece. But you start with an empty canvas, but the painting is already in your mind and heart and soul. (Brian: Right.) You just need to transfer it. What are your thoughts about that?

Brian: Sounds, it sounds difficult, if I'm needing this much time connecting to my feelings in this moment. But it sounds like it'll yield some good juicy stuff.

Michael: When you say difficult, why is it difficult?

Brian: Overriding logical thinking and getting more in touch with feelings, I suppose it's probably a little more difficult for me.

It sounds fun. But like when I say challenging, challenging cause it's not my go-to, I suppose...

Michael: What's your go-to?

Brian: My go-to is pretty much logical, rational thinking, like bullet pointing ideas. Like I'm going to teach you positive neuroplasticity training and I'm going to teach you mindfulness and I'm going to teach you how to create values, alignment, and goals.

Like I've got a bullet point for everything I want to teach people, and it's just a very linear sort of everything that you'll learn from me.

Michael: Yeah. You're not unlocking your power. (Brian: Right.) That's not your power. That's like some things you do, but that's not your power. (Brian: Right.)

It's almost like a safety net. Not saying that it's not helpful. It's something that makes it better. It's like the car has a special thing to make it go faster, but it's not the core. You are the core. Your message, your movie is the core, and I think when you do that, there's going to be a beautiful experience.

Brian: Okay. Yeah. I think this is kind of cool.

Michael: It's your reason for existence. It's the greatest gift you're going to share with the world. And all the negative thinking and all the stuff we talked about, the negative emotions and feelings, past family trauma, intergenerational trauma, you'll be able to truly separate from it because you can't fully separate from the movie that doesn't belong to you if you don't have your own movie. If you're not creating and honing and embracing and honoring your own movie, because it's like, "What then? What do I do after that?" (as in separating from the movies of others)

Brian: Right.

Michael: And your power is so unbelievably healing and so powerful. We constantly have so much stuff happening in our lives – personal lives, work, emotions, the mind, the ego, so much. But that's your superpower, like that's the S on your chest. Like all that stuff (negativity), just like water, just flows right through you, right past you.

Brian: Right. Okay. This is interesting. So I guess in my movie, I'm imagining that I could open up my head and be vulnerable and share my story of overcoming anxiety, share my story of how I was a tortured soul in elementary school and middle school and high school, and how I just suffered immensely from these thoughts and how I became a therapist because of that.

And now that I've learned everything, and I've traveled the Buddhist path and I've taken different vows and studied all of these teachings I've taken. So what I want to do is take decades of suffering and decades of healing and offer those teachings to people so that they don't have to take decades.

They can learn how to cleanse their inner world. Without having to suffer for tens upon tens of years.

Michael: Okay, so let's keep exploring. Let's create kind of a minor plan or schedule. I don't mean fleshing everything out, but I'm just saying one ridiculously small step that will move you closer to your dream and your movie.

And there's (this book I read.) I just read bits and pieces of it. It's like five small steps. I don't even remember the title exactly, but the author was saying, he wanted to lose weight. He wanted to be fit. And normally when people want to do that, they set some extreme goal. I'm going to go work out five times a week, two hours each time.

But when people don't hit that goal, they just give up. And then so his goal was, I'm going to do one pushup a day. And after you do that one pushup, then whatever you want to do after that, that's good for you. Because normally the hardest step is the first step. (Brian: Right.) Because after you do that first step, then it's very easy to do more. (Brian: Right.) So then you build off of that. You can increase a little bit more. Five pushups, 10 pushups.

So what is your one small step to move you closer to your dream and your movie?

Brian: I'm kind of, maybe in the midst of that. Naturally, I may need to add something, but are you familiar with ClickFunnels? (Michael: Yeah.)

Okay. So I just started the one funnel away challenge, so I'm trying to, within the next third, not trying to, that's failure language. I am going to get a funnel out. At the end of this challenge, that's going to have a product that I'm offering. That is my first big attempt, anyway, to market myself.

And again, I've already hired a team, a branding team. I'm working on a logo, so I've already started things in motion for this process. I've got to decide on the logo and everything now...

Michael: Can I ask you a question? (Brian: Yeah.) Have you shared what the product is like? Let's say you give a teaser of it and you don't need to talk about the product in its entirety. It's just about the message. Did you give a snippet of this on social media or email or something in public?

Brian: So I have never done a Facebook live and I am doing a lot of recording into my phone, into my computer. I am planning my first Facebook live. Not to be a perfectionist, but learning from Russell Brunson and learning sales and learning how to carry myself so that I can be more confident when I speak into the camera.

So yeah, I haven't done a Facebook live yet, but in the next week or so, I plan on doing one because I just want to get my message across right, so I don't sound too humble and I don't sound too shy. I'm trying, I'm practicing what that will be like, cause I know once I do that, that inaugural message could, I don't wanna say, make or break me, but...

Michael: Okay. I hear myself in you. (Brian chuckles) Cause like you know, I was doing podcasting, YouTube, and when I did YouTube it was like, "Whoa, you know, like my face is out there." And then I'm just editing. I can edit the intro, edit the outro, edit whatever I want, and just redo it or whatever I didn't like.

And I hear you talking about your first step in ClickFunnels. Your first step is homing in on your message cause that's your Tony Robbins right there. But also like, you haven't done Facebook Live and as you're going to do a Facebook Live, you're thinking, "I need to read up on this, read up on that, to get it right. I want to sound humble. I want to...whatever."

No, just put yourself out there. (Brian: Right.) Like, you already had the decades. Why do you need any more? You need to put yourself out there, and you'll learn stuff along the way.

Like, I'll give you an example. So my wife noticed this in me, and she gave me accountability, and she said, "Every day you need to put yourself out there. You need to aim for fame. So everyday people need to hear your voice, they need to see your face. And the last one, you need to either help other people or make them laugh."

I like holding signs with messages and so I hold this sign while I am holding my son and the sign says, "Success is impossible without play." And on my son's, he's seven months old and on his head is my mom's bra and on my head is my underwear.

Another time, we were walking at a beach that wasn't closed down, and then she's like, "You got to do a Facebook live stream like right now." And I was like, "No, I don't want to." And this is what she does. She just takes my phone. She clicks Facebook live. Boom, like I don't even have any time. And I got upset cause she's making a decision without me. And I was like, "No." I just took the phone and turned it off. And then we talked about it more calmly. She was like, "You got to do it." And I was like, "Okay, okay, let me think about what the title of this Facebook Live should be."

And I said, "Whose movie are you in?" And then, I didn't have anything like crafted, but it's just the message that I always share anyways. And I learned something important about my grandfather. My father who's always working, like he's working all the time, always efficient. And my grandfather at eight years old, I guess he had to move out of his house and away from his family to live on his own, I think because of finance. His mother died, father remarried. Something about that. I don't know what happened, but he had to live on his own at the age of eight so it's like he had to create self-worth through just constantly working and productivity.

He was a doctor, worked at the hospital, came back home (where) he had a clinic. He was working all the time, never took his kids out, always working. And my dad is like that.

So I had learned that recently and shared it. Just something that was personal and I didn't craft anything. And after the end of the video, and after a few minutes, I looked at it (thinking) "Ugh! Only two people liked it...it was so terrible." I didn't want to do it because like we're at the beach. It's really loud, so you won't really hear me.

And I was like, "Oh, whatever." We shouldn't attach ourselves to the likes or whatever. But then like three hours later or a day later, I saw people like, "Oh, this message really helped me." And then more people liked and saw it.

I went on an interview for an online global healing convention. And then the guy who was interviewing me and who was organizing it, he'd actually snuck into my Facebook profile and watched the video and right in the beginning of the video, he told me, "Oh, I saw your Facebook live, and I really enjoyed it."

And I was thinking "Really???" I didn't plan it. I thought I messed up. I was at the beach. It wasn't the right setting. So like, that's what I want you to do, you know, don't put limitations on your creativity, on your message. The message is there. Send it out and you'll learn more stuff along the way.

Brian: Yeah. I guess I'm finding a way to procrastinate probably.

Michael: Just trying to get it right. (Brian: Yeah.) But if you mess up, you'll fail and you don't matter. That's the movie of your past family members. Separate from that and go back to your power because your power is that engine. Remember when you're getting into the feeling of it? You said you want to help people understand the core mechanisms of the thinking mind, of the ego, of these torturous thoughts, of decades and decades of tortuous thoughts seemingly lasting a lifetime, and then you are giving that key to unlock all of that and to be the person that they're really meant to be. You sharing your personal story, like all that stuff.

Brian: Okay. Yeah, I can do that in the next week.

Michael: Okay. Like the Facebook live? (Brian: Yeah.) Alright...

How about within the next three days? Cause I don't want you overthinking the whole process. Like, before the Facebook Live, what are you going to do... to make it good?

Brian: I'm waiting for a tripod to come in the mail, actually from Amazon, but I guess I can just do it on my laptop right here.

Michael: You just hold the phone. That's your tripod. (Brian: Yeah. Yeah. Smiles). I didn't have a tripod when I was doing my Facebook Live. (Brian: Yeah.) Do you hear yourself? "I need the tripod. I need ClickFunnels."

Okay, to make the Facebook live the way that you want to, what are you thinking? Like, let's say I say do it in a week, or do it in three days or whatever. What do you say? Like, "Oh shoot, I need to do this before I..".? What's going on in your mind?

Brian: I just need to practice to get a coherent couple of minutes out. Like I want to get the message out that I want to get out, so that after I do the Facebook live, I'm not like, "God damn, I forgot. I forgot to say this. I forgot to say this."

Michael: When you practice, are you like literally practicing into a video?

Brian: Yeah. Yeah. I'm just doing practice I can watch later. I'm just holding my phone in front of me and talking, and then I'm doing it again and then I'm reviewing it later.

Michael: How about creating just a structure, like, I'm going to talk about this, not verbatim. (Brian: Right) Just like, as I was thinking like, okay, "Whose movie are you in?" I'm going to talk about what I learned about my father, my grandfather.

Let it free flow. Just create a structure. I would for now advise against doing the video because then when you actually do the live stream or as you're recording these videos, repeatedly the ego is going to be like, "Oh, this is not right ... You forgot about this. You forgot about that."

Like some things, I probably left out, but it doesn't matter. (Brian: Right.) You know, because you want to get in touch with the feeling. People want to hear and feel your presence, your passion, and you already have been preparing for decades (Brian: Right.)

So why do you need any more time to prepare? Like you've been shooting free throws for like decades, why do you need to keep practicing? Just go and make it count. And know that what stops you is the movies of others. Okay? And then home in on your message and movie, and just forget about how it will be received.

When you're doing the ClickFunnels, and thinking I need a tripod, who's the audience of your movie, when you're thinking these things?

Brian: People who have severe anxiety that are like, "Oh my God!...."

Michael: Wait, wait, wait. It's you. Right?

When you redo videos thinking, "I don't want to mess up, and if I mess up, then I'm going to feel like a failure... I'm going to feel like I'm worthless," then the audience is you.

When you tap into your power, you're homing in on the message and keep in mind, the message is beautiful for yourself and your own personal life, your family, but the message is how it's going to impact, heal and transform others. When you keep that in the back of your mind or as your vision in front of you, then you unlock your power.

All that negative feeling of "What if I fail? If I fail, I'll be worthless." All that stuff goes down the drain. It becomes like a tiny little mouse squeaking at you. It's like it's negligible and you then feel your power. That's what it's all about. You actually feel your power, your worth, your limitlessness in connection to it all.

Brian: Okay. Stop making it about me. Essentially.

Michael: Yeah. Like when I was trying to write the book, and I was like, "Oh, we lost all these finances" and then like people would find me online through Yelp and when people contacted me, I was just like, "Oh, I gotta like make sure I make this appointment because I need the money."

The purpose of my movie isn't financial, like just getting by, because I will have abundance. I realize I will have abundance because through my message, I can feel it. (Brian: Right.) Abundance is just a natural aftereffect of sharing my message.

Brian: Yeah, this makes a lot of sense. It's something I've been hearing for over a year now, but it's a matter of I'm holding myself back by not getting in front of the camera. I'm holding myself back by not sharing my message. I'm waiting for the perfect time and the perfect copy and the perfect lighting and the perfect shirt to create and I've just got to get out of my own damn way and just talk.

I think the funniest thing is I'm most concerned probably with what will my high school friends think. Oh, they'll think "What's he trying to scam right now?!" Like it's just funny.

Michael: Why? Why is it your high school friends more so?

Brian: Cause they're the friends that I have been around for life, really. I mean, they're my friends. Like, so the friends I met in high school have been my friends since then. I'm 49 years old and they're my closest friends still. I met friends in college. I met friends in graduate school. I met friends here in South Carolina, but my friends that I grew up with in New York, I went to high school with, we have a bond that's just so crazy.

Michael: Are they supportive of what you're doing? (Brian: Oh Yeah!). So I'm curious about how come it matters so much what they think.

Brian: Maybe I'm trying to impress them. I don't know.

Michael: Okay let's say: worst fear, worst-case scenario. What would that be with your high school friends?

Brian: Oh, they just....um...honestly there's nothing. There's no worst-case scenario there. That they don't watch, and that's fine, cause I'm not trying to market to them.

Michael: But then you were worried about it. So there's some underlying feeling around it.

Brian: To think that I am trying to use the pandemic to make money or something like that, or they think that I'm being like everybody else and just trying to get online to make money. That I'm not about helping people. I'm all about making money.

Michael: So maybe not just your high school friends, like everybody else? (Brian: Everybody, yeah.) Everybody thinks you're ....

Brian: Out to make money and I'm not authentic and not trying to help people.

Michael: Okay, and if that came true, everybody thought you were a scam artist, just out to make money capitalizing on their sufferings, how would that make you feel the F.W.P. and why? Failure, worthless or powerless?

Brian: I guess failure. That's the first thing that comes to mind. (Michael: Because?) Because my message is real and if they think that, then I didn't communicate effectively.

Michael: But there's also another element. If everybody thought you were a scam artist, nobody would want to be in your life, like you'd be a virus to stay away from. Like the first feeling is failure, but also there's the feeling of "what if everybody views me as a scam artist?" (Brian: Right.) Then you would be....

Brian: My reputation could get ruined.

Michael: And remember that's from that past family trauma. I don't remember all the details, but your biological father not being in your life because of everybody's obsession with perception (Brian: Right, right, right.) within the Catholic religious world that they lived in. Everything was about image and if you didn't have that image, I don't know, you would go into the gates of hell or something? (Brian: Right.) Is that right? (Brian: I don't know.) I'm just guessing.

Brian: I'm thinking that's what they believed. They believed in a sort of literal hell.

Michael: So that image, you know, image is everything. Reputation is everything.

And so just know that you are in their movie. Separate from that. Come back to your power, your purpose, and the movie that you're supposed to share with the world. That's all that matters.

Brian: Okay. I like that. Creating my own movie. I like that.

Michael: And what would you do to center yourself to come back to your movie when you catch yourself (in the thinking mind)?

Brian: Well, keep telling myself it's not about me. It's about helping people. It's not about me at all.

Michael: And it's not about the movies of your past family members. Cause when it's about "me," when you say "me," it's really about those past family members, that intergenerational trauma. (Brian: Right.) And that's misusing your gift of sensitivity and empathy, internalizing this stuff as your own, and it's – you're just lost in the movies of others. (Brian: Right, yeah.) And then when you catch yourself doing that, then what would you do to center yourself by bringing yourself back into your movie?

Brian: Disconnect from that movie and create a clear screen where I'm the creator of my new movie, my own movie.

Michael: This is perfect. I just wanna know like, what would you actually do? I dunno if I'm asking too many questions, but I'm just curious. Like would you give me an example of what would you actually do?

Brian: I would probably remind myself that I don't want to have to live in their movie anymore. I'm the creator of my own movie.

Michael: And focus on and dive in on actually creating your movie. Not only saying that you will, (Brian: Right.) but actually diving into the process of creating and being a director of your movie, which you will share with the world, and that'll be your anchor.

Cause of course you want to be aware of it, feel it, and then practice it. And then that'll be your constant anchor in all these mental daggers that you feel are being thrown at you.

Brian: Right. Okay.

Michael: Okay. All right. We're about coming to a close. Any last questions, thoughts, or feelings? Feel free to say anything that you want to say or feel or anything that was unsaid.

Brian: Well, it's interesting thinking about how, starting off, I was going to use your process to help you work through things, and then you shifting gears and turning it back on me and being completely unprepared for that, but at the same time continuously telling me to...

In this session, Brian was actually supposed to apply the FIST process to me, as I was going through some difficulties, but I was able to work through them, so I asked Brian if it was okay to continue the process with him in uncovering his movie.

Michael: Maybe that was good. (Brian: Yeah. Right. Exactly.) Otherwise, you're like, I need to be prepared. I need to be in control. You know, I need to make sure that things are perfect. And then, like, shifting that whole thing is like – then you're more in your element.

Brian: Right. So then your repeated redirection to sort of get out of my cerebral sort of thought. Just "I'll do this, this," and my list and I wound up even shutting my eyes to really anchor myself and to go deep in my body to get to what you are asking. And when I was able to do that, you were like, "Yeah, that's what I was talking about."

Like, so it's interesting, the people that I want to help and who I once was, and I guess who I still am, people who live in their thoughts all the time. So it was difficult, but it was, again, almost like I imagined shutting my eyes and going deep into my chest or into my abdomen and just sort of pulling that stuff out.

Michael: Exactly. That's beautiful because I think that's a part of your core message. Getting out of your thoughts. Get into your core, getting to your true self. I think if you put all your decades of experience and then put those decades and start condensing them into this really condensed message. Start brainstorming and it becomes more powerful and you just keep adding stuff to it from what you learn, from what you experienced from the clients that you see. Just keep adding to it and then it's going to be a fun, fun challenge. (Brian: Cool. Cool. Cool.) All right, well, thank you, Brian.

Brian: Thank you. This was great. Yeah, I will, um, I'll work on that Facebook. I won't work on it. I'll just do that Facebook live.

CLOSING THOUGHTS

In essence, the very thing keeping Brian from sharing his message with the world was his intergenerational trauma of being judged and excluded by the world. When you follow your dreams, your most hidden pain and intergenerational trauma will come to the surface, so you can be free of it, but most importantly, transform this pain into the source of your light and the message of your movie to share with the world.

COACHING DIALOGUE WITH SCOTTIE WEBER: FROM ISOLATION TO FREEDOM

(To refer to the details of what was uncovered in the first session with Scottie please refer to <u>page 91</u>)

To briefly mention what was discussed prior to this in Scottie's first session: Scottie's mother had committed suicide the year before. Scottie's mother was also sexually, physically and verbally abused by her own stepfather. Scottie's grandmother told her to be quiet about it because she herself didn't want her relationship to end and feel alone because of it. Scottie's grandmother struggled with feelings of loneliness because her father died of Lou Gehrig's disease when she was just 8 years old. As you remember, Scottie would wake her husband, who has sleep apnea, in the middle of the night to check if he was still alive.

In this second session with Scottie, before we uncover the movie she wants to share with the world, I first check in with her and see what she would like to incorporate for this session. She says due to the pandemic, her fear of being alone and the fear of her husband dying in his sleep because of his sleep apnea has intensified.

Scottie: He's high risk because of COPD and sleep apnea, and I work with the public as a waitress. So I am afraid of bringing the virus home and him getting sick.

Michael: Remember to establish your foundation knowing that "feeling is healing." Before we try to figure it out, establish a foundation by feeling these feelings within your body. Where do you feel the tension in your body? In your throat, heart, or the top of or bottom of your stomach?

Scottie: It's at about the top of my stomach.

Michael: Okay, alright. Just close your eyes for a moment and just feel that tension, the anxiety, the worry, and tell yourself, "Feeling is healing," and you're thereby giving the emotional wound the medicine of love in order to heal. We don't need to figure it out right now. We will later, but for right now, it's about establishing the foundation. Take a deep breath and open your eyes whenever you're ready.

Okay, so now we can apply the PEWF process. The problem of your husband having COPD and sleep apnea brings up feelings of anxiety. Stretch this and think what's your worst fear? Worst-case scenario?

Scottie: Him dying and me being all alone.

Michael: You identified the feeling really well. Now onto "separation," which is about knowing "Whose movie are you in?" I know we talked about this before, but you can see that you are partly in your mother's movie, who was sexually, physically, verbally abused by her stepfather. And her mother did not protect her because she herself felt alone having been through multiple marriages, and did not want to lose this marriage and be alone yet again, and thereby sacrificing her daughter for this feeling that she was holding onto. And your grandmother's feeling of being alone was rooted in her father dying of Lou Gehrig's when she was 8 years old.

So you can see that you're in your mother's movie, your grandmother's movie. I do want to check and see if there is another possibility. I know you had virtually no contact with your biological father, but what do you know about him?

Scottie: I know that he was adopted and that his mother died at an early age as well. I think she had an aneurysm, I believe, or maybe possibly a stroke, but she was young. I think she was only in her thirties or forties, but he and his twin brother both got adopted at fairly young ages too. I'm going to guess between like five and ten years old.

I asked how come Scottie's grandfather did not take over after Scottie's grandmother passed, and she did not know why, and neither did she know of any story about her paternal grandfather.

Michael: We don't need to dig too deep, but just knowing you're in your mother's movie, your grandmother's movie, and now you can incorporate a little bit of your biological father's movie knowing that his mother passed at an early age. Something about the father not being present because he should have taken over. And so if he wasn't present and there was some issue there as well, and then he (your biological father) was adopted. So I see this on both sides, where there was a death of a parent and consequently feeling alone.

So I want you to begin to incorporate and see how you are in your biological father's movie. I'll give you an example.

Here, I share with Scottie the example of Brian, who had the fear of being exposed, judged, and excluded by the world if he were to pursue his dream as a full-time counselor, coach, and entrepreneur. All of which was rooted in the existence of his biological father being kept a total secret from him all his life. His grandparents on both sides were of Catholic faith and forbade his parents from being together since he was born out of wedlock.

Scottie: That definitely resonates with me. I can feel it and see how possibly with my grandmother's father dying of Lou Gehrig's, how she could possibly feel abandoned. The same with my mom and with her relationship with my grandmother when she wasn't protected from being terribly abused. I could see how she could feel abandoned. And the same with my biological father. I can see how his mother passing and being put up for adoption, not just being abandoned by the death, but also by his father. I can see how he could possibly feel abandoned.

Michael: Alright, before we move on to the next phase, I want you to really make this a part of your being. So close your eyes for a moment. And when you experience that feeling in your gut, that feeling of, "What if my husband dies, and I'd be all alone and I'd be abandoned, or his children (from a previous marriage) would abandon me," connect with that fear by feeling it, and then pull up a miniature movie screen in front of your eyes.

Project this feeling from your gut like a projector onto that miniature movie screen in front of your eyes and see how you are in your mother's movie, maternal grandmother's movie, but the very secret one, the hidden one, the unspoken one, was your biological father. Him losing his mother at an early age, and then his father not stepping up, and not taking ownership and saying to his son, "I'll take care of you." No... the father would rather have him given up for adoption.

The secret one is very often the more impactful one. Because it is consciously not known, but subconsciously you can feel it all. Just gently remind yourself whose movie you are in and just see how you are in his movie.

Now you want to use your incredible gift of high sensitivity and high empathy, consciously and correctly, and visualize this movie screen. Don't misuse your emotional antennas by subconsciously zapping yourself in his movie as your own because that makes the movie into a nightmare. Your gift is incredible, but simply watch the movie and don't put yourself in the movie of others as your own.

Now, I move on to asking Scottie about what her movie, her dream, her calling is.

Scottie: I want to make things that inspire other people. That is my dream. And since I'm so nervous about going back to working with the public, I have been having this internal dilemma if I should quit because I've been kind of giving up on my dream. I've had this dream for quite a few years, and there's been multiple opportunities to take it, but I haven't really gone for it.

Michael: You said there's multiple opportunities to take it. How so?

Scottie: Like my husband and I ran a restaurant and I said, "I want to quit because I want to make my crafts full time." I like to make hand-bound journals and make little journal prompts in there and sell those to inspire people. I made a few, but because it wasn't a stable income, it upset me, and it scared me to not have a stable income, so I went out and got a steady-paying job that turned out to be extremely toxic. Then I quit that because it was too toxic, and I was like, "I'm going to go back to creating (arts and crafts)," and still it wasn't a stable enough income, so I went on and got a job as a waitress, and that's still hard on my body too...

Michael: You said not having a stable income upsets you? Because why?

Scottie: Well, yes, I said upset. I feel like it is something that comes up from growing up in poverty and then being fairly poor growing up. And you know, cause when you're living in poverty, you do anything it takes just to survive.

Michael: Before we tie in your upbringing, I just want to know... the thought of not having a stable income brings up what kinds of thoughts, fears, and feelings running through your head?

Clients I work with very often quickly tie in a current struggle with their past, but without identifying their true feelings and pain being brought up in the current struggle and problem. We do this in order to avoid feeling our negative feelings and pain. My suggestion to you is that before you tie in your past with your current struggle, first identify what feelings you are experiencing in the moment using the PEWF process. Afterward, you are ready to tie in your past by asking yourself, "Whose movie are you in?"

Scottie: I don't quite want to say "death," but if you don't have money, you don't have electricity or heat or internet access. And because I live on a farm, internet access is very important to me because it's my connection with the outside world really.

Michael: If you were to stretch this fear of not having a stable income into your worst fear, what would it look like? Also, what would you fear would happen because of having no stable income or having very little income or no income? Stretch that to your worst fear, worst-case scenario, and tell me what does that look like?

Scottie: I can imagine being taken to court and sued or the bank account being overdrafted on top of that. You get an overdraft fee and overdraft fee and overdraft fee and just never being able to climb out of that debt or ever being able to get ahead again.

Michael: So your worst fear is to forever be in debt or is it to become homeless? ... I know the logical mind will tell you, "Oh, that's not possible," but it's the logical mind that reasons your way out of it so you don't feel the uncomfortable or the negative feeling.

But it's always the logical mind trying to prevent the worst fear from happening, because if the worst fear were to happen, it would bring up this uncomfortable feeling within yourself. So we're just here trying to identify that feeling and cutting the head off the snake. Just think about it and really stretch it to your worst fear, worst-case scenario and really stretch it out. Even if you think it's not possible, stretch it all the way.

Scottie: Being thrown in jail because of not being able to pay debts. We were taken to court for not being able to pay debts and then being thrown in jail. Because my freedom is very important to me, that would really be very, very worst-case scenario. Family and friends not being able to get a hold of me cause I don't have the internet.

I ask Scottie if her worst fear came true, how would it make her feel the FWP and why (Failure, Worthless or Powerless). Scottie says she would feel powerless because she would have no control over her life and situation and feel alone as well.

Scottie: It's definitely feeling alone. I'd feel alone if I was in jail. I'd feel pretty alone if I didn't have internet access. Definitely powerless.

Michael: (Feeling that) powerlessness comes from the need to be in control, and control is a coping mechanism to prevent something bad from happening. Because if that worst fear were to happen it would bring up a negative feeling in you which you are trying to avoid feeling through the need to be in control.

Imagine, if you didn't have that control, that coping mechanism, what would you fear would happen because of it? Also, what does powerlessness look like to you? Absolutely and utterly powerless. Give me a visual. What does that look like?

Scottie: Sitting in a jail cell. Totally and completely locked in a box.

Michael: I just want to clarify a bit: what is terrifying about being locked in a box and being in a jail cell?

Scottie: I mean, you're completely blocked out from the outside world. No connection to anybody. You're all alone. It'd just be myself in a jail cell for – and I wouldn't be able to tell how long I was going to be there or why I was there, or, you know.

Michael: Got it, got it. I think you kind of hit it on the nail. So you said blocked out from the outside world, utterly alone, just trapped in a box, completely severed from all other connection. You can see that, as you're trying to create your own movie and share it with the world, the barrier to that is the movies of others. It is being in and living in and immersing yourself in the movies of others, which is more specifically the feeling of feeling alone.

So yes, money is important to everybody, but it's more of a surface issue for you, because if you don't have money, you don't have a stable income. Then what if you get sent to court, you go to jail, you'll be completely severed from the world. You'd be alone without any interaction.

Scottie: Right. That would kind of feel like abandonment. That same abandonment, that it seems to be kind of on both sides, maternally and paternally. It's still that aloneness and abandonment. I can totally see that I'm in those people's movies.

Michael: And we want to create an anchor, an anchor for your life, for your source of power and peace, especially when things get rocky, especially when you feel alone. And creating and being that director of your own movie is that anchor, is the calm in the eye of the storm. So I want you to clarify what this anchor really looks like and feels like.

You say you want to create arts and crafts that inspire others. Let's uncover and define in what way do you want to inspire others. By the way, there's going to be a little bit of an element of the very thing that you're struggling with. The reason why you struggle with this so much is because that is a huge part of what you're meant to share with others. The healing through that, as difficult as it is, is because you're meant to go through it and the healing of that and sharing that with others is one of the things you're meant to do.

Have that in the back of your mind as you're creating and being a director of your own movie and have the audience in mind. No movie was created to not be watched by others. Your movie is a box office hit. Visualize and envision your movie being played in a massive theater with a packed audience.

Keep that in mind. Gently remind yourself and ask yourself, "Who is the audience of your movie?" Because when you are thinking, "Oh, if I don't have a stable income, then I'll go to court and be sent to jail. I'll be completely severed, alone and abandoned." When you have thoughts like that, then the audience of your movie is your unresolved *feelings, your emotional pain, and very importantly, your biological father, as well as your mother, your grandmother. But then they're in no way helped by watching this movie. That's not the way to help them – by living in their movie as your own.*

So really visualize who's the audience of your movie, knowing the audience of your movie is others and the world. Especially now, more than ever. I think what's happening in our world (due to the pandemic and lockdown), like, you know, small businesses all over are having to close down. But I'm thinking in order for them to survive and thrive, but it's not just them, anybody, is to think global.

Don't think of yourself as a small business. Don't think of your gifts and talents as something that's small or just to make ends meet. It's something that's meant to be shared with the world or to a specific audience of the world. It doesn't have to be each and every person, but it is to a specific audience of the world. So think about who's your audience for your movie and what impact do you want to have on them.

Scottie: The audience would be other people like me that feel like sometimes they feel alone. I feel if I could create some art that would maybe resonate with them and inspire them to create art, because when I make art, I feel existence is wonderful, and when I create, I feel close to the Creator... So if somebody else can feel inspired to create too, you know, that would be what I would want.

Michael: Almost like it's therapeutic. It's therapeutic art and craft that is therapeutic.

Scottie: And over these last six weeks, it's really come up for me that art should be that way. That art should be made just for the sake of art. And once I finally meditated on that. Holy cow! Like, just so much inspiration. Just, you know, doodling for the sake of doodling, just changed everything. But it's because of that fear of, I guess abandonment or, you know, being locked away, being cut off from everybody that I've had to monetize my inspiration and move past that.

Michael: I'd like to define, uncover and clarify what your movie is and what you want to share with the world. And so what I heard so far was arts and crafts that inspire others. But not only are you creating arts and crafts for others, but also it sounds like (you're) empowering them to do the same for themselves, to create art that is therapeutic for them. Is that right?

Scottie: Yes, definitely. Like more specifically, like recently I've been hand binding and creating these journals and like make them super pretty, right? And then, including on the first page, a list of journal writing prompts. You know, cause to me, journaling is very therapeutic.

And I stumbled on a bunch of really awesome prompts, and I wanted to share that with them so that they could in turn heal themselves. It's as beneficial to them as it has been to me too.

Michael: Can you give me an example?

Scottie: If you... can you imagine... I know this is kind of – it's going to be kinda weird. But it's like, can you imagine, if on your first day of high school, if your mother took you out to lunch, super special, what would that day look like? Or something like that. Or, you know, just things like that. I got a bunch of stuff.

Michael: Keep going. I want to hear them.

Scottie: Like, what is, you know, like what does your future look like? Can you see what it looks like? If you had a perfect life, what would that look like and what would that look like in a year? And what would that look like in five years? Or, if you could imagine yourself as a child, what would be one thing that you would want a grownup to come to you and tell you?

Michael: Yeah. Awesome. Awesome. You can embellish this more if you like. In what ways do you want to give art that is therapeutic to others or to empower others to use crafts and arts in a therapeutic way? When you answer this question, I want you to just let your imagination run wild.

Scottie: So for me, like a part of making art, growing up poor.. I've always been creative, because growing up in poverty, I didn't always have art supplies. And recently I've been getting into my journals that I'm talking about too. They are using everyday ordinary objects, and then adding layers and textures just through found objects. So it doesn't cost any money to make this stuff, right? You just have to buy the glue and the paint, you know? It's not expensive. You don't have to have money to create art.

Michael: So are you selling this artwork or are you teaching other people how to create this kind of journal or this art?

Scottie: Both.

Michael: Okay. Is it kind of like an online course?

Scottie: Well, it was an in-person class two years ago, but the kind of life changed a little bit, but I'm really trying really hard to (go back to teaching them) because of this uncertain time that we're living in. I might have the opportunity to teach these classes in person.

I've always wanted to do an online class, and I've never given myself the chance to pursue it, but it is definitely on the agenda. But if you know this pandemic stuff...

Michael: How do you feel about creating an online course?

Scottie: Like super excited. I mean, a little intimidated, but I don't think that anything is unlearnable. I'm sure there's going to be a learning curve because I'm not too tech-savvy. But it is exciting cause it feels like I'm following what I am supposed to be doing.

Michael: Yeah, you don't need to flesh out all the details, but I would like to hear some examples. What do you think your online course would be teaching and while you are answering this question, in the back of your mind, I want you thinking about what is the purpose of your movie for others? What is the impact it's going to have on others?

Because with an online course, there's so much that you can delve into, so much that you can teach and empower with. (Scottie: Right.) And so many people that you can affect because it's not limited to the people that you see in front of you.

Scottie: True, true...I'm not sure why this keeps coming up, but it's like that freedom thing keeps coming up. That, you know, this art is accessible to everyone, and you have the freedom to be able to create. Art is not confined to that little box (deemed by society or museums.) There's so much room. There's so much freedom.

Michael: Perfect. Perfect.

Scottie: And like anything can be used, you know, ANYTHING can be used. So I think that showing other people in this online class that there's no confinement, there's no restrictions.

Michael: And they have the freedom to express their soul and doing so is therapeutic and empowering. (Scottie: Yeah absolutely.) And it's going to help others. When people are free to express themselves, it's going to help others.

Scottie: For sure.

Michael: Can you give me some more details or content examples for what this online course would entail? I would love to have a visual of what you are wanting to create and share with others and be able to feel it. This way it's more tangible for you, giving more of a sense of direction.

Scottie: I taught an online sewing class about a month ago showing people how to make face masks. But this specific online class that I've been wanting to teach for about two years now, it's called "junk journaling." And basically you can take anything and everything, like a scrap of yarn or a junk letter in the mail or a magazine or buttons or ribbon or a cute little package of tea. Then you kind of like collage it together and you can color and then you can journal on it. Or you can write little inspirational quotes, or you can make little pocket tags, or you can take stickers or whatever.

And it's kind of like an aesthetic thing, where you can sew it all together or you can glue it all together. There's just so many possibilities, but it's something where you basically turn trash into treasure. And I like the renewable aspect of it, you know? Not just the consumer society and plastic disposable society that we live in. It's like using those things for art to inspire other people is why it's so fascinating to me.

Michael: And, in this class, you're teaching people how to do that. (Scottie: Yes. Yes. Yeah.) And, I just want you to clarify for yourself: this will have what kind of impact for others?

Scottie: It would definitely show people that you don't have to be rich or have fancy equipment in order to make art or write down your thoughts and your feelings. You can literally turn anything into something special. It's about your intention. That's what makes it special.

Michael: Got it. Got it. So tell me what's one small step that you can take to move yourself closer in this direction?

Scottie: I definitely should write out an outline because I do have all these ideas on what I want to include. If I sat down for like a half an hour and just made an outline of what I wanted to include and what maybe could be left out or what I could expand upon, that would be beneficial. I should do that.

Michael: And brainstorm, just the way you create this art and have the freedom to do so, making something out of nothing. Infuse that same energy when you're creating the class. So you don't have to think of an outline just yet. That's the finished product. But just feel free to brainstorm, put pieces together, rearrange, and then organize as you go.

Scottie: Yeah, for sure.

Michael: By when would you want to complete that outline?

Scottie: I mean, that's really like a small step. So I should probably, since I've been given this opportunity with the pandemic and being shut down and stuff, I would like to have it done by the end of the month for sure. (Keep in mind, this session took place Thursday, May 7th, 2020 and Scottie would have three weeks to complete this outline)

Michael: How about starting? When would you like to start?

Scottie: Um, probably this weekend. Yes.

Michael: Why not sooner?

Scottie: Well, like I think I need to probably clean my house tonight and get some sleep because my life is kind of changing up a little bit, and I might be working late tomorrow, and I know that I'm not going to be able to get anything done. So I work tomorrow, and I know I won't be able to get anything done if...

Michael: Because I sense the energy that you need to get it done right. It's so important for you, so you want to get it done right. Don't think about that right now. Getting it done right and perfect, okay? It's just like you said, doodling just to doodle. It's just spending like 10 minutes. You got 10 minutes today, right? (Scottie: Yeah). Just spend a little time. Kind of piece some things together. Just one small step. Cause when you say, "the end of the month," that seems like a looong time. I'm not saying that you take a long time, but it sounds like you're trying to perfect it and make sure you get it done right.

Scottie: Of course, that's the way that I am. I take pride in everything that I make, so of course that's exactly... I mean, I feel a little called out cause that's definitely true.

I then shared with Scottie how I was seeking perfection in writing this book, and I originally had five people's examples of going through the FIST process together in my book, but it was so time-consuming and literally draining me and obviously it would be terribly confusing to the reader. Therefore, I simplified everything by just choosing one person's example, Monica's, to explain the FIST process and then including everybody else's examples into condensed summaries.

Michael: The perfection is what is hurting you and it for sure hurts me. (Scottie: Sure). Because then it's out of fear. You're creating out of fear because you want to make it right because you don't want to fail because you don't want to end up in jail if you have no money, and you don't want to feel alone. So just remember that art is freedom, right? You keep coming back to your core value of freedom. These are freedom journals.

Scottie: Absolutely. Oh man. Definitely, creating it and making sure it's perfect is creating it out of fear instead of the exact opposite of what I want to accomplish. And I do believe that when you are on the right path or doing the thing that you're meant to be doing, that it should be free and easy and fun and just absolutely sunshiny and rainbows because it's what you're passionate about. Yeah, that really resonates with me.

Michael: This is your purpose and I don't want to force anything onto you, but a thought just came into my head. What if you were to call them freedom journals?

Scottie: Yeah, definitely.

Michael: Because that speaks to what you want them to do. Just be free. On top of that, it's a reminder for you to know this is not about thinking, overthinking, or perfecting. It's about freedom. And it dispels everything: the fear of being in a jail cell, the fear of being alone. You don't feel that anymore because you're connecting to your power, which is your freedom.

Scottie: Yes! That's really brilliant. I'm definitely gonna brainstorm more on that. I really liked the connection between my deepest fear and then also the inspiration that it can go the very opposite direction.

Michael: And I think it's going to help others tremendously. When you call them freedom journals, then your message becomes infused with everything you are creating for others, and it gets imprinted on the back of their minds as they're creating, making it therapeutic for them. They're probably feeling a lot of pain, feeling alone, trapped, stuck, abandoned, but FREEDOM, FREEDOM, FREEDOM is how you express your message at its highest level. When you do that, you feel your limitless self-worth and you tap into your power. That's how you truly help others and gain the peace that you deserve.

Scottie: I really like it a lot. I love how it touches on so many different points that are meaningful to me and can be meaningful to other people too. I'm sure I'm not alone, that other people would relate to that as well.

Michael: Yeah. For sure. Alright, we're about coming to a close. It was a real pleasure. Any last questions, thoughts, or feelings?

Scottie: I feel very empowered. Thank you so much.

Michael: Awesome. Awesome. Awesome.

Scottie: I didn't realize all these connections like that. I didn't realize the connection on my biological father's side. Cause when we had our first session, I really was kind of focusing on my mother and grandmother's side. And I never really thought about my father's side, that those guys are all... it's going down the chain. That same thing. I appreciate the insight.

Michael: I have a feeling that you are experiencing all of this, this huge weight and burden and struggle and emotional pain and feeling all these feelings of loneliness, which are coming through you intergenerationally, because you're meant to help other people in this light, so that's why your movie is that important. You were meant to share your movie, this specific movie with others. Intergenerationally it set this whole thing up, and that shows why you experienced this pain – because you are meant to help other people heal in this way.

Scottie: Absolutely. For sure. I absolutely see that because after I feel it myself, then I can learn how to process, move past it and help other people. And maybe it's not quite as tangible as the kind of work that you're doing. But I think the kind of work that I want to do absolutely can be inspirational and beneficial as well.

Michael: I mean, it's tangible for sure in its own way, you know. I can feel the healing and freeing energy of your movie and how it totally pertains to everything that you went through and that the generations before you went through and how powerfully it just puts everything, gives closure and just really heals all of that for yourself, your past family members, and ultimately all others. So it's like it was all meant to be in your movie. That's as tangible as you can get.

Scottie: Yes, definitely.

Michael: Alright. Well, thank you, Scottie. That was a lot of fun.

Scottie: Michael, I really appreciate it.

CLOSING THOUGHTS

This session with Scottie was a classic example of the power of transforming your greatest pain into your source of light. Scottie's intergenerational trauma was about feeling alone and abandoned. Scottie's movie was about transforming this intergenerational trauma of loneliness into her "freedom journals." So many of us struggle with feelings of loneliness and abandonment and worthlessness because of it. We can find our souls locked and confined in the very jail cells Scottie talked about, severed from the world. Freedom is a beautifully empowering concept that is not only the complete antithesis to feeling alone but will allow you to set free the beauty and power of your soul to share with the world.

Think about what your core pain is and what your intergenerational trauma is. Afterward, transform this pain into your source of light and into your movie. You are experiencing this pain and intergenerational trauma for a reason, and that reason is to learn a powerful lesson and message that will transform the world.

COACHING DIALOGUE WITH ELENA HARDER: LIBERATING YOURSELF FROM THE TRAUMA OF RELIGIOUS EXCLUSION

This coaching dialogue with Elena contains a two-part session. The first session was about discovering, "Whose movie are you in?" and the second session was about creating and being the director of her own movie to share with the world.

At the beginning of the first session, Elena talked about this pain of invisibility and worried that her healing work would never see the light of day. She also repeatedly talked about how one of her worst fears is to be a narcissist, when nothing could be further from the truth. This fear of being narcissistic comes down to making others feel that they are invisible, when actually that is how Elena feels inside.

In turn, this feeling of invisibility manifests as feeling disrespected by her son and starts with something seemingly small: how her son likes to fart on her while sitting on her:

"This morning, my son was sitting with me and I was trying to focus on doing something work-related and he comes and sits on my lap and I'm like, 'Well, you can sit here, but like, don't wiggle...' So he's sitting relatively still. He like intentionally farted on me and I go, "Dude!" and then he goes like (waves his hand at me) making sure I smell it.

He's like nine. He just thinks it's hilarious. And I'm like, 'I'm trying to focus. You can sit here, but like, do not fart on me. That's so rude.' You know? And then he did it again like four or five times.

I think it has more to do with, like, I asked you not to and you're not respecting what I've asked."

Elena's father also has this issue of feeling invisible. One time, Elena's son didn't listen to something his grandfather had told him to do, and his grandfather smashed a bowl by throwing it onto the floor:

Elena: A couple years back, we were sitting outside eating food and Alex (Elena's son) *didn't stop doing something that he (Elena's father) asked. My dad picked up a bowl and just smashed it on the ground. It's like he did it once with a bowl and once with like his favorite mug, just like: spsh!! rah!!! Everything exploded.*

And my dad's like a wonderful human being, generally a super peaceful dude, but you know something, something hits him the wrong way. I've seen that happen a couple of times. Scary. Love you dad. If you're listening later.

Michael: There's no judgment on this. A lot of this comes from somewhere. It's not true about who we really are.

Elena: Yeah. And he would understand more than most.

Elena's father grew up with a very abusive father who, not surprisingly, also felt invisible. For example, her father's brother would be the one who would not listen to his father's controlling orders, and he would get constantly beaten for it because if people didn't listen to Elena's grandfather's orders, he himself would feel invisible.

Elena's grandfather was a pastor and came from a family of pastors probably fearing that their message would be invisible and fall onto deaf ears, just as Elena worries that her message will never see the light of day.

Elena originally said her father had to be invisible to avoid being beaten, and yet underneath her grandfather's abusive rage were his own violent fears that he and his message were invisible.

ELENA'S MOTHER

Elena's mother experiences a lot of anxiety, namely worrying about the health and well-being of her children, and even worrying if her children will die. This fear is rooted in the intergenerational trauma of Elena's great-grandmother. During the communist takeover in Ukraine, Elena's great-grandmother was separated from all of her children. Her children were scattered all over, and she remained cut off from them for 20 years and didn't know anything about them. As if things couldn't get any worse, Elena's great-grandfather was suddenly pulled out the front door one day, never to be seen again.

"Her husband was pulled out the front door by soldiers and never seen again."

After talking about this, Elena sees how she has inherited this trauma in her own life. She lives in Canada, and she has fears about the US military taking her from her home so that she disappears without a trace:

"One of my fears was the US military is going to show up at the front door and like, take me and I'll never be seen again. Like, that was totally like a worry that crossed my mind."

ELENA'S MOVIE

In the second session with Elena, we focus on finding out what her movie is that she wants to share with the world. I want to preface this by saying that in the beginning, she starts with a message that is – and I don't mean this out of ill will – very flowery and without true specifics or a true core. That is because the flowery part of her message is actually serving to cover up something deeply hidden and painful.

This dialogue with Elena is a prime example of how, when you follow your dream and share it with the world, it brings to the surface your deepest and most hidden wounds. And yet, it is the very process of healing these wounds that becomes the message and the beacon of light you shine onto the world.

Elena: The movie I want to share with the world is a message of hope. It's an experience of moving from surviving to thriving, being able to completely let go of past identity, who we previously identified ourselves with, and be in this new experience, and be like, "Wow, this is really different. This is really different than what was happening before."

Michael: Yeah. Can you give me more details? Tell me more about what is the movie that you want to share with the world and what's the impact that you want it to have on others? And I want you to really feel it as well, as you describe it... not just explain it but allow yourself to feel and allow me to feel it.

Elena: So there's a place of taking the tools that I have experienced that work and (then it's about) sharing them with others and getting to see how a little daily practice lights up their life and changes the way that they're feeling. And so that they feel really beautiful and loved and then they know that they created that themselves.

There is a desire for that which is so magnificent in their lives that they then turn around and go to friends like, "You need to come and be a part of this. This is so cool. And it's really working for me."

Michael: What is the impact – specific impact – you want for others? And then how does this relate to the struggles, healing, and transformation that you personally went through? What's the movie you want to share with others and what is its specific impact on others?

Elena: The specific impact is accelerating the conscious evolution and the journey of self-love for other people. Instead of 10 years, they can do it in a year. They don't have to go through all the mistakes and don't have to go through all the bullshit and don't have to spend so much money on like $50,000 worth of things and they'll just go, "Oh!" Like, you don't have to go do research. "I'll just listen to what Elena says that I need to do, and I'll do those things."

You can observe how Elena does not state the true impact of her message but reduces the impact of her message and healing process by simply saying they're more time-efficient.

And "Wow, the first one that I did worked really well, so I'll just do some of these other things, and they're a little bit strange, but like, I feel so much better. So who gives a crap?"

Like, "Who cares how strange it is? It feels so much better," and not like, "Oh, I feel so much better for like five minutes or ten minutes or an hour while I'm doing it." But like, "Things are changing in my life outside of that." So that they can really see that they're creating their reality, that they know how to modify that, rather than getting stuck in, like, "I know I create my reality, but like I'm creating all this shit that I don't really want...Why? I don't know."

And it's like, "Well, this is why. Why is because your subconscious is out of alignment with your conscious desires, and so you're creating from your subconscious desires, and it feels like shit." That's what the whole world is doing right now. So many people who are lonely already. They are just like so much more lonely.

Feel connected to people. Feel loving. Feel alive. Feel happy, feel stable. Feel safe, feel secure. So many things.

Michael: Okay, and so you want to share your message through this 50-author collaborative book launch?

Elena: Oh my gosh, I wanted to write my own whole book. But I've been working on that for seven years. So when a collaborative book launch came up, I was like, "Yeah, that gets me one step closer to being a published author."

Michael: So this book involves collaborating with 50 other authors?

Elena: Yeah. So we each write a chapter. There's 50 chapters, 50 authors, which means that instead of me promoting my book, there's 50 people promoting our book.

Michael: What about creating your own book?

Elena: I'm 30,000 words into that, and that's probably the next phase. I have 30,000 words written in my manuscript cause I wrote it as it was happening along the way... I have lots of that written already. I've edited it several times.

Michael: What is your mindset or approach as far as your book that you're writing? What is your plan for it?

Elena: The one that I'm writing?? (Michael: Mhm.) My plan right now is to not flake on the group book launch that's happening this month. If I manage to do that, then I can think about tackling the next piece. Probably still with JB, who's the lady organizing this first one and has launched 12 collaborative books last year or something which is a mind-boggling accomplishment to me right now.

Michael: Yeah. Okay. But, this book launch, this collaborative book launch is good, but I want you to just take a moment and really mentally, emotionally, spiritually focus your energies on your book. Because this is your message, your platform, your reason for existence, and what you're meant to share with the world. This book is a major stepping-stone to creating your message and sharing it with the world. What is your plan for it?

Elena: Like five years from now when it's already happened, and looking back at it, that kind of thing?

Michael: Not looking back on it five years from now. Just saying like, okay, you finished this collaborative book launch, and now you have all the time you need to focus on your book and finishing it. What's your plan to complete it and to share it?

Elena: I don't have a plan... The plan is to not fuck up this month. Sorry, that's my answer. It's like, don't fuck this one up. Don't fuck this up.

Michael: Why "Don't fuck up this one"? Because why?

Elena: Because I've created dozens of launches over the last seven years for myself, and I haven't executed on any of them beyond two weeks in. I was like, (sarcastically mimicking a small, griping voice), "Oh, I am not getting the results I want. I'm just going to quit." So to actually go through within this one, it's like, "Wow!" And that will expose me to thousands more people. I'm giving a talk at a summit. I have more plans for more summits. I have more plans, like I want 10 more podcasts where I'm featured in the next two months, three months probably.

Michael: That's good. It's helpful. But then to hear that you don't have plans for your own book, that's...

Elena: Michael, I had plans for my own book for like five or six years, and I continued to not action on them. So I'm not dreaming about anything that far in the future that I currently don't particularly believe I will action on or trust that I'll continue to action on.

Michael: So you don't believe that you will finish your book?

Elena: The evidence does not point that way currently.

Michael: Because if you... okay, don't take this the wrong way, but if you don't take your book seriously, then all this other stuff will not have an anchor. It's not going to *give you the abundance, the purpose that you were meant for, that you were created for. And if you keep putting it off, you're pushing away your base, your source for everything.*

It's not just the book. You're going to do other great stuff along this path, if you pursue that path (of writing your book and focusing on sharing your message with the world.) What are your thoughts and feelings thus far, or questions?

Something is set off in Elena, making her sob profusely.

Elena: (sobbing) I'm just crying... it hurts. It's okay, I get it. It's part of the process. I don't like what you just said (sobbing). Okay, we'll keep going.

Michael: What part of what I said? (Elena still sobbing.)

Here, Elena takes some time to collect herself emotionally and allows herself to just cry it out. I try to get her to center herself emotionally and reframe her experience of having these painful feelings.

Okay. Take a moment. With your eyes closed, tell yourself, "Feeling is healing." Whatever it is, whatever pain, emotional pain, difficulty, struggle, that you're feeling right now. You're meant to experience this and feel this because this is part of your movie. You going through this, you experiencing this, and you eventually overcoming it, and healing through it, will be a huge part of your message. (Elena still sobbing)

Elena: Okay. Yeah. I'm thinking, "Why would I try again?" and feeling despair.

Michael: Remember, these feelings are weeds. We've got to cut the head off the snake. So let's continue to explore it, but I just want you to feel safe as you do so. Okay? Because this thing is always there. It's hidden. It's so hidden that no matter what you're trying to do elsewhere in your life, if this is still here – if the head of the snake is not cut off – then it's always going to be your barrier. It's always going to be these hidden chains of yours.

Remember, if we go back to the PEWF process, we have cut the head off the snake and identify the weed. "Why would you try again?" is the thought. The emotion is despair. What is your worst fear, worst-case scenario?

Elena: Feeling worthless.

Michael: Before identifying what the feeling is, let's say you complete your book, and yet nobody reads it, or that you just never complete it.

Elena: I put all the effort in. I ignore the people around me in the process, and the thing I want to happen doesn't happen.

Michael: Ignoring people in the process? What do you mean by that?

Elena: I'd always be on my computer. I'm not being present for my son. "Michael, I'm editing. I don't have time for you, right now." "No, I don't want to play. I'm working."

Michael: Oh, so you're saying if you write the book, then it'll take away from you being present in other people's lives?

Elena: Yeah... and what if it doesn't work anyway? Then it's just like...

Michael: Okay, let's say you had unlimited time to spend with your friends and family, unlimited time to work on your book. What is your worst fear? Worst-case scenario? An example can be, like, so you actually did complete the book and nobody reads it, or you never complete it. Stretch this to your worst fear. Worst-case scenario.

Elena: Yeah. It's probably that nobody reads it.

Michael: Is that it?

Elena: Yeah, or somebody does read it, and it completely discredits me from ever being able to, like, do anything professionally or successfully. Cause I was too vulnerable or too...

Michael: I think what you are saying is that your worst fear is to be discredited forever in the eyes of the world. (Elena: Yeah.) If your worst fear came true, how would that make you feel the FWP and why? Failure, worthless, or powerless? Remember, we're just cutting the head off the snake. So these feelings are not true about who you really are. (Elena: worthless.) So worthless, and why?

Elena: Because I tried and it didn't work, cause the vision I had never came to pass, which means that maybe I was just crazy or something... Delusional... delusional... uhhh!

Michael: As you experience all these feelings, like nobody reads it, or you're discredited, so you never will be able to do this work ever again, completely exposed, and your image and reputation are tarnished forever, whose movie are you in?

Elena: My grandpa's.

Michael: The one that was a pastor, right? (Elena: Yeah.) Can you give me a visual of how he felt this feeling? I know your father would get angry, like if your son wasn't listening, and he would throw and smash the bowl onto the floor.

Elena: It's a lack of integrity. There's this piece of living one thing and saying another thing. Like standing in front of 200 people and saying (Elena mimics an imposter voice), "You should do this. These are the words of God. God's love moves through all of us..."

But what he doesn't say is, "Please don't find out I beat my kids and drink to hide my own secret pain and disconnection from God." It's like a lip service kind of thing.

Michael: So he was terrified of being exposed for what was really going on? Is that what you're saying?

Elena: Yeah. Yes. (Michael: Okay.) And he, with the exception of his immediate family, he totally successfully hid that. There were hundreds of people at his funeral being like (speaking in a sarcastic tone), "He was such an amazing man!"

And my dad tells this story of being like, "What the fuck? Like how is that even possible?" Like he could say one thing, and like, my experience could be so different.

Michael: So he was an alcoholic, is that right?

Elena: Oh, for sure. Yeah. Both of them. (Michael: Both of them?) I love you, Dad... My dad and my grandpa.

Michael: Okay. So he was creating this illusory image, hiding what was really going on. But at that time he was still an alcoholic. Yet alcoholism is still a coping mechanism to numb some type of pain, and that was not just because of the situation that he was in, but it's coming from something that happened earlier in his life, something that happened in his childhood or to his parents.

(Here Elena talks about how her grandfather's mother died at early age, but it didn't really feel like trauma or an intergenerational trauma tied to what Elena was feeling. So I then applied the PEWF process to the grandfather to see what his core feeling was, so I could then tie it to some kind of intergenerational trauma.)

Michael: You said your grandfather's primary emotion was anger or worry, fear and anxiety? (Elena: Anger.) Did he experience any anxiety, worry, or fear? (Elena: I don't know).

Michael: Okay, and what problem or situation would bring up strong feelings of anger in him?

Elena: Not being listened to.

Michael: Can you give me an example?

Elena: My Uncle Dan as a teenager...

Michael: Would not listen to your grandfather, and then he would beat your Uncle Dan, right?

Elena: Yeah. Yeah. And then, like, the being quiet in church thing is huge. Oh my gosh. (Elena now talks about how her son likes to wiggle and fidget at church, and it triggers her and her father's compulsive need to be quiet in church.)

Michael: What do you mean by that?

Elena: You can feel, like, the not wiggling and not being loud in church, like as a participant... Like sitting in the pews or whatever, when my son is wiggly, and he has been raised in a completely different way, and we never go to church, but when we do go, he just likes to wiggle and fidget. And the other day he was lying on the floor under the pew, just like wiggling because that's what he needs to do.

And like, you can just feel the force of trauma, like oozing through me and my dad, just being like, "We're not going to do what we want to do, which is just like grab him and then like throttle him until he's dead and stops making sounds" Which we would never do, but like you can feel it. It's like this intense, intense force that comes through when we're in that situation. Intense force... I can totally see, like, Grandpa when me and dad are reacting emotionally like that.

Like when my son wiggles, there's so much internal pressure of just like, (speaks in evil sinister voice) "This is not okay! This is not okay! Make him stop! Make him stop!" There is this pressure of this violent reaction.

Michael: Okay. Wiggling in church or wiggling in public, or something like that?

Elena: In church specifically. Like other places, it doesn't bother me at all, but there, it's just like "Ahhhhh!!!!!" (freaking out in anger). I can feel the trauma down the family line.

Michael: Got it, got it. And if he's wiggling in church, what part of that is bothersome to you? What do you fear would happen because of his wiggling in church?

Elena: We'll be asked to leave and maybe never be able to come back.

Michael: Okay. Got it. Completely excluded.

Elena: Yeah, yeah. Excommunicated totally. And that's something that the Mennonite faith did regularly in order to maintain accordance with the beliefs that were being taught, for sure. A social pressure thing like the Mormons do, but the Mennonites, which is the religious faith that all four of my grandparents come from, would all use this as one of the ways to control people and make sure that they were all adhering to their cultural and religious rules.

Michael: What is the Mennonites faith?

Elena: It's a Christian and Baptist tradition, sort of like Lutherans, but different, sort of like Amish, but different. Named after Menno Simons who decided to do something different in relation to the church.

Michael: Got it. Got it. Do you know of any past family trauma for your grandfather or his parents? I know that was a part of the culture of the religion, like, you're going to be excluded if you do something wrong that goes against the church, but do you know anything they experienced firsthand? Because I'll give you this interesting story...

I then continue to share Brian's story of how he had the dream of being a full-time counselor and entrepreneur sharing his message with the world like Tony Robbins. However, he didn't want to pursue it out of fear of being exposed, for one, as a scam artist taking advantage of COVID-19.

Brian's fear of being judged and excluded by the world was rooted in the complete secrecy surrounding the existence of his biological father, since his grandparents on both sides didn't want his parents to be together, since Brian was born out of wedlock. Brian's parents were then forced to separate, and Brian was not informed of his biological father's existence until two years before his mother passed, when she at last revealed to him that his father was not his biological father.

Elena: When you shared that story, I was like, "Oh, that happened to my aunt." She conceived out of wedlock and was excommunicated from the church, publicly and loudly.

Michael: Wow.

Elena: She's also the only other single mom in our family line, and her daughter went on to become a single mother as well, with an alcoholic father.

Michael: So your aunt is your dad's sister, right?

Elena: That's my mom's sister. Again, both of Mennonite faith.

Michael: All right, so coming back to your base, with you writing your own book or the decision to do so, the decision to complete it, the decision to share it, and that fear and intergenerational fear, pain, and trauma of "What if I get excommunicated just as my aunt was." That was the whole environment, the culture, and the world that they came from. And so you're worried that – let's say somebody reads it and because you're too vulnerable or whatever, you get discredited forever – that you're never able to do this work again.

And so I just want you to close your eyes for a moment. Feel that feeling in your body, your true emotional antenna, and then picture a miniature movie screen in front of your eyes.

First, where do you feel this feeling in your body? Is it your throat, your heart, the top or the bottom of your stomach? The feeling of like, "Oh, I'll be discredited forever. What's the point of trying again?" Where do you feel that in your body?

Elena: In my throat.

Michael: Okay, that's very interesting. Your throat is your center of self-expression and your voice. Feel this feeling in your throat knowing that "feeling is healing" and then project that feeling, that tension, that pain, or that intergenerational trauma, onto this miniature movie screen in front of your eyes and then visualize, first, yourself, writing your book and feeling like, "Why would I try again?" And also the fear of "I'll be discredited forever." And then change the scene and see the true movie, which is your whole family really, on both sides. This is not just your grandfather. This is on your mother's side as well, which is the trauma of public and total excommunication that your aunt experienced.

I think that was the hidden one. I think your father and your grandfather were so out in the open with their alcoholism that you could see their pain very clearly, but the aunt is the hidden yet most impactful one.

But besides that, I just want you to know that you are in your father's movie, your grandfather's movie, your aunt's movie, all these family members that come from this Mennonite religion and that world. And just visualize this movie, using your emotional antennas, your gift of high sensitivity, and high empathy, consciously and correctly, so you can see the movie. But do not zap yourself subconsciously into the movies of your past family members as your own.

Now change the scene of that movie. Change the whole scene of everything. You see a big screen, a big movie screen, a theater screen, and it's your movie, and the theater is full. What is your movie that you want to share with the world? What is the impact you want to have with others, and how is it empowered by the healing that you're going through with this intergenerational pain and trauma of feeling like if you do something wrong, then you'll be excluded from the world?

Elena: I deeply understand that, that woman on the screen talking to the people, she deeply understands the pain of trying to create a new culture. The fear of being excluded by speaking what you would want to say.

And she's there, clearly speaking about how we can't let those things stop us from creating what we want to create, can't let those things hold us back when we know in our hearts what we want and what's right for us. And that if it feels like it's coming from love and from connection and beauty, then that's what we should follow, and we should use our voices to be loud and proud and create change in our lives.

Michael: To be authentically and boldly visible on a platform.

Elena: I like loud and proud, but yeah (Elena chuckles).

Michael: Like on a public platform for the world to see and to stand there boldly and authentically and with your soul naked. Truly yourself, just as you are.

How does that resonate? Cause this pain of "What if I am exposed and excluded from the world?" – this pain is bleeding through the generations, making you feel you cannot be yourself and that if you make one wrong turn, then you'll be completely excluded from the world.

And so I think part of your message – at least from what you tell me, it feels like a big part of your message – is transitioning and transforming from that and then standing boldly, authentically, and nakedly to the world and sharing the beauty of who you are, the beauty of your message, the beauty of your voice.

Cause my feeling is that through all your experiences, and through the experiences of your past family members through the generations, you are primed and ready and you have the power and the tools to help people do that for themselves.

Elena: Yeah, for sure.

CLOSING THOUGHTS

As you can tell, from the beginning of the session to now, there was a major shift and transformation in how Elena described her movie and calling. It was absolutely beautiful to hear how Elena described her movie and calling, and how centered and aligned she was with the truth of her soul.

Once again, it was Elena's greatest pain, her intergenerational trauma, that was the single greatest barrier to her following and embracing her dreams. However, her dreams and greatest gift to the world are based on transforming this same pain into the message of light she is meant to share with the world. Whatever pain you are feeling, accept it and stop resisting it, for pain is your greatest teacher.

COACHING DIALOGUE WITH STACEY GROSS: "AM I A NARCISSIST?"

This is my second session with Stacey where we begin to identify what her movie is. Here is a refresher of Stacey's first session:

Stacey discussed how she struggled with social anxiety and feelings of loneliness and needing to be accepted by others. She also heavily doubts and "picks apart" the work she releases out into the world with her podcast and writing. Ultimately, a lot of her fears of failure and being judged and then excluded by others were rooted in her emotionally suppressed father being the unwanted "accident" child. Having said that, in this second session, Stacey's mother's intergenerational trauma comes to the surface.

At the beginning of this session, Stacey shares how her movie is about the healing power of storytelling. When I tell Stacey that turning her struggle into her transformation is a big part of her movie, and ask her what she still struggles with, she answers:

Stacey: I struggle with second-guessing myself. I struggle with being overly concerned with the opinions of others or feedback of others. I prefer a traditional publishing route because I like the validation that comes with someone saying, "This work is worthy of being printed and shared," rather than self-publishing. The most important part of anything that I do is that I don't want it to be self-centered or navel-gazing.

Michael: I just want to explore what you said about second-guessing and caring about other people's perceptions. Stretch that to your worst fear, your worst-case scenario. What does that look like?

Stacey: Absolutely. I can tell you, without a doubt, it's that I am a narcissist and have no idea that I'm completely narcissistic... I have no insight and I think that I do, and everyone can just sort of see right through that. It's just a completely narcissistic endeavor. That would be my greatest fear. Being a narcissist and not even being aware of it.

Michael: Let's identify the feeling, the weed. If that worst fear came true, what do you fear would happen because of it? If people find out that all the while she's been a narcissist, and she's not even saying anything valid or helpful. What do you fear would happen because of that?

Stacey: It would be a completely devastating blow to anything positive that I think – that I feel about myself. That there was no value the whole time. You know, I think that I'm creating a podcast that's helping other moms, or I think that I'm writing a memoir that is going to impact someone else in a positive way and it turns out it was just me being the star of my own show. Do you know what I mean? There was no universal value in it whatsoever.

Essentially my greatest fear would be that I am, in fact, a narcissist, which would mean that everything that I thought I was doing, or every value that I saw in what I was doing, was invalidated.

Stacey talks about how being a narcissist would invalidate everything she did, which is really about her feeling that her identity would be invalidated.

Michael: I hear you kind of holding onto that term "narcissism." What is it about narcissism that really irks you? Of course, it's an inappropriate behavior, but you have a strong focus on it. I wonder if it's because people who are narcissists make you feel like you don't matter, but then that feeling was already there. It's not true about who you really are. But I first want to identify that feeling.

Stacey: Yeah. That feeling for me originates very early in life. I have a mom, and I know we discussed this in the last interview, and I love her. She's a wonderful person, but in a lot of ways, she doesn't have a lot of insight into... she likes to be in control, or she likes to make unilateral decisions, for how even the schedule of our week is going to go.

And then she'll dictate that. She'll hand that down to everyone, and it sort of makes me feel as though how I would maybe schedule the week is not important. She's made the decision, and we're all gonna follow now.

Michael: Got it, so she's very controlling.

Stacey: Yeah. And I don't think she does it necessarily to be intentionally dictatorial. But I think that's just her nature.

She doesn't like any kind of uncertainty. She likes to know exactly what's going to be happening and when.

Michael: Can you give an example?

Stacey: Well, I mean, she'll get a hold of me at the beginning of the week and say, "Now this is going to happen this day and I'm going to do it this way." And she wants it very concretely, rigidly planned, and it's better if it's according to her plan. Because that way she has control over it. Losing control, I think for her, is scary.

Michael: Can you give me a specific example?

Stacey: Sure. So I got a text a few days ago. She was watching the girls, and she was planning for me to pick them up, and how, and when, and you know, how that would all go down. And it was, "You will pick them up on Thursday," or I can't remember the day, but "You will pick them up this day. Then you will take them home. Then you will do this with them, and then the next day this will happen and then you will, etc., etc." And that's how it was worded. So it was very much like, I am dictating to you what's going to happen.

Stacey points out that the root of her mother's struggles was not knowing her mental health issues earlier. We go deeper into the family's past and talk about how Stacey's grandmother was not accepted by Stacey's grandfather's parents since she came from a poor background.

Michael: Your grandmother was not accepted because of the poverty she came from? (Stacey: Right.) And your mother internalized that feeling of exclusion, which is like, "I don't matter. I'm worthless." But the way she internalizes this and replays this in her own life is: "I need things a certain way, and they have to be this way because, if they're not, I'm not valued."

Stacey: I think. Yeah, that makes sense.

Michael: And then coming back to base, which is you feeling that "narcissism is my worst nightmare" or "what if I'm a narcissist?", because you being a narcissist would make other people feel like they don't matter.

Stacey: And I think that I felt like I didn't matter for a long time as a kid... But I want to be very careful to – to be clear that I don't think that it was intentional on her (Stacey's mother's) part. But I did feel that way because she had to expend so much energy on maintaining control, maintaining an image. And if I didn't fit in with that image, then it wasn't good.

Michael: What was this image that she would try to make you fit?

Stacey: Upstanding. Attractive. Normal.

Michael: Give me an example when you were growing up.

Stacey: Normalcy. And I don't know how to really say that in a concrete way, but everything had to look very nice. Everything had to be in its place. Everything. So when it came to me, my hair had to be washed, brushed and cleaned. My face needed to be cleaned. My clothes needed to be cleaned and pressed. I needed to stand straight. I needed to look pretty. I needed to look nice.

Michael: Because if you didn't have that image, you would be looked down upon and judged by all others?

Stacey: Exactly. Yes. And so I was sort of an extension of her and existed to maintain that for her. So her concern with other people not accepting me, or not thinking that I looked nice or normal, would speak to her.

Michael: I feel – okay, there are two things I want to say. I feel it is twofold. One, for sure, the way she's treating you is making you feel like you don't matter because she's projecting this idealized image onto you (and making you feel you can never live up to it.) But also her control issues, or obsession with image is rooted in this feeling, this intergenerational pain of feeling worthless, and that's what you're subconsciously internalizing. And that's the movie.

Something else I want to explore is... I just asked about your mother, but your grandmother, was her family heavily affected by the Great Depression?

Stacey: Oh yeah. My grandparents grew up in the Depression. My grandma, I remember her saying, "I'm a 1940s grandma," but they had lived through the Depression, and so they, my grandparents were parentified quite a bit. Especially my grandmother.

Michael: How were they parentified?

Stacey: So my grandmother had to drop out of school before, maybe, sophomore year to take care of her siblings. Her mother was addicted to some substances. There was a lot of dysfunction, chaos, and trauma between the siblings. And so she watched her parents deal with the trauma of going through the Depression and it affected her. My grandmother, I almost feel like she internalized a lot of their experience of the Depression.

Michael: From what you know, tell me more about your grandmother's family. You said the kids had to drop out of school, her mother was a drug addict, siblings were fighting...

Stacey: Yeah. I can remember stories about – so there were a number of siblings, six or seven I think, but certain sisters would be sold or traded to brothers' friends as teenagers for sexual favors. My other aunt, my grandmother's sister, also dropped out of school or would skip school for several days at a time to help her mom clean. Her mom would feed her "black beauties." She would feed her speed to make her clean, so that she would stay home and clean the house.

Michael: Wait... feed her drugs so she would clean?

Stacey: She (Stacey's great-grandmother) would feed her pills. And my grandmother's sister was probably between 12 and 15. And her mom would feed the girls speed so that they would clean the house and they would stay home.

Micheal: They wouldn't clean the house if she didn't give them drugs?

Stacey: I don't know. Apparently. She felt that they did a better job if they were all strung out. Yeah. I mean, it's intense. It's intense stuff. A lot of dysfunction.

Now I return to the subject of Stacey's grandmother and see how her feelings could be connected to her upbringing by applying the PEWF process to her. Stacey said her grandmother would experience anxiousness at times.

Michael: Can you give me an example? Like, firsthand, something you saw that made her anxious.

Stacey: She would be anxious if anything was out of place. She didn't like the house messed up ...You know, I never saw her anxious, because she was so good at controlling everything.

I remember one time I had lied to her. I was spending the night at her house. I was pretty young, and I had lied to her about something, brushing my teeth or something, and she found out that I hadn't, and she came right in and spanked me. I mean, really hard, and was like, "You will not lie to me!" That, I can only imagine, was anxiety over something...

Michael: Like, if you lied to her, it makes her feel like she doesn't matter.

Stacey: Maybe. Yeah.

Ultimately, as horrific as the behavior of the great-grandmother and the grandmother's brothers was, their behavior was all about themselves, in total disregard and at the expense of others. This kind of narcissistic behavior is rooted in a person feeling worthless, because narcissism is rooted in a person's void within themselves, which underlies their need to make it all about themselves.

However, throughout the session you will see Stacey repeatedly holding onto the pain of her mother's need for control over her well-being – and not also see in addition to that, how Stacey's own feelings of invalidation were in many ways the intergenerational pain of feeling "I don't matter" that her mother, grandmother, and including great-grandmother all felt.

Michael: All right. Let's come back to how you think all of this relates to being featured in the movie that you will share with the world.

Stacey: I think that, for me, I felt very invalidated as a kid, and I never want anyone else to feel that way. Part of what I had to do, because of my mom's mental health issues, was I had to learn how to read her emotions. I had to learn how to read her emotional state at any given point in order to successfully navigate with as little conflict as possible. And so it became second nature.

Michael: With this experience of feeling invalidated by your mother growing up, and then you want to do what?

Stacey: I want to validate other people by listening to and sharing their stories, or by sharing my story in such a way that it puts their minds at ease about an issue that they're struggling with. So when I do podcasts about parenting and I talk about my struggles or my fears with parents or my experiences with parenting, it's to let someone else out there who's struggling know you're not the only one.

Michael: Cause when you talk about invalidation, I feel like there's this pain on two levels. One level of pain is how a parent mistreats a child. The other pain, which is a core level of pain, is the pain that a child feels subconsciously in their parent and unknowingly internalizes as their own. Hidden. And so when you say "invalidated," your grandmother and her sisters were invalidated. They were drugged to clean the house. Their brothers would sell them off for sexual favors. I think you may be feeling their invalidation. That invalidation is like a worst nightmare.

Stacey: It's intense.

Michael: It's horrific. And your mother's behavior, I think, stems from that. She needs control because if she doesn't have control, she doesn't matter. And people who felt like they didn't matter were your grandmother's siblings who were being drugged and being sold for sexual favors.

Stacey: I'm not sure if I'm going to be quite on track with what you're thinking, but I definitely look at my grandmother's mother, who would keep them home from school and have them clean. And I see extreme narcissism and so I guess part of my biggest fear is: "Am I maybe a narcissist?" or "Am I that kind of a monster person?"

Michael: The narcissism, as bad as it is, it's a symptom rooted in the feeling of worthlessness. So I think your mother internalizes this through your grandmother. For example, your mother needs to have things a certain way: you need to do this on Monday, you need to do this on Tuesday, and this on Wednesday, and this is how you're going to do it, and this is when you're going to do it, and if you don't do it, then she feels like she's worthless. So the root of the narcissistic behavior is worthlessness.

Stacey: Being that I'm so concerned with narcissism, I think at a deeper level, I'm concerned with a sense of worthlessness, and being invalidated as a kid did make me feel worthless.

Michael: But that whole narcissist thing is rooted in the feeling of worthlessness. (Stacey: Right.) Which is this intergenerational pain and trauma we've talked about.

For example, your grandma getting infuriated and telling you, "You lied to me??!!" over not brushing your teeth because she feels worthless. On your grandfather's side of the family where it was all about the image and status. Your grandmother and her siblings were made to feel worthless by your great-grandmother. But I'm pretty sure your great-grandmother engaged in all this toxic behavior and made everything about herself because she, too, felt worthless.

Maybe it was more compounded by the era, because the Depression ripped everything from everybody. (Stacey: Right.) They're ALREADY poor. Now you're even poorer than poor. (Stacey: Yeah.) They did that to survive. I mean, what they did was really bad, but it was a form of survival, you know? (Stacey: Right.) They couldn't go to school because they had to survive. You know?

I feel like we can relate it to what we are feeling right now with what's happening now. (Michael referring to COVID-19 and the economic collapse). Emotionally, this is ripping our hearts out. All these small businesses are being forced to close down. Like I had a haircut recently... I know I'm not supposed to get a haircut, but I had a haircut. I went to my hair stylist's garage. He owns two or three salons and when I saw him, he was very down and very depressed because everything that he'd built for his whole life had been taken away from him. I could feel it the whole time he was cutting my hair.

I went to my hair stylist's garage. He owns two or three salons and when I saw him, he was very down, and very depressed because everything that he built for his whole life was taken away from him. I could feel it the whole time he was cutting my hair.

I just want you to see that it's not about narcissism, which is happening more so at the surface. It's a behavior rooted in a feeling. (Stacey: Right.) The feeling is...

Stacey: The feeling is worthlessness.

Michael: Yeah. Or the fear of, "What if I'm a narcissist? Then I will make other people feel worthless." But that's how you feel inside about yourself all the time. But that's not true about who you really are. It's just an intergenerational feeling.

Stacey: Yeah. Yeah. That definitely makes sense.

Michael: So after hearing all this, what do you think about what your movie is? And what do you want to share with the world?

Stacey: I think that for me it boils down to... I want to reach that one person who's feeling worthless or feeling valueless or invalidated and completely spin that around for them. And let them know that they do matter, that they do have worth. That they have enough worth. That it's worth fighting for themselves to see themselves go forward.

Michael: And what is the vehicle through which you will help them feel that way? Because it's not just you telling them, "You do matter." (Stacey: Right.) It's your message. It's your movie that they will watch. You don't have to tell each and every person in the world because movies are meant to be watched by the world.

Stacey: It's a memoir. It's a story. It's good storytelling, a character and a plot and just a story that connects with them so that, through the people they see on the page or in the story, they can have that experience vicariously... that awakening or understanding.

A memoir that talks about attachment and anxiety.

Michael: What is attachment?

Stacey: Attachment, so when I say attachment, I mean, early experiences with primary caregivers. And so how that influences us as we age, whether we feel secure with other people or we feel competent within ourselves. On a fundamental level.

Michael: Got it. Got it. But also including not only the attachment, but like your mother's control comes from this feeling of worthlessness. Your grandmother being mad at you saying, "You lied to me!" because she feels worthless. The great-grandmother doing all this crazy stuff, you know? Her children were made to feel worthless, absolutely, like beyond worthless... like, to the point where it was evil, but then she also probably felt worthless.

After Stacey sees how her feelings of invalidation that she thought was primarily caused by how her mother raised her, was primarily an intergenerational trauma of invalidation, we come back to defining her plans for her memoir.

244

Michael: Okay, so tell me about what your plans are for writing this memoir. After you complete the book, what is your plan?

Stacey: Well after that, I'm going to submit it. I'm hoping for a good response, even if I don't win the manuscript competition. So the professor who invited me to submit, it's a journal that he works for, and they're trying to publish their first book. Even if it's not selected for this particular competition as a winner, I still would send it out for review and work on publication.

Michael: How about self-publication?

Stacey: Um, self-publication is, is good. Um, but again, um...

Michael: I remember you saying that you didn't want to self-publish, because you wanted the validation of your work through a publication company, right?

Stacey: I like to know that I am for sure putting something out there that's going to be helpful. If it's not going to be helpful or someone isn't going to look at this and say...

Michael (interjects): Sorry, sorry... You don't need to know that. You don't need to know...

Stacey: I do!

Michael: Because your memoir comes from your soul. Without your soul, you wouldn't be helpful, you wouldn't be empowering and inspiring, because that is why you exist. So there's no question about that. I already heard your story and felt its power.

You just need to get feedback on honing it... like, as if you were putting on an outfit: "Should I match this color with this color?" The core is there. You just need to fine-tune it because it's going to be a way to heal yourself. Furthermore, it's going to be a tool for you, and that's how you know it's going to really help others. But you don't need that validation.

That need for validation is intergenerational, like through the generations of your family. Everybody wanted validation. And the whole point of the book is to help people overcome this need for validation, right?

Stacey: I think, yeah...

Michael: These people are afraid to be themselves, and your message is about telling others, "Why do I need 'you' to say I'm okay. I don't need your approval." You know? "The Creator created me. So that's the only validation I ever need."

Stacey: Mhm, yeah. I think part of it, too, comes from... you know, when I was in my master's program, there was a lot of talk about how this is the approach (for publication), and it was a different time too. It was at the beginning of this era of self-publishing, which was considered sort of cheating, like you're a cheat and you're cheating the process.

Michael: You want feedback for sure, but you don't absolutely have to have publication to validate your work and make sure it's okay. I asked my wife, I asked a coach, for feedback because I was struggling with writing my book... because initially what I did for my book, in order to show the PEWF process, I picked five people to go through the process together.

So I had five different examples, but it was so confusing to describe how this person went through this, and this person went through that, and then say, "Okay, now let's go to the next step with the same five people." It was like, "Wait, what happened?" as you were reading it.

So instead, I just highlighted one person for each step of the PEWF process, and used examples from my own life too, and that made it so much easier. And I included the actual dialogue that I thought was important, and I highlighted that and made it easy. Then I summarized everybody else.

So of course you're going to need feedback. But you don't need validation. You're already the shit, you know? That's the name of my first book: "You Are the Fucking Shit: Heal Your Anxiety, Anger, and Depression from the Ground Up." You already are the shit.

That's the reason why you're struggling – or experiencing this and struggling with it – it's because it's a part of your book to show people how to work through this. So what are your thoughts and feelings now?

Stacey: Yeah, that makes sense. That does make sense.

Michael: I'm not saying should you publish or self-publish, but when you said, "Well, if I don't have that publication, then that means it's not as good or it's not as valid." That's coming from a feeling.

Stacey: Right. Yeah. It's that fear of, "Well, maybe I'm just being completely narcissistic. This wasn't selected as a winner, and so it must not have value, but I'm going to force it to have value by putting it on Amazon myself." You know what I mean? So I guess that's just what I struggle with.

For Stacey, her fear of being a narcissist subconsciously deflects and avoids underlying feelings of invalidation and worthlessness. It's not that being a narcissist would cause feelings of invalidation, but that it would just bring up feelings of invalidation that she already had about herself. Remember, this feeling of invalidation is in many ways her intergenerational trauma.

Michael: That's a part of your book. So when you write your memoir, say what you're struggling with. Say what you're feeling. And then you keep on working at it – creating your own tools because that's the engine of the book.

Stacey: Yeah, that makes sense. I hadn't really thought about that process once it's finished. I've been focused on, well, "I'm going to get it submitted and then that will be the end of the process." But it's not. So it's good to start thinking ahead to that. What will be my next steps with that?

Michael: Kind of like Elena... She's doing this collaborative project, and she's like, "This is it! This is it!" And I said, "What about your book? Your message and purpose relies on that." And she started balling. She was like, "I don't want to hear it. I'm crying. It just hurts. I don't want to hear what you're telling me." But she was cool with it, and was like, "It's okay. I know it's part of the process." But she's crying, crying, crying, and then that's the elephant in the room.

Your elephant is saying, "If I self-publish, then I'm forcing it, then I'll be narcissistic and/or people won't want to hear it. I don't matter." That's the elephant. But that's also the beacon of light you are going through, that you are featuring, that is going to make the memoir come to life.

Stacey: Yeah, that's true. That is true.

Michael: Think about the audience, the audience of your movie. When you think, "Well, if I don't go through a publishing company, and I force it through self-publication, then I will feel like I'm a narcissist or a fraud, or that I don't matter because I'm completely wrong and my message means nothing," then the audience of your movie shrinks to only you and your unresolved feelings, although they're not true about who you really are. The audience becomes only you, or your past family members.

When the audience is you, you're not helping anybody. You're feeding into the insecurity. You're feeding into the intergenerational trauma (Stacey: Right.) Think about the audience of your movie.

Stacey: Right. By self-publishing, it's taking the responsibility of validation upon myself and saying, "No, I don't care what anyone else thinks. This does have value." You know what I mean?

Michael: You just know. Like, I haven't published my book and what if I were to say "Until it publishes, then it has value." (Stacey: Right) And so as I'm talking to you right now what if I were to be like (Michael mimics insecure mannerisms and tones), "Uh, you know, like this is how you do it... The PEWF process goes like this... Oh, you know, think about the purpose of your movie." And then I was like, "Oh, you have to publish. And then, and you're like, validated, then you are good to go." No, no... If I were to do that, then my work with others would not work.

Michael: You just know. Like, I haven't published my book, and what if I were to say, "Until it's published, it has no value." (Stacey: Right) And so, as I'm talking to you right now, what if I were to be like (Michael mimics insecure mannerisms and tones), "Uh, you know, like this is how you do it. The PEWF process goes like this. Oh, you know, think about the purpose of your movie." And then I was like, "Oh, I have to first publish, and only then, my work is validated." No, no. If I were to do that, then my work with others would not work.

Stacey: Right, right. That's true.

Michael: Obviously, there are many times that I doubt myself, thinking, "Oh no, what if it fails?" But that's something that I incorporate into the message of the book. (Stacey: Right, right.) You've got to own it, because you got to own your beauty, your power, your message. It all lies within you.

Why put it into the hands of somebody else's approval? You are denying something that's already beautiful. Niagara Falls is just beautiful. (Stacey: Yeah, that's true.) It doesn't need anybody's validation. It just is.

Stacey: Yeah. I never thought about that. I have a very different view of self-publishing right now than I did before. Yeah, it's empowering to say, "I'm going to be the one to decide whether this has value or not."

Michael: You don't even need to decide. It's not a decision to be made. It already has value. Like I said, Niagara Falls doesn't need to decide if it has value or if it's beautiful or not. It just is. (Stacey: Right, yeah.)

Alright, cool. We're about coming to a close. Any last questions, thoughts, or feelings?

Stacey: No. This has been an interesting conversation. Yeah. I definitely have a different view of what the process is going to be when it's finished. I've always thought of that – finishing it and submitting it – as the terminus of the project.

Michael: What I've realized in doing this for myself and for others... I initially thought you heal all that pain, that intergenerational trauma, and then it's about the true self. It's about sharing your message with the world. It's the beauty, it's the flowery positivity, the light.

Not really. When you go after your dream, your purpose, and you share your movie with the world... When you go into that process, the most hidden source of pain comes up. The most secret one, the one that's really controlling you. That one comes up and then that becomes part of your light. It's the vehicle for the light which you share onto the world.

So it's a very powerful process. You're not writing it to write it, or to complete it. This is a transformative process for you, and then it's going to be transformative for others. This process of healing and shining your light, while you're writing your book, will bring about a process of transformation for yourself. And that transformation is what you're going to share with others. That's your divine message.

So it's a very powerful process. You're not writing it just to write it or to complete it. This is a transformative process for you, and then it's going to be transformative for others. This process of healing and shining your light, while you're writing your book, will bring about a process of transformation for yourself. And that transformation is what you're going to share with others. That's your divine message.

Stacey: Yeah, that's true.

CLOSING THOUGHTS

It hadn't dawn on me until after the session but the reason why Stacey was so fixated on the thought of being a narcissist, was because she fully identifies herself as the servant. Her whole existence is dedicated to others, and in particular, her loved ones. If she was indeed a narcissist, then she, as the servant, would have no reason to exist and feel utterly worthless because of it. Stacey's self-identification as the servant is in many ways a coping mechanism to avoid feeling the feelings of invalidation and worthlessness she inherited and internalized from her past family members. This ties back to why Stacey didn't want to own her light and power by self-publishing because she needed that feeling of validation outside of herself to mask the feelings of invalidation and worthlessness she continually feels from within.

Time and time again, you can see how your greatest pain is both your single greatest barrier to you following your dreams but also what will propel your message and light onto the world. You, and the generations before you, have experienced this pain, trauma, and struggle, so you can both heal and transform the world through the lessons you learned from pain.

CHAPTER FOURTEEN:

Channel Your Pain into Your Beacon of Light

If you attempt to heal your pain in isolation, you will be at it for an eternity, because your life is not only about healing pain, but also about transforming pain into your beacon of light.

What does that mean? In order to truly heal your pain, you need to know the purpose of pain. The purpose of you experiencing your pain and intergenerational trauma is for you to transform it into a movie in which that you will share with the world. That is why pain exists and that is why you exist.

You may want to "resist" your negative feelings, thoughts, and emotions and just want to put an end to it all. However, if you do so, you will never truly and completely heal your pain and separate from it, because pain only exists for you to transform it into light.

It is true that the journey of shining your light and sharing your movie with the world will bring up your deepest and most hidden wounds and truly force you to face your pain head-on. The truth is, as much as you hate this pain and suffering, the reason why you are seemingly stuck in this vicious cycle of pain, negative thoughts and feelings, is because you want to. You find it more comfortable to do this rather than to shine your light. It is only when you shine your light onto the world, that you are forced to face both your pain and ancestral pain head-on.

That is why we end up choosing a life sentence of avoiding, projecting, and numbing our pain through our many addictions. The question remains: What is our drug of choice? Is it social media? Our phone? Alcohol? Overeating? Overworking? Control? Or is it the most pervasive and common drug of all? Thinking, thinking, and overthinking. We can willingly get lost in our thoughts because they give us the illusion that we are seeking a solution, when all that we are really ever doing is using constant thinking as a drug to numb, distract us from and project our pain.

OUR PAIN IS OUR LIGHT

Choose to face your pain, and in doing so, choose your light. Transform your pain into light, because the universal truth and God's truth is that our pain is our light.

You may not be able to see it, but just like a diamond in the rough, this pain and suffering you feel just needs your polishing for its message to shine. Pain is your hidden treasure because pain is your greatest teacher. In turn, if you choose to ignore the lessons that pain is trying to teach you, you will have sacrificed the purpose of your existence and have nothing to offer others.

Pain only becomes true pain when you avoid it. True pain is the avoidance of your light.

Anytime you catch yourself belittling yourself, doubting yourself, being unsure of yourself, and simply punishing yourself with endless negative self-talk, take a moment to imagine if Picasso were to do that to himself when he was learning to paint. If he were to not choose his God-given purpose by expressing his gifts through painting and art, he would have deprived the world of his God-given gifts and the impact he was destined to make. You are doing the very same thing when you put yourself down and doubt yourself, your gifts, your purpose, and the movie you are meant to share with the world.

As a matter of fact, Picasso's most famous paintings were born out of channeling his pain into art, which is the movie he was meant to share with the world. For example, many of his most famous works came out during what is called his "Blue period," which was motivated by his best friend's suicide, as well as his feeling like an outcast in society. His most famous work of all is *Guernica* (1937), depicting the horror of Nazi bombings during the Spanish Civil War of a town in his home country of Spain.

You must awaken your inner Picasso and channel your pain into your movie to share with the world, and you will change the world forever.

Don't choose to drown yourself in your fears, pain, and frustrations. Imagine if Niagara Falls could actually talk and all that it ever said was, "I'm so ugly! I'm so ugly!" You are doing the same thing with your negative self-talk.

Quit it now! Just as it is ludicrous for Niagara Falls to say how ugly it is, it is ludicrous to doubt yourself because you would not exist if you did not have this greatness you were destined to share with the world. You exist only for one reason, which is to share your movie with the world.

Don't ever limit, doubt, or judge yourself. Don't do that to yourself. Don't do that to others because you are depriving all of humanity of your beautiful purpose. Don't do that to God because this is why you were created. That is the essence of what sin is; to not choose your light by avoiding your pain. Choose your light by transforming your pain into your beacon of light.

ANSWER YOUR CALLING

As I'm writing this now, over 40 million Americans have lost their jobs since the coronavirus pandemic. Small businesses are being shut down in record numbers. Robert Kiyosaki, author of *Rich Dad Poor Dad*, predicts that this will be the greatest global recession in human history. He has talked about this era bringing the end of the "industrial age" where you worked by giving your time in return for money. According to Kiyosaki, the traditional route of doing what you are supposed to, such as getting a college degree, becoming an employee, and waiting for your pension, is a path of guaranteed instability and powerlessness. Kiyosaki goes on to say that the answer to your future and the answer to your abundance comes from your "intellectual property."

Your intellectual property can be a digital product that you use to serve the world, such as an online course, a book, a podcast, a YouTube channel, an online community, you name it. The world is your oyster and you are only limited by your imagination.

When you tap into your intellectual property, you are no longer an employee serving a corporation, or a small business serving a community. Instead, you end up serving the global community of humanity with your light, movie, and purpose.

Ultimately, you need to right your own ship, not the ships of others. You are not a follower, but a leader. You lead with your light. Especially in such uncertain and tumultuous times as these, it is more important than ever to answer your calling. Answering your calling is how you not only protect yourself and your family in this brave new world, but it is also your golden ticket to abundance, joy, and peace. I am living proof of that. The more I have followed my calling, the more abundance, peace, joy, and health I have attracted into my life.

As I am writing this paragraph, I have recently moved out of my parents' house and currently live in the Czech Republic with my wife and child. I didn't foresee all of the different changes I would experience while living here. I made the choice to raise my counseling session fees significantly right before coming, yet I have more clients and make almost twice as much money as I did before. It feels amazing that I am able to now fully provide all of the necessities and comforts for my family nucleus, instead of depending on and living with my parents. My body feels a lot healthier, and I sleep better now. All of these transformations have manifested because I kept continuing to answer my calling and work through all of my pain. The more you do that for yourself, the more abundance, peace, joy, and health you will attract in your own life. That is a universal law, for when you tap into the power of the Universe, you tap into your universal abundance, peace, joy, and power. Answer your calling and mountains will be moved for you and for the rest of the world.

You may be jobless in this current climate and still need to provide for your family. However, no matter how many jobs have been lost, or what is happening in our world, your reason for existence can never be taken away from you. God created you for this very purpose and ultimately, God is in control.

I know you may wish things could return to the way they were before, but let's take a moment to see how things were truly were before the Coronavirus hit. Yes, it is true that our economy was booming. When you would go out for a drive you could see all the multitude of businesses and seemingly endless ways to make money. But, the question is: are all of these millions of people who have lost their jobs, including you, answering their calling? You may have lost your job, and your livelihood, but you can never lose your reason for existence, your higher purpose.

With all this free time that you have staying at home, or if you are jobless, capitalize on it by discovering what your calling is. Your calling is your reason for existence and your source of infinite power; a power that is far greater than whatever is happening in our world. Your calling, your dream, and your movie are the most certain things you can ever hold onto in the face of all the uncertainty we are experiencing in our world right now.

Your calling and your movie are your anchors for everything. They are the oxygen that your soul breathes and depends on. Nothing else matters. Take yourself off the life support of mindless busyness and constant thinking and connect to your eternal source of by answering your calling, which is really God's calling for you.

You may think, how can little ol' you change the world? But you can! It is why you were created. Otherwise, you would not exist. When you are living out your movie and your dream and sharing it with the world, you are aligned with your greatest power. You can truly feel within the fabric of your soul why you were created. You can see and feel the infinite expansion of your limitless self because your movie is limitless and knows no boundaries.

Can you feel that infinite power within you and how that very power is oozing out of your soul into the world and into the Universe? Take a moment to envision of all this as your reality because it's your destiny and your birthright.

Your power and light are not defined and confined by what you see immediately in front of you. Knowing your movie, your purpose, and your light, connects you to the true world, which is the spiritual world. In the spiritual world, everything is possible because you know why the Creator created you. In the spiritual world, your soul is limitless, and its power knows no boundaries. The spiritual world is the maker of our material and physical world.

In so many ways, the material world is the current manifestation and reflection of our ancestral pain, fears, and trauma. Our material world has no choice but to transform itself when we shine our beacon of light by sharing our movies with the world, because the world transforms as we transform.

When we collectively follow our dreams and share our movies with the world, the world will, in turn, experience an unprecedented transformation that will send reverberations until the end of time. We can no longer live in this cycle of intergenerational pain within ourselves and within our world by continuing to live a life of avoiding our pain. Avoiding pain, who is our greatest teacher, is avoiding our light.

That is the very reason why I wrote this book. It is my dream to create a movement where we collectively share our dreams with the world and change the world forever.

Yes, this pandemic and economic collapse, excuse my language, suck a$$. Despite the toll this has taken on us, this is actually a moment, an opportunity for humanity to transform. These times are calling on you and virtually forcing you to step up to the plate to answer your calling. Yes, it may seem we are facing the era of the death of small business and the death of stable, reliable employment, but it is truly the death of your small self and the rebirth of your global self, your highest self self, and your light.

Are you ready to answer your calling?

Or are you going to continue to choose to ignore the call and lose yourself in the mindless scrolling of social media, nonstop busyness, and perpetual fear, worry, anger, frustration, depression, and sadness?

Are you going to continue being mad about the world only to deny your power to transform it?

Are you going to continue to lose yourself in overthinking just to avoid feeling, when what you are truly avoiding, above all else, is your greatness and your light?

Your light may feel intimidating because it feels like it can blind you, but what you are really feeling scared of is the massive power of your infinite light. But once you feel the power of your light, you will never go back and be fooled by the familiarity, the comfort, and ultimately, the illusion of the ego and the thinking mind, which fools you into thinking that darkness and pain are your enemies when in actuality they can be your greatest teachers in life. Moreover, the lessons you learn from your darkness symbolize the key that will unlock the mystery of transforming our world.

We can do this, and we must do this together. We have two choices in front of us and the same two choices for humanity as a whole. One, we can continue to choose the avoidance of suffering and pain, which only results in the never-ending and vicious cycle of pain and ancestral trauma. Or, we can end it all by choosing our light and the light of humanity – transforming our darkness into light and collectively sharing our movies of transformation with the world.

Whatever you need to get done today, or this week, or this month, or this year, forget it all, because none of it matters, if you don't have the anchor of your movie, your purpose, your dream, and reason for existence. None of it matters. Your movie is the anchor for everything that you will ever do in your life. This is all that matters.

Everything else you want in your life comes from the anchor of your blockbuster movie. You want abundance? You want to attract the right relationships and people into your life? You want peace, joy, and above all else, God, in your life? When you begin to embark on your journey by saying "YES, I will answer my calling," you will not only have all the peace, joy, and abundance you can ever ask for, but more importantly, you will have the power to transform the world.

Are you ready to embark on the true reason why you were placed on this earth? Let's do it, and let's do it together. Because when we do it together, we feed off each other's infectious energy and power into a synergistic and symbiotic force that that world and human history have never bare witness to.

You are the fucking shit! We are the fucking shit! It's time to own our power, to own our beauty, our peace, and limitless selves. Close your eyes for a moment and feel all of this within your body and now envision your power, your beauty, your peace shining infinitely onto the world, onto the universe, changing the world forever.

Choose your birthright. Choose your power. Choose your beauty. Choose your reason for existence by choosing to share your movie with the world. Choose it now. Not tomorrow. Not next week. Not next month. Not next year, but NOW.

NOW.

NOW.

For nothing else matters when this is all that has ever mattered and ever will.

Get your butt off that couch. NOW!

Feel your feelings and heal it all. NOW!

Get a pen and paper and craft out your dream and your movie which you want to share with the world. NOW!

Stand into your power and birthright. NOW!

Transform your pain and intergenerational trauma into your beacon of light. NOW!

Don't think about the destination. Embrace the journey, because the true destination is the journey when you simply make the choice to answer your calling NOW.

The power does not come from reaching your desired destination and the validation you feel you will attain from getting there. Rather, the power is accessible NOW, and forever because you were created by the Creator to share the power of your movie with the world and to leave a legacy that transforms the world forever.

ALL IS ONE

We are constantly resisting and wanting to defeat and put an end to all this "darkness" in ourselves, in our lives, in others, and in our world. So much so, that it has become our constant mode of being and the only life we know. But wanting to resist and defeat this darkness is completely denying how darkness is your most powerful vehicle to become the light that you were created to be. In other words, beautiful things can come out of darkness if it is channeled in the right direction.

Are you bothered by what's happening in this world and find yourself wanting to resist and fight it? The darkness of this world only exists for you to transform into light. First and foremost, it requires you to transform your own darkness into light and shine that light onto the world. Only then will the darkness of this world transform itself into light. However, resisting the darkness of this world is what creates true darkness, and is the very definition of hell on earth.

God placed the darkness in this world and in your life for you to recognize it and channel it towards transformation. Darkness only becomes the true darkness that you know so well when you resist darkness. When you resist it, you are pushing away God's gift and vehicle to know and become the light that you were created to be.

YOU ARE ONE WITH IT ALL

When you know that you are one with it all, you see the gift in everything in your life and in this world. You become empowered beyond your wildest imagination. When you know you are one with it all, you become one with God; allowing God's energy, love, wisdom, and peace to naturally flow through you and shower over you.

Your eyes, both physical and spiritual eyes, become awakened and now see the empowering truth that God is walking with you, supporting you, guiding you, every single step of the way. You have nothing to worry about. Close your eyes now and take a moment to feel within your core the absolute truth of this all.

When you know this, nothing, and I mean absolutely nothing, can ever stop you. When you know this, abundance, peace, and joy becomes your birthright and it becomes the constant reality and truth of your life and of our world. It was always there, but you chose to resist darkness thereby blinding you from your light and the light of God supporting, guiding, and walking with you every step of the way.

Spread your arms out wide like a phoenix spreading her wings and feel the God-given empowerment of knowing and embracing that you are one with it all. Resisting is the disguise of the devil's clothing. Everything is "God", so when you become one with it all, you become one with God.

YOU BECOME WHAT YOU RESIST

You become what you resist because resistance is the projection of pain to avoid feeling pain.

You may ask, "How can that be?"; especially when you are fighting and resisting evil? All evil, pain and darkness stems from within ourselves.

Essentially, pain comes from within. Thus how is it possible to fight it outside of yourself? When you try to fight it outside of yourself, you are thereby denying and avoiding the existence of pain that lies within.

As you already know, you only avoid what you think is real. Avoiding your painful feelings is subconsciously telling yourself that they are true. Therefore, resistance creates all pain and suffering because the ultimate pain and suffering is the avoidance of pain and suffering.

A REVOLUTION OF TRANSFORMATION

I became immersed in the teachings of Robert Kiyosaki, the author of "Rich Dad Poor Dad," after losing half of our savings in stocks. I really enjoy his teachings because he teaches financial education and empowerment by combining it with emotional and spiritual empowerment. In many of his interviews, he talks about what he learned from his mentor R. Buckminster Fuller, who told him that your life is about "What God wants done?" Meaning, the ultimate purpose of your life is what God wants done through you.

My dream is to create a revolution of transforming darkness into light for our world. I'm sure it sounds like an impossible feat for anyone. But when I ask myself the question, "What does God want done?" that is my answer each and every time and most importantly it feels right to my soul.

Join me in this revolution.

Know that this revolution is not a revolution of resisting the darkness of this world or the darkness within ourselves or others. Love does not trump hate. Just as light does not defeat darkness. It cannot, because light only comes to existence when you transform darkness into light.

As a matter of fact, if you try to use "love" to trump hate or light to defeat darkness then what you are using is not love or light, but darkness itself. The opposite of love is not hate but fear. Fear is the avoidance of pain. However, remember pain is your greatest teacher and your greatest vehicle for transformation into the light that you were created to be. Therefore, if you avoid pain, you are avoiding your light and denying the world of that light. Likewise, if you resist pain and darkness you are resisting your light, and ultimately resisting God. God placed darkness into your life and into the world in order for you to transform yourself into the light that you were created to be.

You are not meant to resist the world, you are meant to transform the world. You transform the world, yourself, and all others by transforming darkness into light; from within and from without.

Once again, if you try to defeat, resist or avoid darkness, you won't see the purpose of darkness, which is to be transformed into light. You will never know, experience, and feel what light truly is, the true power of light, and the light of who you really are.

ARE YOU TRULY "THAT" POWERFUL?

You may question your destined ability to do all of this.

Close your eyes and feel the ocean of infinite abundance, power, wisdom, and peace within your soul. This infinite abundance within you is a never-ending stream of creativity, insight, and inspiration that flows out of you and into the world.

Tap into that inner abundance at all times to create and share your movie with the world. Imagine your abundance as that Superman "S" on your chest where your limitless power, wisdom, peace, and creativity infinitely flows from.

That "S" on your chest is your connection to God.

That "S" on your chest is the reason why you were created for the world.

Honor and embrace your reason for existence and share that with all of humanity.

Feel the infinite abundance, power, peace, wisdom, love, and creativity flowing out of the "S" on your chest.

Whatever you are doing in your life, honor the "S" on your chest and let it guide you at all times. This is why you were placed on this earth. This is the very breath of your soul.

Feel the immense power and the immense gift of who you are. That is your connection to humanity because your connection to humanity is your gift to humanity.

Nothing is impossible when you connect to this, and to the "S" on your chest. As a matter of fact, everything that is impossible becomes possible from this place. "What God wants done?" through you may seem impossible to you, but that is the true magnitude of your light, of your existence and ultimately of God. "Impossible" is the word and the illusion created by the ego in order for you to stay small. Staying small is the death sentence for your soul, for your soul is limitless and eternal.

When you are doing something that is "impossible" you are tapping into the magnitude of your light and you are aligned with the infinite power of God.

SOAR AND THE WORLD WILL SOAR WITH YOU

Remember that the world suffers when you stay small. Are you going to watch the world go up in flames while you stand on the sidelines?? You have a moral right to honor humanity by honoring that "S" on your chest and sharing your movie and light with the world because humanity depends on this inner light. Humanity depends on all of us honoring each other's S's on our chests.

When I say watch the world "go up in flames," I don't mean to resist or fight the darkness of our world, because darkness is the absence of your light. Furthermore, you cannot fight corruption, because corruption is the physical manifestation of the unhealed and untransformed darkness within ourselves. Corruption is the absence of your light. Remember, the world can only transform itself, when you first transform yourself. If you choose to "fight corruption," you are saying something outside of yourself must transform but you do not. With this mentality, corruption will always exist, because corruption is the absence of your light and the absence of your transformation.

The darkness of this world only exists for you to transform it into light, and making this transformation happen requires you to first transform your own darkness into light and transform the illusion of your small self into your infinite and eternal self.

If you continue to stand on the sidelines, and not honor the "S" on your chest, settling for society's and your family's definitions of happiness and not your own, the world will suffer because of it, and you yourself will suffer too. Don't try to find happiness. Find yourself. Find your calling, because that is what can become your never-ending source of joy, peace, power, and even happiness.

Find yourself, and happiness will find you.

Find yourself, and abundance, love, peace, and power will be knocking on your doorstep.

If you dare not to answer your calling, there is no other purpose to your life, except for the illusion of purpose. When I ask clients what their dream is, many respond by saying that they just want to "be happy," but that's just about yourself and you are depriving the world of your light. As a matter of fact, if you choose to deprive the world of your light, your darkness will never be healed and transformed.

Again and again, strive to connect to the "S" on your chest. That is your heart chakra, and your heart chakra is your connection to humanity. Your connection to humanity and to God is your movie that you are meant to share with the world.

Humanity is waiting for your movie premiere. We are all standing in line for it, and the red carpet is being rolled out just for you. Prepare for your movie premiere; envision it, act on it and launch your movie premiere with the world.

This is not a time for perfection because perfection is the pursuit of failure. Seeking perfection is denying the perfection of who you already are. Let all of that go and launch your movie premiere.

I know you may feel scared, thinking, "What if I fail? What if I'm judged?"

In writing this book, I am answering my calling, and as I'm heading towards its completion, I wrongly perceive this book as my one shot to answer my calling. Suddenly I am overcome by all the thoughts of what will happen if I mess up. I fear that I may lose my chance to answer my calling for good.

Consider the opposite, and think:

"What if my movie does change the world?"

"What if my movie heals all of the darkness within myself?"

"What if my movie changes my life, others, and the world forever?"

Your light is the oxygen that the world depends on. Don't deprive it any longer, for the world – you included, is suffering more and more if you continue to "stay small," "play it safe," and "stay in your comfort zone."

Do you realize how fucking great you are? Do you realize how bright your light truly is? Do you realize that if you immerse yourself in that light, it can transform you? It's as powerful as the sun casting its light for all of the earth and the universe. The sun that all the planets of our world revolve around and depend upon for its life-giving sun energy. Without the sun, life would not be possible. Without your light, which is your movie premiere, you will only experience hell on earth, which is the pain of feeling worthless for not fulfilling the reason why God created you.

Is it really so terrible not to answer your calling? Absolutely! You may not be aware of it because you are so used to staying small. You are more than your physical body. You hold an entire universe inside of you, and it is up to you to unlock its infinite power.

If you don't honor the sun that you are, which is your movie, you are not alive. Your life is just an imitation of life – a matrix.

Everything that matters is riding on this. Do you really want to waste it all away by mindlessly scrolling on social media, checking your email, watching the news, and ultimately getting lost in your infinite thoughts and negative thinking?

You are the sun to the galaxy around you. Stop eclipsing the light of your sun by playing small. Most importantly, awaken the "S" on your chest which is the sun that the galaxy depends on.

Don't ever question your power.

Does the sun ever question its power to shine its life-giving energy that the galaxy depends upon? That would be ridiculous, and just as ridiculous as you questioning your own power. Don't ever dare question your power and the power of your movie, because humanity depends on it. Too many lives are at stake for you to throw it all away, only to drown yourself in pain, fear, and resistance.

Join me now and answer your calling and we shall do it together. We shall shine our light onto the world together by answering our calling. When we do it together, we can support each other and be inspired by each other. Most importantly, create a movement together and a revolution of healing and transformation that the world has never bare witnessed to.

This is not a revolution to follow a singular leader like Martin Luther King. This is a revolution by humanity and for humanity.

This revolution is God's calling for us all. This is not a revolution to topple the world but to transform our world forever.

This revolution is about humanity coming together as one by shining our light together.

This is a revolution of awakening – an awakening to our purpose, to our reason for existence, for nothing else matters.

This is a revolution of letting go of our pain and fear, and ultimately letting go of the illusions of fear, which tells us that pain and darkness are our enemies.

This is a revolution through which we become aware that pain is our greatest teacher, that we can use the lessons we learn from pain as our vehicle for transforming darkness into light and pain into love.

This revolution is a reunification with our creator in God.

This is a revolution where we awaken from the illusions of the matrix and step boldly and bravely into our light.

We must come together as humanity because that is what makes us whole, alive, and free. Coming together does not mean in any way that we lose or sacrifice our sense of self. Sacrificing your sense of self for the "greater whole" is sacrificing the greater whole, because the "me" is the greatest gift to the "we."

When we become obsessive in our will to serve others at the expense of ourselves then we do so from a place of pain and feeling of worthlessness. We desperately want to assist and comfort others because we don't want them to feel what we feel all the time, which is a feeling of worthlessness. That is the role of the "servant."

Those who take on this role know no other identity than that of consuming themselves with serving and protecting others, because if they don't or fail to do so, then they don't have a reason to exist, making them feel worthless.

Often, in expending all their energy on helping others, the servant ends up enabling and disabling them by overprotecting them from danger as helpless victims. The truth is, you only truly help others not when you overprotect them, but when you empower them to the point where their light becomes activated and lets them know that nothing can stop them.

Light your torch while leading and inspiring others to light their own torch to lead others in turn.

What are you waiting for? Inspiration? Don't seek inspiration. Be the inspiration that you seek. When you do that, you set your soul ablaze as a torch for the world to follow, and then allow others to blaze their own trail.

This revolution obviously won't happen overnight, but it will be a domino effect that will eventually snowball into an avalanche of healing and transformation. Ultimately, this is a revolution from within and from without.

Don't think solely about being "practical" and think "I need to pay the bills" and "I have mouths to feed." Being practical may feed the mouths of your family, but being practical doesn't feed their souls. Contrarily, answering your calling feeds the souls of our world.

You may begin to doubt your calling, thinking, "How can I share my light in a world filled with so much uncertainty?" Yet, it is in this time and world of uncertainty that God is busting through your door for you to answer your calling – because it is only your light, your dreams, your purpose that are the most certain things you can ever hold onto in this time of uncertainty.

Staying small, playing it safe, and being practical out of fear and familiarity, is protecting yourself against a hurricane with a toothpick umbrella. On the contrary, when you share your light and your movie with the world, you become a hurricane of transformation.

You may ask how you can be truly connected with others when you are very likely staying at home and practicing social distancing. However, these things will never break our connection to each other.

Feel our connection to each other now. Feel the power we share together that is born out of our connection to each other. Feel our moral responsibility to each other, which is honored by sharing our movies with the world.

Our light, our movies, our dreams and our purpose are our ultimate connections to each other. This connection to each other is what we ultimately dedicate each and every day and each and every moment to. We serve humanity with our light and tireless dedication to our movie. Our movie is our connection to each other because it is how we serve each other.

I want you to physically stand up right now. (If your disability prevents you from physically doing so, let your soul stand up now.)

Stand tall.

Stand into your light.

Stand into your power.

Stand into your movie premiere.

Stand into your connection to all others.

Stand into your reunification with God.

Stand into the Universe.

Stand into the power of your sun, the "S" on your chest, that gives life to the entire galaxy.

Stop playing small and stand tall into your limitless self.

Rise up from the ashes like the phoenix that you truly are.

Spread your wings out wide and allow your soul to soar limitlessly and endlessly.

SOAR and you will know the true essence of your soul.

SOAR and you will know your true existence.

SOAR and nothing will ever stop you.

Soar and you be one with God.

Soar and you will instantly break free from the chains of your small self.

Soar and you will be one with your limitless self.

Soar and you will transform darkness into light.

Soar and the world will soar with you.

HELP SHARE THIS BOOK'S MESSAGE WITH THE WORLD

I wrote this book to help you, your family, and the world heal and transform. If you were impacted by this book, please consider leaving an honest review on Amazon to help me share this book's message with the world.

The link to my Amazon author page is:

www.amazon.com/Michael-Hsu/e/B07KDGPVPB

STAY CONNECTED WITH MICHAEL HSU:

Visit my site at: www.healfromthegroundup.com

Check out Michael's podcast Heal From the Ground Up on iTunes

Find Heal From the Ground Up on Facebook and Instagram

Index of Acronyms Used in this Book

F.I.S.T.

Abbreviation for FEEL - IDENTIFY- SEPARATE - TRUE SELF & TRANSFORM:
a process that heals the root of your pain and transforms it into the source of your
light.

P.E.W.F.

Abbreviation for PROBLEM - EMOTION - WORST FEAR & WORST-CASE
SCENARIO - FEELING ABOUT THE SELF: The "I" in the F.I.S.T. process stands
for "identify" which uses the P.E.W.F. process to identify your core negative feelings.

F.W.P.

Abbreviation for FAILURE - WORTHLESS - POWERLESS: specifically identifying
your core negative feelings with the last stage of the P.E.W.F. process in identifying
"Feeling About the Self"

Bibliography

https://www.newyorker.com/magazine/2015/06/29/the-great-divide-books-dalrymple

Alternative Medicine Definitive Guide to Cancer W. John Diamond, M.D., W. Lee Cowden, M.D. with Burton Goldberg. p 617

https://en.wikipedia.org/wiki/Great_Chinese_Famine

It Didn't Start With You, Mark Wolynn pages 36-37

Dias and Ressler, "Parental Olfactory Experience Influences Behavior and Neural Structure in Subsequent Generations."

https://en.wikipedia.org/wiki/Economic_history_of_Argentina

https://www.macrotrends.net/countries/ARG/argentina/poverty-rate